Apologetics,
Fundamental Baptist Bible Doctrines

A Versa Curriculum Book For Students and Teachers

By Dr. Keith D. Thibo

King's Kids Baptist Press

22648 Grosenbach Road, Washington, Illinois 61571 (309) 698-2000

SECOND EDITION

Editing, Heidi Rodberg and Gina Kincaid

Design and Final Editing, Joe Mitchell

1.1 Introduction

Strictly speaking, apologetics is the defense of or a rational explanation for our Christian faith. Carrying it a step further, apologetics is the logical, systematic, and Biblical defense of justly held doctrines and convictions. It is not apologizing for what we believe, but systematically and capably defending what our beliefs are using Bible commands, principles, and statements. One studying apologetics would become well versed in truths of great doctrines such as the deity of Christ, the inspiration and preservation of Scriptures or eternal security. This book is written on a general survey level, not on a seminary level.

A well-meaning Baptist pastor of some fame once said that *"doctrines divide"*. Thus, the Christian School and Bible college associated with his church did not emphasize the study of doctrine. As a result, an inordinate number of graduates lost their way and ended up in pursuits and religious circles that were not fundamental. The word fundamental refers to those doctrines which cannot be changed and still have Christianity. For example, one could not do away with the virgin birth of Christ and still have Christianity.

Independent, fundamental Baptists are more than just fundamental, they are biblically based in all their doctrines.

1.2 Fundamental Doctrines

There are 10 fundamental doctrines which are essential to Christianity. To take away one of these is to no longer have Christianity. What are these doctrines?

✓ Creation as Literally Set Forth in Scriptures

✓ The Inspiration of Scripture

✓ The Incarnation and Virgin Birth of Jesus Christ the Son of God

✓ The Deity of Jesus Christ

✓ The Vicarious and Blood Sacrifice of Christ on the Cross for our Sins

✓ The Death, Burial, and Resurrection of Christ

✓ Salvation by Grace through Faith in Christ Alone

✓ Eternal Life for the Saved in a Literal Heaven

✓ Eternal Damnation for the Lost in a Literal Hell

✓ The Return of Christ

These fundamental doctrines are the pillars which hold up Christianity and cannot be removed. To remove any of these fundamental doctrines is to no longer have Christianity.

Thus when a person or group refers to themselves as "fundamental," they are saying that they hold these doctrines to be true and Biblical.

It is vitally important that those of Baptist or Baptistic faith understand that Biblical doctrines extend well beyond those considered to be the fundamental ones. Eternal security of the believer is a good example. The Bible clearly teaches that once a person is saved they cannot lose their salvation.

Class Discussion Questions

1. What other doctrines would you consider to be Biblical that we have not yet mentioned?

This book will examine all fundamental doctrines and other doctrines Baptists hold to be Biblical and true.

1.3 Why Study Bible Doctrines?

You might be thinking, "But I'm not called to be a preacher or a teacher. Why do I need to study Bible doctrines?" In answer it should be noted that you do not know all that God will call you to do in the future. Secondly, all Christians are called to full time Christian service even if they are not called to do it occupationally. In other words, we are all to be serving God all of the time.

(John 4:24) God is a Spirit: and they that worship him must worship him in spirit and in truth.

(3 John 1:4) I have no greater joy than to hear that my children walk in truth.

Without a mastery of Bible doctrine a Christian can neither stand for nor upon the truth. We would be tossed around with every false belief invented by man. Someone once said that "he who stands for nothing will fall for everything."

(Ephesians 4:14-15) That we henceforth be no more children, tossed to and fro, and carried about with every wind of doctrine, by the sleight of men, and cunning craftiness, whereby they lie in wait to deceive; But speaking the truth in love, may grow up into him in all things, which is the head, even Christ:

God is not interested in designer religion. If we are to know God; if we are to walk with God, if we are to serve God, we must do so in God's way.

1.4 Five Reasons to Study Doctrine

1. Studying these things is a major part of God's instruction to us.

(2 Timothy 2:15) Study to shew thyself approved unto God, a workman that needeth not to be ashamed, rightly dividing the word of truth.

(2 Timothy 3:16-17) All scripture is given by inspiration of God, and is profitable for doctrine, for reproof, for correction, for instruction in righteousness: That the man of God may be perfect, throughly furnished unto all good works.

God wants us to know Him so that we might greater love Him and worship Him. God wants us to know Him so that we might greater glorify Him and serve Him.

2. Studying these things enables us to separate truth from error.

The Mormon religion teaches that God was once a man and passed through the steps of Mormonism to become a god. They further believe that good Mormons will become gods in eternity. In other words, they believe in many gods. Is this truth or error? If you correctly believe this to be in error than you must be ready to explain the wording of Genesis 1:26 which states, *"And God said, Let us make man in our image, after our likeness."*

Before you jump on the ecumenical unity band wagon, it is important to note that God commands that there are things we are to divide over. Liberal love talk says, "united we stand, divided we fall." The "we" is the problem in their statement. There is no such group in the Bible as an all inclusive "we".

There are issues that God commands us to divide over.

✓ The issue of false doctrine

(Romans 16:17) Now I beseech you, brethren, mark them which cause divisions and offences contrary to the doctrine which ye have learned; and avoid them.

✓ The issue of disorderly walk

(2 Thessalonians 3:6) Now we command you, brethren, in the name of our Lord Jesus Christ, that ye withdraw yourselves from every brother that walketh disorderly, and not after the tradition which he received of us.

✓ The issue of fellowship

(Ephesians 5:11) And have no fellowship with the unfruitful works of darkness, but rather reprove them.

✓ The issue of vain philosophy

(Colossians 2:6-8) As ye have therefore received Christ Jesus the Lord, so walk

ye in him: Rooted and built up in him, and stablished in the faith, as ye have been taught, abounding therein with thanksgiving. Beware lest any man spoil you through philosophy and vain deceit, after the tradition of men, after the rudiments of the world, and not after Christ.

3. Studying these things prepares us to give an answer of our faith.

As believers we are the defenders of the faith and God's spokesmen for sound doctrine.

Class Discussion Questions

1. If Jesus is called the light of the world (Jn 8:12) and we are called the light of the world (Mt 5:14-16), do we have a contradiction in Scripture?

2. God created two great lights in the sky. How is it that the moon is called a light? What lesson do we see here?

If we are not prepared to do this then we cannot be the light of the world.

4. Studying these things helps us to accredit our Christian Testimony.

If we do not know what we believe, why would the lost listen to us?

5. Studying these things helps us to do God's work in God's way.

Have you ever wondered why so many churches do so many things differently than others? Have you ever wondered why churches of different denominations are so drastically different? How can you be sure to do things Biblically and according to the way God commanded? The answer is simple. We read it earlier.

(2 Timothy 2:15) Study to shew thyself approved unto God, a workman that needeth not to be ashamed, rightly dividing the word of truth.

One of the first things that is distinctive of all Bible believers is that the Bible is the final rule of faith and practice in all matters.

Illustration

John Wesley once received a note that read, "The Lord told me to tell you that He doesn't need your book learning, your Greek, or your Hebrew." Wesley answered, "Thank you sir. Your letter was superfluous, however, I already knew the Lord has no need for my book learning, as you put it. However, although the Lord has not directed me to say so, on my own responsibility I would like to say to you that the Lord does not need your ignorance either."

This Week's Memory Verse

Study to shew thyself approved unto God, a workman that needeth not to be ashamed, rightly dividing the word of truth. (2 Timothy 2:15)

Chapter One Quiz & Memory Verse Fill In Study Sheet

Why Study Bible Doctrines?

1. Define Apologetics: The _____, _____, and _____ defense of justly held _____ and _____.

2. List the five reasons given as to why we study doctrines:

_____

_____

_____

_____

_____

3. There are ten doctrines which constitute the fundamentals of Christianity. Name 5 of them.

_____

_____

_____

_____

_____

Write out this week's Bible verse from memory.

2 Timothy 2:15

_____

_____

_____

_____

_____

Finish the Phrase

God is a Spirit: and they that worship him must _____

I have no greater joy than to hear that my children _____

Study to shew thyself approved unto God, a workman that needeth not to be ashamed

_____

All scripture is given by inspiration of God, and is profitable for doctrine _____

And God said, Let us make man in our image, _____

Now I beseech you, brethren, mark them which cause divisions and offences contrary to the doctrine which ye have learned; _____

And have no fellowship with _____

Beware lest any man spoil you through philosophy and vain deceit _____

Then spake Jesus again unto them, saying, I am the light of the world: he that followeth me shall not _____

_____

Ye are the light of the world. A city that is _____

Let your light so shine before men, that they may _____

_____   _____
_____   _____
_____   _____
_____   _____
_____   _____
_____   _____
_____   _____
_____   _____
_____   _____
_____   _____
_____   _____
_____   _____
_____   _____
_____   _____
_____   _____
_____   _____
_____   _____

BEST POINT MADE

_____   _____
_____   _____
_____   _____
_____   _____
_____   _____
_____   _____
_____   _____
_____   _____

Proverbs Chapter One

What were the main themes of this chapter?

_____

_____

_____

_____

What were the instructional points meant to bring you closer to God?

_____

_____

_____

_____

What were the instructional points meant to protect you from spiritual destruction?

_____

_____

_____

_____

What things in your life could use strengthening?

_____

_____

_____

_____

_____

Was there anything in this chapter that was of help in serving the LORD?

_____

_____

_____

_____

Did you learn anything new about the LORD?

_____

_____

_____

_____

Were there any suggestions made whereby you can be a greater blessing to others?

_____

_____

_____

_____

_____

_____

2.1 Introduction

You might have asked yourself at some point in your life, "Who is God"? Many people ask themselves that question. But have you ever tried to answer the question, "What is God"? We must consider that there is a major difference between knowing who God is; and knowing what God is; just as there is a major difference between knowing who God is and knowing God.

2.2 What is God?

People who claim to have seen God are not a few. Their endless books and interviews create a hodgepodge of confusion and contradiction among those unfamiliar with Scripture. Truth can have but one authority. For the truth of God, that source is the Bible. All other sources are brought forth from the imaginations and philosophies of man. We previously cited the following text:

(Colossians 2:6-8) As ye have therefore received Christ Jesus the Lord, so walk ye in him: Rooted and built up in him, and stablished in the faith, as ye have been taught, abounding therein with thanksgiving. Beware lest any man spoil you through philosophy and vain deceit, after the tradition of men, after the rudiments of the world, and not after Christ.

What is God? Even with the Bible as the sole authority, one cannot just go to a single chapter and verse for such an explanation. The answer as to what God is, is derived from a preponderance of Scripture statements. From these statements we know what God wanted us to know about Him. Gathering these Bible statements we know the following truths:

✓ God is the sole creator, preserver, and final disposer of all things.

By Him alone all things exist and have their being. By Him alone all things are either eternal or temporal. If it exists at all, God created it, regardless of the universe or dimension in which it exists. You exist because God willed it.

(Colossians 1:16) For by him were all things created, that are in heaven, and that are in earth, visible and invisible, whether they be thrones, or dominions, or principalities, or powers: all things were created by him, and for him:

(Revelation 4:11) Thou art worthy, O Lord, to receive glory and honour and power: for thou hast created all things,

and for thy pleasure they are and were created.

✓ God is Spirit.

(John 4:24) God is a Spirit: and they that worship him must worship him in spirit and in truth.

God is not limited to time or space. He does not leave somewhere to go somewhere else. He has none of the limitations of humanity. He has none of the limitations of animate or inanimate objects. He is not a spirit in the sense of a created spirit. He has no corporeal substance. God is immaterial, immortal, invisible; the totality of intelligence, knowledge, and wisdom. Yet, God is not a ghost.

God does take on forms that reflect who and what He is. If God had never taken on form, how is it that we were created in His image?

The scriptures refer to God's head, eyes, hands, fingers, nostrils, etc. He rests, but He does not get tired. Yet, He is invisible when He chooses to be. These things are hard to sort out by human intellect. All Bible statements are true and do not contradict each other from God's point. You can be very secure and content to know that God is so complex that you cannot comprehend Him. If you could, God would not be big enough to be your God.

✓ God is Light.

(1 John 1:5) This then is the message which we have heard of him, and declare unto you, that God is light, and in him is no darkness at all.

This means that God is absolutely pure and holy without any presence of evil or darkness. He is the light that overcomes the darkness. He is the source of all light both physical and spiritual. This light also reflects God's own glory.

(Revelation 21:23-24) And the city had no need of the sun, neither of the moon, to shine in it: for the glory of God did lighten it, and the Lamb is the light thereof. And the nations of them which are saved shall walk in the light of it: and the kings of the earth do bring their glory and honour into it.

✓ God is a consuming fire.

(Hebrews 12:29) For our God is a consuming fire.

God is a consuming fire to all those who refuse to listen to Him. Such an identity invokes fear. It is a terrible thing to fall into the hands of an Almighty God.

✓ God is one God who is triune in His existence. He is referred to as the Trinity.

God the Father

All agree that the Bible recognizes the Father as God. Few would debate this point. But the Son of God is also recognized as God, as is the Holy Spirit.

Class Discussion Questions

1. Which ones of the following cults do not believe in the Trinity?
    Mormonism?
    Jehovah's Witnesses?
    Christian Science?
    The Bahai faith?

2. What world religions would reject the truth of the trinity?

The Son of God

(Isaiah 9:6) For unto us a child is born, unto us a son is given: and the government shall be upon his shoulder: and his name shall be called Wonderful, Counsellor, The mighty God, The everlasting Father, The Prince of Peace.

(John 1:1) In the beginning was the Word, and the Word was with God, and the Word was God.

(John 1:14) And the Word was made flesh, and dwelt among us, (and we beheld his glory, the glory as of the only begotten of the Father,) full of grace and truth.

(Titus 2:13) Looking for that blessed hope, and the glorious appearing of the great God and our Saviour Jesus Christ;

The Holy Spirit

(Acts 5:3-4) But Peter said, Ananias, why hath Satan filled thine heart to lie to the Holy Ghost, and to keep back part of the price of the land? Whiles it remained, was it not thine own? and after it was sold, was it not in thine own power? why hast thou conceived this thing in thine heart? thou hast not lied unto men, but unto God.

There are numerous ways to illustrate how God can be one God and yet be three personages; how they can be the same and yet different. Take H_2O for example. Is it water? Is it ice? Is it steam? Are these the same thing or are they different? Actually, they are the same and they are different. Consider yourself. You are a trinity made up of body, soul, and spirit. These are all different, but there is only one you.

Again, if God was small enough and simple enough for you to comprehend and understand, He would not be big enough to be your God.

2.3 The Eminent Attributes of God

A closer examination of God's attributes will not only assist you in knowing who and what God is, but how this relates to your personal life. Keep in mind, that God has not told us everything about Himself. There are Heavenly things that we are not capable of understanding and these have not yet been shared with us. (Jn 3:12) Everything God has told us about himself is important for us to know or He would not have told us these things.

We will begin with God's Eminent Attributes. Attributes are inherent characteristics and qualities. Eminent refers to those things which operate within a defined dominion. These are the inward attributes of God's being. Transcendent means to operate outside of and beyond the limits of ordinary experience. These are the outward attributes of God's being.

The Eminent attributes of God related to *Spirituality*

✓ LIFE - God is a living God; the source of His own being and all other living things. He cannot stop living. He cannot cease to live.

(Jeremiah 10:10) But the LORD is the true God, he is the living God, and an everlasting king: at his wrath the earth shall tremble, and the nations shall not be able to abide his indignation.

(Genesis 2:7) And the LORD God formed man of the dust of the ground, and breathed into his nostrils the breath of life; and man became a living soul.

(1 John 5:11) And this is the record, that God hath given to us eternal life, and this life is in his Son.

Illustration

The Amazon River is the largest river in the world. The mouth is 90 miles across. There is enough water to exceed the combined flow of the Yangtze, Mississippi, and Nile Rivers. So much water comes from the Amazon that they can detect its fresh water currents 200 miles out into the Atlantic Ocean. One irony of ancient navigation is that sailors died for lack of water while caught in windless waters of the South Atlantic. Adrift without wind, they were helpless and dying of thirst. Sometimes other ships from South America who knew the area would come alongside and call out, "What is your problem?" And they would exclaim, "Can you spare us some water. Our sailors are dying of thirst!" And from the other ship would come the cry, "Just lower your buckets. You are in the fresh water currents of the mighty Amazon River." The irony of tragedy around us today is that God, the fountain of life, is right here and people do not recognize Him!

✓ PERSONALITY - God is a personal being with personal emotions and characteristics. These combine to give God personage.

The Eminent attributes of God related to *Infinity*

✓ SELF-EXISTENCE - God exists by reason of His nature, not by His will to exist. He cannot take His life nor can it be taken. God cannot will Himself out of existence. He is what He is.

(Exodus 3:14) And God said unto Moses, I AM THAT I AM: and he said, Thus shalt thou say unto the children of Israel, I AM hath sent me unto you.

✓ IMMUTABILITY - God has always been and is absolutely indestructible and unchangeable. He is the same today as He was eternally back and will be eternally forward.

(Psalm 102:27) But thou art the same, and thy years shall have no end.

(Malachi 3:6) For I am the LORD, I change not; therefore ye sons of Jacob are not consumed.

What has changed about you in the past ten years? Man is on a journey of changes. God is on no such journey. He does not change.

The Eminent attributes of God related to *Perfection*

✓ TRUTH - All truth is found in God and in Him are no untruths. In fact, He is truth. He is the truth, the whole truth, and nothing but the truth. All truth emerges from God.

(Deuteronomy 32:4) He is the Rock, his work is perfect: for all his ways are judgment: a God of truth and without iniquity, just and right is he.

(Psalm 100:5) For the LORD is good; his mercy is everlasting; and his truth endureth to all generations.

✓ LOVE - God's love is and always has been voluntary, rational, and deliberate. God's love toward us is manifested through God's mercy and grace.

(1 John 4:16) And we have known and believed the love that God hath to us. God is love; and he that dwelleth in love dwelleth in God, and God in him.

Yet, his love is not irrespective of its moral qualities. It is an error to believe that God is love in the sense that it has no moral boundaries. God is also a God of anger, justice, judgement, and wrath.

✓ HOLINESS - God is totally absent of all sin and iniquity.

(Exodus 15:11) Who is like unto thee, O LORD, among the gods? who is like thee, glorious in holiness, fearful in praises, doing wonders?

✓ JUSTICE - God can never be unfair or incorrect.

(Psalm 89:14) Justice and judgment are the habitation of thy throne: mercy and truth shall go before thy face.

(Isaiah 45:21) Tell ye, and bring them near; yea, let them take counsel together: who hath declared this from ancient time? who hath told it from that time? have not I the LORD? and there is no God else beside me; a just God and a Saviour; there is none beside me.

Class Discussion Questions

1. Is God fair in sending people to Hell who have never heard the gospel?

2. In what way does Romans 1:18-28 shed light on this question?

3. In what way does Matthew 7:7-8 broaden our understanding this question?

Illustration

Missionaries in the previous century have told many stories of people walking straight out of the jungles after traveling 100's of miles looking for the true and living God. One such man back in his native village looked up to the Heavens and said, "God if you are there, show yourself to me and I will worship you." God directed his way to a missionary station over 100 miles away.

✓ GOODNESS - God's goodness is and always has been great toward men.

(Psalm 34:8) O taste and see that the LORD is good: blessed is the man that trusteth in him.

(Psalm 31:19) Oh how great is thy goodness, which thou hast laid up for them that fear thee; which thou hast wrought for them that trust in thee before the sons of men!

Class Discussion Questions

1. What is the essence of Psalm 68:19?

2. In what ways has God been good to believers who seem to experience a continuous line of hardships?

This Week's Memory Verse

Fear ye not, neither be afraid: have not I told thee from that time, and have declared it? ye are even my witnesses. Is there a God beside me? yea, there is no God; I know not any. (Isaiah 44:8)

The Doctrine of God, His Eminent Attributes

1. Name the five things listed as "God is ..."

    _____

    _____

    _____

    _____

    _____

2. Name the two eminent attributes of God related to *Spirituality*.

    _____

    _____

3. Name the two eminent attributes of God related to *Infinity*.

    _____

    _____

4. Name the five attributes of God related to *Perfection*.

    _____

    _____

    _____

    _____

    _____

Write out this week's Bible verse from memory.

Isaiah 44:8

_____

_____

_____

_____

_____

Finish the Phrase

For by him were all things created, that are in heaven, and that are in earth, ___ _____

For thou hast created all things, and for thy _____

God is a Spirit: and they that worship him must worship him in _____

God is light, and in him is _____

For our God is a consuming _____

In the beginning was the Word, and the Word was with God, and the Word _____

But the LORD is the true God, he is the _____

And the LORD God formed man of the dust of the ground, and breathed into his nostrils the _____

And God said unto Moses, _____

For I am the LORD, I change _____

He is the Rock, his work is perfect: for all his ways are judgment: a God of _____

His truth endureth to all _____

God is love; and he that dwelleth in love dwelleth in God, and God _____

Justice and judgment are the habitation of thy _____

O taste and see that the LORD is _____

BEST POINT MADE

Proverbs Chapter Two

What were the main themes of this chapter?

_____

_____

_____

_____

_____

What were the instructional points meant to bring you closer to God?

_____

_____

_____

_____

_____

What were the instructional points meant to protect you from spiritual destruction?

_____

_____

_____

_____

_____

What things in your life could use strengthening?

_____

_____

_____

_____

_____

Was there anything in this chapter that was of help in serving the LORD?

_____

_____

_____

_____

_____

Did you learn anything new about the LORD?

_____

_____

_____

_____

_____

Were there any suggestions made whereby you can be a greater blessing to others?

_____

_____

_____

_____

_____

_____

_____

3.1 Introduction

In the previous lesson we were looking at God's Eminent Attributes. We said that His attributes were inherent characteristics and qualities. Eminent referred to those things which operate within a defined dominion. These were the inward attributes of God's being.

We now turn to the Transcendent Attributes, meaning to operate outside of and beyond the limits of ordinary experience. These are the outward attributes of God's being. (Transcendent Attributes are sometimes referred to as God's Transitive Attributes.) These attributes reveal the magnitude of God's being.

3.2 The Transcendent Attributes of God

The transcendent attributes of God related to *Time and Space*

✓ ETERNITY - God's nature is without beginning or end and is not subject to the laws of time.

(2 Peter 3:8) But, beloved, be not ignorant of this one thing, that one day is with the Lord as a thousand years, and a thousand years as one day.

(Psalm 90:2-4) Before the mountains were brought forth, or ever thou hadst formed the earth and the world, even from everlasting to everlasting, thou art God. Thou turnest man to destruction; and sayest, Return, ye children of men. For a thousand years in thy sight are but as yesterday when it is past, and as a watch in the night.

Illustration

If you were to take a yard stick and hold it horizontally in front of you, you would see the Divine Dimension Principle. The zero mark would represent the beginning of time. The other end of the yard stick would represent the end of time. God holds the past, present, and future in his hand all at the same time. Though God does not live in the dimension of time, He can interact with any point in time any time He chooses. God encompasses time.

Time does not exist in the Divine Dimension. We sometimes say that God lives in the past, present, and future all at once. This is not exactly correct since these are terms which describe the passing of time. God never gets older. After the rapture of Christians and after we have received our glorified bodies we will not age.

When we understand that God exists in a Divine Dimension, it is easier to harmonize Bible teachings like "election" and "whosoever will". To God, in His dimension, "before the foundation of the world" and "today" are one and the same. In His dimension it makes no difference whether He chooses to save a soul today or before the foundation of the world because it is the same to Him.

Class Discussion Questions

1. Since no one ages in the Divine Dimension, do you think babies who die on earth will be babies in Heaven?

We live in the age of speed. Jets are faster, race cars are faster, and computers are faster. Sometimes people say that the older you get the faster the years go by. Of course, this is not true. Time will plod on at the same pace it always has until time is no more. Before you know it, your life will be spent. It is as though it is human nature to lose track of time. You may think that you have a long time to serve God, but you do not. Have you ever stopped to think about why most older people wish they had the opportunity to live their lives over again? Live your life for God today and tomorrow you will not wish you could go back and change it.

(James 4:14) Whereas ye know not what shall be on the morrow. For what is your life? It is even a vapour, that appeareth for a little time, and then vanisheth away.

Jesus said, "I must work the works of him that sent me, while it is day: the night cometh, when no man can work."

✓ IMMENSITY - Immensity is infinity as it relates to space. Just as God is not subject to the laws of time He also is not subject to the laws of space. He is bigger than space. *"It is more correct to say that space is within God."* Emery Bancroft.

Have you ever looked up at the stars at night and said to yourself, "it never ends out there?" No wonder the psalmist said, "Such knowledge is too wonderful for me; it is high, I cannot attain unto it."

Many years ago a Russian cosmonaut circled the earth in a tiny capsule called the Soyuz space craft. It had a tiny window in it so that the cosmonauts could look out and peer into space. Upon Soyuz's return, the Russians declared that they had looked out the window of the craft at the emptiness of space. Since they saw nothing of God or Heaven, they promptly declared that there was no God and there was no Heaven. These are likely the same kind of guys that cannot find their socks in the morning.

The transcendent attributes of God related to *Inclusion*

✓ OMNIPRESENCE - God is present everywhere at the same time. All of Him is everywhere at the same time. God cannot leave one place and go to another. He is already there.

(Psalm 139:7) Whither shall I go from thy spirit? or whither shall I flee from thy presence? If I ascend up into heaven, thou art there: if I make my bed in hell, behold, thou art there. If I take the wings of the morning, and dwell in the uttermost parts of the sea; Even there shall thy hand lead me, and thy right hand shall hold me.

(Jeremiah 23:23-24) Am I a God at hand, saith the LORD, and not a God afar off? Can any hide himself in secret places that I shall not see him? saith the LORD. Do not I fill heaven and earth? saith the LORD.

Impossible as it may sound, in terms of time, God is everywhere at once throughout all eternity all at the same time.

Omnipresence gives depth to God's promise that He will never leave us, nor forsake us.

(Hebrews 13:5) Let your conversation be without covetousness; and be content with such things as ye have: for he hath said, I will never leave thee, nor forsake thee.

God is always there for us. His watch care never ceases. He is constantly attending to our needs. No part of the universe is ever out of God's direct control. Nothing cataclysmic in our solar system can happen unless God orders it. There is coming a time when God will in fact order things like this. That time is called the Tribulation, but Christians will not be here for that.

It is more important for us to know we are never out of God's presence.

✓ OMNISCIENCE - God knows everything. If God does not know it, it is unknowable. If God does not know it, it is non-existent.

God knows everything: past, present, and future. He knows what science does not know.

Scientific conclusions are perpetually changing. New conclusions invalidate old conclusions. How is it that the earth has gone from millions of years old to billions of years old? Well, it hasn't. The earth is about 10,000 years old or so. It gets even more ridiculous. Is chocolate good for you or bad for you? Is real butter better for you than oleo? New scientific conclusions on this have reversed themselves once again. Do certain fats in our food really clog your arteries? Oops, they're changing their minds again! Does all of this mean that man really does not know anything for sure? No, it does not mean that.

Class Discussion Questions

1. Who do we believe when man's conclusions, whether scientific or philosophic, contradict what God says?

When man says something contradictory to what God has said, man has drawn a false conclusion. Paul said, "let God be true, but every man a liar."

The will of God in our lives is of paramount importance. Have you considered that since God does know everything we would be wise to seek God's direction for every decision we make? Keep in mind that God knows what is behind you and what lies ahead for you.

(Psalm 33:13-15) The LORD looketh from heaven; he beholdeth all the sons of men. From the place of his habitation he looketh upon all the inhabitants of the earth. He fashioneth their hearts alike; he considereth all their works.

(Matthew 6:8) Be not ye therefore like unto them: for your Father knoweth what things ye have need of, before ye ask him.

(Proverbs 3:5-8) Trust in the LORD with all thine heart; and lean not unto thine own understanding. In all thy ways acknowledge him, and he shall direct thy paths. Be not wise in thine own eyes: fear the LORD, and depart from evil. It shall be health to thy navel, and marrow to thy bones.

While God knows your needs before you even ask Him, asking keeps us in fellowship with God. Asking keeps us reminded that it is God who provides for us. Asking keeps us reminded that we have a dependent relationship with God, not an independent relationship to God. God has a divine will for you.

(Romans 12:2) And be not conformed to this world: but be ye transformed by the renewing of your mind, that ye may prove what is that good, and acceptable,

and perfect, will of God.

Class Discussion Questions

1. What are some of the big things for which we should seek the will of God?

Historic preacher George Mueller gives us essential insights into determining God's will. He had these things to suggest to us when searching for God's directive:

> I seek in the beginning to get my heart into such a state that it has no will of its own to a given matter. Nine tenths of the trouble with people is just here. Nine tenths of the difficulties are overcome when our hearts are ready to do the LORD's will, whatever it may be. When one is in this state, it is but a little way to the knowledge of what His will is.

> Having done this, I do not leave the result to feeling or simple impression. If I do, I leave myself open to great delusions.

> I seek the will of the Spirit of God through, or in connection with, the Word of God. The Spirit and the Word must be combined. If I look to the Spirit alone, without the Word, I lay myself open to great delusions also. If the Holy Ghost guides us at all, He will do it according to the Scriptures and never contrary to them.

> Next, I take into account providential circumstances. These often plainly indicated God's will in connection with the Word and Spirit. I ask God to reveal his will to me aright.

> Thus through prayer to God, the study of the WORD, and reflection, I come to a deliberate judgment according to the best of my ability and knowledge, and if my mind is thus at peace and continues so after two or three more petitions, I proceed accordingly.

While Mueller was not writing Scripture, you will find that this method is always effective.

We said that God knows everything and if God did not know it, it was unknowable and did not exist. But knowing everything is one thing; being powerful enough to do something about it is another.

✓ OMNIPOTENCE - God is all powerful. He can do anything that is consistent with His nature and that He desires to do.

Non-thinkers ask questions like *"Can God make a rock too heavy for Him to lift?"* Foolish questions come because foolishness is bound into the heart of man from his childhood. God says, "But foolish and unlearned questions avoid, knowing that they do gender strifes." (2 Tim 2:23)

God is almighty. He told this to Abram before God renamed him Abraham.

(Genesis 17:1) And when Abram was ninety years old and nine, the LORD appeared to Abram, and said unto him, I am the Almighty God; walk before me, and be thou perfect.

READ Genesis 18:9-14

It is clear that God brings about things that nature, if left to itself, cannot bring about.

The basis of our petitioning God is that He can and does intervene in life situations. The miracle working God of the Bible is the same God today and always shall be. He is all powerful!

Everything God does is centered in His purpose, plan, and pleasure. Nothing God does is pointless and is always consistent with His will.

Class Discussion Questions

1. Why do some Christians not get the Divine intervention that they pray for?

2. Are there Bible verses that shed light on this?

In this lesson we have learned that God is:

    Eternal
    Immense
    Omnipresent
    Omniscient
    Omnipotent

These are some of the things God wanted you to know about Himself. These are some of the ways in which God relates to us.

This Week's Memory Verse

Am I a God at hand, saith the LORD, and not a God afar off? Can any hide himself in secret places that I shall not see him? saith the LORD. Do not I fill heaven and earth? saith the LORD. (Jeremiah 23:23-24)

Chapter Three Quiz & Memory Verse Fill In Study Sheet

The Doctrine of God, His Transcendent Attributes

1. Name the two transcendent attributes of God related to *time and space*.

_____

_____

2. Name the three transcendent attributes of God related to *inclusion*.

_____

_____

_____

3. Which attribute teaches us that God is all knowing?

_____

4. Which attribute teaches us that God is not subject to the laws of space?

_____

5. Which attribute teaches us that God is everywhere at the same time?

_____

6. Which attribute teaches us that God is without beginning or end?

_____

7. Which attribute teaches us that God is all powerful?

_____

Write out this week's Bible verse from memory.

Jeremiah 23:23-24

_____

_____

_____

_____

_____

Finish the Phrase

But, beloved, be not ignorant of this one thing, that one day is with the Lord

_____

Before the mountains were brought forth, or ever thou hadst formed the earth and the world, even from _____

For he hath said, I will never _____

Can any hide himself in secret places that I shall not _____

For your Father knoweth what things ye have need of, _____

Trust in the LORD with all thine heart; and lean not unto thine own _____

In all thy ways acknowledge him, and he shall _____

And be not conformed to this world: but be ye transformed by the renewing of your mind, that ye may prove what is that good, and acceptable, and _____

Is there anything too _____

Am I a God at hand, saith the LORD, and not a God _____

For what is your life? It is even a vapour, that appeareth for a little time,

_____

BEST POINT MADE

Proverbs Chapter Three

What were the main themes of this chapter?

_____

_____

_____

_____

What were the instructional points meant to bring you closer to God?

_____

_____

_____

_____

What were the instructional points meant to protect you from spiritual destruction?

_____

_____

_____

_____

What things in your life could use strengthening?

_____

_____

_____

_____

Was there anything in this chapter that was of help in serving the LORD?

_____

_____

_____

_____

Did you learn anything new about the LORD?

_____

_____

_____

_____

Were there any suggestions made whereby you can be a greater blessing to others?

_____

_____

_____

_____

_____

_____

_____

4.1 The Preexistence of Jesus Christ

One of the greatest misconceptions among men is that the Son of God had origin (a point of beginning). This erroneous idea of origin is often tied to what some have called the Nativity. To say that Christ had origin is to say that He was created. To say that He was created is to destroy the foundation of Christianity. Plainly put, one cannot be a Christian and believe that Christ had origin.

The New International Version and other contemporary versions engage this false doctrine in their text. Compare the KJV to the NIV.

(Micah 5:2 KJV) But thou, Bethlehem Ephratah, though thou be little among the thousands of Judah, yet out of thee shall he come forth unto me that is to be ruler in Israel; whose goings forth have been from of old, from everlasting.

NIV "... out of you will come for me one who will be ruler over Israel, whose origins are from old, from ancient times." The blasphemy made here is of their own invention. Christ had no origin. He was not created. In fact, Jesus participated in creation as did the Father and the Holy Spirit.

(Genesis 1:26) And God said, Let us make man in our image, ...

(Colossians 1:16-17) For by him were all things created, that are in heaven, and that are in earth, visible and invisible, whether they be thrones, or dominions, or principalities, or powers: all things were created by him, and for him: And he is before all things, and by him all things consist.

The Bible clearly teaches the existence of the Son of God throughout eternity back. A third and equal part of God, He existed as spirit and was not bound in body to one place as a body of flesh is. Do you remember the words of Jesus?

(John 17:4-5) I have glorified thee on the earth: I have finished the work which thou gavest me to do. And now, O Father, glorify thou me with thine own self with the glory which I had with thee before the world was.

4.2 The O.T. Appearances of Christ

Before the Son of God took on the form of a man, there were numerous appearances of Jesus Christ in Old Testament times. We call these appearances of Christ "Christophanies". A similar term is

"Theophany", meaning the appearance of God.

One of those incredible moments happened when king Nebuchadnezzar looked into the fiery furnace in which he had thrown Shadrach, Meshach, and Abednego. Having only thrown three into the furnace, imagine the king's shock when he saw four men walking around in the furnace without being burned. And who was the fourth?

(Daniel 3:24-25) *Then Nebuchadnezzar the king was astonied, and rose up in haste, and spake, and said unto his counsellors, Did not we cast three men bound into the midst of the fire? They answered and said unto the king, True, O king. He answered and said, Lo, I see four men loose, walking in the midst of the fire, and they have no hurt; and the form of the fourth is like the Son of God.*

What did the Son of God look like? It does not say, but there is no doubt the king knew who it was!

How exciting it must have been for the Jewish people who had looked forward to the birth of the Messiah! Under inspiration of the Holy Spirit, Isaiah expressed this anticipation.

(Isaiah 9:6) *For unto us a child is born, unto us a son is given: and the government shall be upon his shoulder: and his name shall be called Wonderful,* *Counsellor, The mighty God, The everlasting Father, The Prince of Peace.*

There were other appearances of Christ in the Old Testament. Christ appears on earth as the *Angel of the Lord* in 68 Bible references.

Class Oral Reading

Selected members of the class will now orally read the following texts to the rest of the class:

Genesis 16:7-13
Genesis 22:11-15
Exodus 3:2
Numbers 22:22-35

As other Christophanies, Christ appeared as *The Angel, Angel of Jehovah, The Angel of the Covenant, and The Messenger of the Covena*nt.

In each case the above figures are ascribed as deity, yet different from Jehovah. Christophanies and Theophanies do not serve as a ground for polytheism (the belief that there are many gods). We have already noted in a previous lesson that there is only one God and you were presented with Bible texts for this truth.

The Son of God did arrive on earth just as the prophets foretold.

(Micah 5:2) But thou, Bethlehem Ephratah, though thou be little among the thousands of Judah, yet out of thee shall he come forth unto me that is to be ruler in Israel; whose goings forth have been from of old, from everlasting.

(Psalm 2:7) I will declare the decree: the LORD hath said unto me, Thou art my Son; this day have I begotten thee.

4.3 The Incarnation of Jesus Christ

The incarnation of Christ means that the Son of God became flesh.

(John 1:1-3,14) In the beginning was the Word, and the Word was with God, and the Word was God. The same was in the beginning with God. All things were made by him; and without him was not any thing made that was made. (vs.14) And the Word was made flesh, and dwelt among us, (and we beheld his glory, the glory as of the only begotten of the Father,) full of grace and truth.

The eternal Son of God became flesh without diminishing his divine nature. God calls Adam the first man. When the Son of God took on flesh, He became the God-man for the first time in eternity.

This was the plan of God for our redemption before the foundation of the world. The Son of God would come in the flesh to accomplish our salvation in part by condemning sin in the flesh.

(Romans 8:3) For what the law could not do, in that it was weak through the flesh, God sending his own Son in the likeness of sinful flesh, and for sin, condemned sin in the flesh:

(1 John 4:2-3) Hereby know ye the Spirit of God: Every spirit that confesseth that Jesus Christ is come in the flesh is of God: And every spirit that confesseth not that Jesus Christ is come in the flesh is not of God: and this is that spirit of antichrist, whereof ye have heard that it should come; and even now already is it in the world.

We conclude then, that the incarnate Son of God was fully God and fully man. "For in him dwelleth all the fulness of the Godhead bodily." (Colossians 2:9) To deny the incarnation of Jesus Christ is heresy.

4.4 The Virgin Birth of Jesus Christ

It was necessary that the Christ be born of a virgin, not just to fulfill prophecy, but to accomplish His mission. Jesus Christ was born of the virgin Mary by the Holy Ghost.

(Matthew 1:20-23) But while he thought on these things, behold, the angel of the Lord appeared unto him in a dream, saying, Joseph, thou son of David, fear not to take unto thee Mary thy wife: for that which is conceived in her is of the Holy Ghost. And she shall bring forth a son, and thou shalt call

his name JESUS: for he shall save his people from their sins. Now all this was done, that it might be fulfilled which was spoken of the Lord by the prophet, saying, Behold, a virgin shall be with child, and shall bring forth a son, and they shall call his name Emmanuel, which being interpreted is, God with us.

We are sinners because we inherited our sin nature from our father, who inherited it from his father and from fathers all the way back to Adam.

(Romans 5:12) Wherefore, as by one man sin entered into the world, and death by sin; and so death passed upon all men, for that all have sinned:

Jesus had no earthly father, thus He inherited no sin nature. Because of Adam, we faced death, but now in Christ, we can have life.

(1 Corinthians 15:21) For since by man came death, by man came also the resurrection of the dead. For as in Adam all die, even so in Christ shall all be made alive.

4.5 The Deity of Jesus Christ

The God-man was exactly that, all God and all man. We call this the Deity of Christ.

✓ The prophets foretold it.
(Isa 9:6; Micah 5:2)

✓ The demons admitted it.
(Mt 8:28-29; Lk 4:33-35)

✓ The Son of God declared it.
(Jn 5:18; 10:30; Phil 2:6)

✓ The resurrection of Christ proved it. (Rom 8:34)

✓ The Apostles proclaimed it.
(Jn 20:28; Tit 2:13)

✓ The gospel requires it.
(Rom 10:9-13; Heb 11:6)

The Scriptures attest to the deity of Christ by demonstrating that Jesus possessed the attributes of God.

Class Oral Reading

Selected members of the class will now orally read the following texts to the rest of the class:

Mt 9:4, 28:20; Jn 1:4, 5:26, 14:6, 17:5; Acts 1:24; Eph 1:23; Col 2:3,9; Heb 1:11, 7:16,26, 13:8; 1 Jn 3:16; Rev 3:7

The attributes of God in these texts were many. Name some of them from these oral readings.

The Scriptures attest to the deity of Christ by ascribing the works of God to Jesus.

The Scriptures attest to the deity of Christ by giving Jesus honor and worship due only to God.

If our God's triune existence seems hard for you to grasp at first, it was hard for the apostles of Christ, too.

(John 14:1-10) Let not your heart be troubled: ye believe in God, believe also in me. In my Father's house are many mansions: if it were not so, I would have told you. I go to prepare a place for you. And if I go and prepare a place for you, I will come again, and receive you unto myself; that where I am, there ye may be also. And whither I go ye know, and the way ye know. Thomas saith unto him, Lord, we know not whither thou goest; and how can we know the way? Jesus saith unto him, I am the way, the truth, and the life: no man cometh unto the Father, but by me. If ye had known me, ye should have known my Father also: and from henceforth ye know him, and have seen him. Philip saith unto him, Lord, shew us the Father, and it sufficeth us. Jesus saith unto him, Have I been so long time with you, and yet hast thou not known me, Philip? he that hath seen me hath seen the Father; and how sayest thou then, Shew us the Father? Believest thou not that I am in the Father, and the Father in me? the words that I speak unto you I speak not of myself: but the Father that dwelleth in me, he doeth the works.

The "light came on" for Philip that day. No wonder Jesus had previously said, "I and my Father are one". (Jn 10:30) After the disciples saw the resurrected Saviour, their faith was complete. However, Jesus has a special compliment for believers today. He said, "Thomas, because thou hast seen me, thou hast believed: blessed are they that have not seen, and yet have believed."

This Week's Memory Verse

Jesus saith unto him, Have I been so
long time with you, and yet hast thou
not known me, Philip? he that hath
seen me hath seen the Father;
(John 14:9a)

Chapter Four Quiz & Memory Verse Fill In Study Sheet

The Doctrine of Christ, The Person of Christ

1. What is a Christophany? _____

_____

2. What does the incarnation of Christ mean? _____

_____

3. Concerning the deity of Christ -

      The prophets   _____

      The demons   _____

      The Son of God   _____

      The Resurrection   _____

      The Apostles   _____

      The Gospel   _____

4. The Scriptures attest to the deity of Christ by demonstrating that Jesus possessed the _____ of God.

5. The Scriptures attest to the deity of Christ by ascribing the _____ _____ to Jesus.

6. The Scriptures attest to the deity of Christ by giving Jesus _____ and _____ due only to God.

Write out this week's Bible verse from memory.

John 14:9

_____

_____

_____

_____

_____

Finish the Phrase

And God said, Let us _____

And he is before all things, and by him all things _____

For unto us a child is born, unto us a son is given: and the government shall be upon his shoulder: and his name shall be called _____

Hereby know ye the Spirit of God: Every spirit that confesseth that Jesus Christ is come in the flesh is _____

And every spirit that confesseth not that Jesus Christ is come in the flesh is not of God: and this is that spirit of _____

For as in Adam all die, even so in Christ shall all be made _____

Let not your heart be troubled: ye believe in God, believe also _____

For in him dwelleth all the fulness of the Godhead _____

He that hath seen me hath seen the ___

Behold, a virgin shall be with child, and shall bring forth a son, and they shall call his name Emmanuel, which being interpreted is, _____

BEST POINT MADE

Proverbs Chapter Four

What were the main themes of this chapter?

_____

_____

_____

_____

What were the instructional points meant to bring you closer to God?

_____

_____

_____

_____

What were the instructional points meant to protect you from spiritual destruction?

_____

_____

_____

_____

What things in your life could use strengthening?

_____

_____

_____

_____

Was there anything in this chapter that was of help in serving the LORD?

_____

_____

_____

_____

_____

Did you learn anything new about the LORD?

_____

_____

_____

_____

Were there any suggestions made whereby you can be a greater blessing to others?

_____

_____

_____

_____

_____

5.1 Introduction

Christians take very little time to try to understand the humanity of Christ. They do not relate well to a God incarnate with human limitations. They are more comfortable with the idea that the Son of God merely walked the face of the earth in the form of a man. To them the term "God-man" is a contradiction. After all, the term does not actually appear in the Bible. Nevertheless, the humanity of Jesus Christ is a wonderful fact that helps us to see more clearly Jesus as the perfect Lord and Saviour.

5.2 The Humanity of Jesus Christ

✓ Christ called himself "man" and was called by the same.

(John 8:40) But now ye seek to kill me, a man that hath told you the truth, which I have heard of God: this did not Abraham.

(Acts 2:22-24) Ye men of Israel, hear these words; Jesus of Nazareth, a man approved of God among you by miracles and wonders and signs, which God did by him in the midst of you, as ye yourselves also know: Him, being delivered by the determinate counsel and foreknowledge of God, ye

have taken, and by wicked hands have crucified and slain: Whom God hath raised up, having loosed the pains of death: because it was not possible that he should be holden of it.

(Romans 5:15) But not as the offence, so also is the free gift. For if through the offence of one many be dead, much more the grace of God, and the gift by grace, which is by one man, Jesus Christ, hath abounded unto many.

(1 Timothy 2:5) For there is one God, and one mediator between God and men, the man Christ Jesus;

Class Discussion Question

How does John 1:1-4, 14 reflect upon Christ's humanity?

✓ The genealogies of Jesus speak of His natural human descent.
(Mat 1:1-17)

Jesus is referenced to as the "Son of David, the Son of Abraham". This is an important point for two reasons.

First, this identity for the Christ was prophesied.

(Genesis 22:18) And in thy seed shall all the nations of the earth be blessed; because thou hast obeyed my voice.

When the people hailed Jesus as the Son of David, it angered the Pharisees.

(Matthew 21:15-16) And when the chief priests and scribes saw the wonderful things that he did, and the children crying in the temple, and saying, Hosanna to the Son of David; they were sore displeased, And said unto him, Hearest thou what these say? And Jesus saith unto them, Yea; have ye never read, Out of the mouth of babes and sucklings thou hast perfected praise?

Secondly, the title "Son of David" clearly establishes Jesus as Jewish. Certainly this establishes His humanity.

(Galatians 3:16) Now to Abraham and his seed were the promises made. He saith not, And to seeds, as of many; but as of one, And to thy seed, which is Christ.

The question might come to mind, how was Jesus a descendant of Abraham and David seeing that Joseph was not His father? The answer is clearly in Mary. She was of the Tribe of Judah and of the lineage of David. Notice what the angel first said to her.

(Luke 1:30-33) And the angel said unto her, Fear not, Mary: for thou hast found favour with God. and, behold, thou shalt conceive in thy womb, and bring forth a son, and shalt call his name JESUS. He shall be great, and shall be called the Son of the Highest: and the Lord God shall give unto him the throne of his father David: And he shall reign over the house of Jacob for ever; and of his kingdom there shall be no end.

✓ His title as the "son of man" speaks strongly of his humanity.

(Mark 10:45) For even the Son of man came not to be ministered unto, but to minister, and to give his life a ransom for many.

✓ He was subject to the laws of human nature.

Jesus gave up much to come to earth. He exchanged a palace for a stable. He was born into this world through the natural birthing process when his mother *"brought forth her first born son, and wrapped him in swaddling clothes, and laid him in a manger"*. Jesus exchanged the place where He knew only honor and praise for a place where His own would receive Him not. He had never previously suffered anything and He certainly had never been forsaken by the Father.

The Son of God gave up more than just his throne in Heaven while on earth. He also voluntarily set aside the full use of the "omnis" (Omnipresence,

Omnipotence, Omniscience). These self-imposed limitations were very real and were not a "charade", as Professor Ben Witherington III rightly pointed out.

✓ After the virgin birth, Jesus proceeded through human stages of development.

(Luke 2:40) And the child grew, and waxed strong in spirit, filled with wisdom: and the grace of God was upon him.

(Luke 2:46-49) And it came to pass, that after three days they found him in the temple, sitting in the midst of the doctors, both hearing them, and asking them questions. And all that heard him were astonished at his understanding and answers. And when they saw him, they were amazed: and his mother said unto him, Son, why hast thou thus dealt with us? behold, thy father and I have sought thee sorrowing. And he said unto them, How is it that ye sought me? wist ye not that I must be about my Father's business?

(Luke 2:52) And Jesus increased in wisdom and stature, and in favour with God and man.

5.3 Christ's Humanity Summarized

Christ's humanity can be summarized in 11 categories:
1.   Birth (Lk 2:11)
2.   Growth (Lk 2:40,52)
3.   Fatigue (Jn 4:6)
4.   Hunger (Mt 4:2)
5.   Thirst (Jn 19:28)
6.   Indignation (Mk 10:14)
7.   Compassion (Mt 9:36)
8.   Sorrow (Mt 26:37)
9.   Temptation (Heb 4:15)
10.   Suffering (Heb 5:8)
11.   Death (1 Cor 5:3)

5.4 Why a Saviour that was both Deity and Humanity?

✓ **First ... To Make Him a Personal Saviour**

Jesus wanted to be to us all that our human flesh would desire in a personal Saviour. A Saviour who knew our sufferings and pains first hand. A Saviour who knew our heartaches and griefs first hand. A Saviour who knew our sorrows and rejections first hand. A Saviour who knew what it was to be powerfully tempted of Satan. While He knew all of these things before He came to us... He wanted man to accept this truth by seeing it.

Why a Saviour that was both Deity and Humanity?

✓ **Secondly ... To Make Him a Perfect Mediator between Man and God the Father**

Listen to this great quotation by an unknown author used in several old catechisms.

"The union of the two natures in one person is necessary to constitute Jesus Christ as a proper mediator between man and God. His two fold nature gives him fellowship with both parties. His manhood allowed him to experience our infirmities, as well as our temptations." (Heb 2:17,18; 4:14-16) Both his deity and his humanity combine to move the hearts of man. (Heb 7:25)

(1 Timothy 2:3-5) For this is good and acceptable in the sight of God our Saviour; Who will have all men to be saved, and to come unto the knowledge of the truth. For there is one God, and one mediator between God and men, the man Christ Jesus;

A mediator is one who mediates. He serves as a go-between to work with opposing sides in order to bring about an agreement or settlement. The goal of a mediator is to resolve a dispute. God had a dispute with us because of our sin. As a holy God who is also a just God, He cannot accept our sin. Sin is a transgression of the law of God (1 Jn 3:4) and a rebellion against the will of God. It prevents man from bringing God glory, honor, and pleasure. Simply, our sin stood between us and Him.

All people are sinners and there is nothing that we can do to resolve this conflict. Without a mediator we face only eternal damnation. No man or priest can fill this position or take on the roll of a mediator for your sins between you and God.

(Hebrews 9:15) And for this cause he is the mediator of the new testament, that by means of death, for the redemption of the transgressions that were under the first testament, they which are called might receive the promise of eternal inheritance.

(Hebrews 4:12-16) For the word of God is quick, and powerful, and sharper than any twoedged sword, piercing even to the dividing asunder of soul and spirit, and of the joints and marrow, and is a discerner of the thoughts and intents of the heart. Neither is there any creature that is not manifest in his sight: but all things are naked and opened unto the eyes of him with whom we have to do. Seeing then that we have a great high priest, that is passed into the heavens, Jesus the Son of God, let us hold fast our profession. For we have not an high priest which cannot be touched with the feeling of our infirmities; but was in all points tempted like as we are, yet without sin. Let us therefore come boldly unto the throne of grace, that we may obtain mercy, and find grace to help in time of need.

Why a Saviour that was both Deity and Humanity?

✓ Thirdly ... To Make Him the Only Possible Sacrifice for our Sins

(Hebrews 9:12-14) Neither by the blood of goats and calves, but by his own blood he entered in once into the holy place, having obtained eternal redemption for us.
For if the blood of bulls and of goats, and the ashes of an heifer sprinkling the unclean, sanctifieth to the purifying of the flesh: How much more shall the blood of Christ, who through the eternal Spirit offered himself without spot to God, purge your conscience from dead works to serve the living God?

(Romans 5:8-9) But God commendeth his love toward us, in that, while we were yet sinners, Christ died for us. Much more then, being now justified by his blood, we shall be saved from wrath through him.

A Poetic Tribute by an Unknown Author

"In the beginning was the Word. The Word was made flesh and dwelled among us. We beheld His glory, ... the glory of the only begotten Son of God. The Word, who is Christ, is the beginning. He is the beginner of the beginning. He is the beginner in whom the beginning began. In fact, He is the beginning before the beginning began. Thus, He is the beginning who did not begin. He did not start, for He had nowhere to come from. He will not stop, for He knows no eternal boundaries He is the eternal logos of forever and ever. He has nowhere to go, for He occupies the immensity of space. He does not look around for His eyes are in every place. He is older than time, yet younger than the future. He is Christ! The son of the living God. He thought it not robbery to be equal with God. How could He, for He was God. He is what He was. He was what He is. And what He is He always will be. And when ten billion years have burned into the ashes of forever, His face will still be beaming with the bliss of eternal and divine youth."

(Colossians 2:8-9) Beware lest any man spoil you through philosophy and vain deceit, after the tradition of men, after the rudiments of the world, and not after Christ. For in him dwelleth all the fulness of the Godhead bodily.

This Week's Memory Verse

Beware lest any man spoil you through philosophy and vain deceit, after the tradition of men, after the rudiments of the world, and not after Christ. For in him dwelleth all the fulness of the Godhead bodily. (Colossians 2:8-9)

The Doctrine of Christ, The Humanity of Christ

1. Christ called Himself a _____ and was called by the same.

2. The _____ of Jesus speak of His natural human descent.

3. His title as the _____ speaks strongly of his humanity.

4. He was subject to the laws of human _____.

5. After the virgin birth, Jesus proceeded through _____

    _____.

6. Why a Saviour that was both Deity and Humanity?

    To make Him a _____

    To make Him a _____

    To make Him the only possible _____

Write out this week's Bible verse from memory.

Colossians 2:8-9

_____

_____

_____

_____

_____

Finish the Phrase

For there is one God, and one mediator between God and men, _____

And Jesus increased in wisdom and stature, and _____

For the word of God is quick, and powerful, and sharper than any _____

Seeing then that we have a great high priest, that is passed into the heavens, Jesus the Son of God, let us hold fast our _____

For we have not an high priest which cannot be touched with the feeling of our _____ *but was in all points tempted like as we are, yet without sin.*

Neither by the blood of goats and calves, but by his own blood he entered in once into the holy place, having obtained eternal _____

BEST POINT MADE

Proverbs Chapter Five

What were the main themes of this chapter?

_____

_____

_____

_____

What were the instructional points meant to bring you closer to God?

_____

_____

_____

What were the instructional points meant to protect you from spiritual destruction?

_____

_____

_____

_____

What things in your life could use strengthening?

_____

_____

_____

_____

_____

Was there anything in this chapter that was of help in serving the LORD?

_____

_____

_____

_____

_____

Did you learn anything new about the LORD?

_____

_____

_____

Were there any suggestions made whereby you can be a greater blessing to others?

_____

_____

_____

_____

_____

_____

6.1 Six Descriptive Terms

(2 Corinthians 13:4) For though he was crucified through weakness, yet he liveth by the power of God. For we also are weak in him, but we shall live with him by the power of God toward you.

There are six terms that describe what Christ did for us on the cross. When you understand these terms, you understand the depth of Christ's sacrificial work for us.

✓ ATONEMENT ... to forgive and cover up so as to remove the condemnation of sin

(Romans 6:23) For the wages of sin is death; but the gift of God is eternal life through Jesus Christ our Lord.

(Romans 4:6) Even as David also describeth the blessedness of the man, unto whom God imputeth righteousness without works, Saying, Blessed are they whose iniquities are forgiven, and whose sins are covered.

Sin brought about a two-fold judgement. First, death and an eternal separation from God. This death is both physical and spiritual. Secondly, sin brought about a broken relationship with God.

(Isaiah) 59:1) Behold, the LORD'S hand is not shortened, that it cannot save; neither his ear heavy, that it cannot hear: But your iniquities have separated between you and your God, and your sins have hid his face from you, that he will not hear.

In the Old Testament we see the picture of Christ's future atonement in the use of the scapegoat on the Day of Atonement. The Day of Atonement took place each year on the tenth day of the seventh month.

Two goats were chosen. (READ Lev 16:1-19) The first goat was killed and its blood shed as a sin offering. First, atonement was made for the sins of the priest. Secondly, atonement was made for the Tabernacle itself because God considered it fouled by the sins of the people. Thirdly, atonement was made for the people. The priest took the blood and entered the Holy of Holies. There he sprinkled that blood on the Mercy Seat. This pictured the Divine covering of the people's sins. God's wrath was then appeased. The second goat was called the scapegoat. (READ Lev 16:20-22) The priest symbolically placed the sins of the people upon the head of the live goat. The goat was then taken far into the wilderness and released. As the goat wandered off, the sins of the people were carried away forever. The Day of Atonement took place on the same day of every year. God had painted a picture for Israel of Messiah yet to come. He would become the scapegoat for the sins of all mankind.

(Isaiah 53:3-6) He is despised and rejected of men; a man of sorrows, and acquainted with grief: and we hid as it were our faces from him; he was despised, and we esteemed him not. Surely he hath borne our griefs, and carried our sorrows: yet we did esteem him stricken, smitten of God, and afflicted. But he was wounded for our transgressions, he was bruised for our iniquities: the chastisement of our peace was upon him; and with his stripes we are healed. All we like sheep have gone astray; we have turned every one to his own way; and the LORD hath laid on him the iniquity of us all.

(Psalm 103:12) As far as the east is from the west, so far hath he removed our transgressions from us.

(Micah 7:19) He will turn again, he will have compassion upon us; he will subdue our iniquities; and thou wilt cast all their sins into the depths of the sea.

Our sins were put upon Jesus Christ and (as our scapegoat) He carried away our sins.

"Gone, gone, gone, gone
yes my sins are gone.
Now my soul is free and in my heart's a song.
Buried in the deepest sea,
yes that's good enough for me.
I shall live eternally, praise God,
my sins are gone."

✓ RECONCILIATION ... to make equivalent

Sin made us unable to fellowship with a holy God. In Christ's atoning sacrifice, He forgave, covered, and took away our sin making it possible for God the Father to fellowship with us again.

Illustration

When a checking account is opened the bank asks the owner of that account to reconcile their check ledger to the bank's monthly statement. If the balance does not agree, the mistake must be found and adjusted to correctness. Bringing the statement and the ledger into agreement is called reconciling. When the two agree they are equivalent and are considered to be reconciled.

The blood of Christ covers the error of our sin in a way that God only sees the righteousness of Christ in us. In Christ we become reconciled to God.

(Ephesians 2:14-16) For he is our peace, who hath made both one, and hath broken down the middle wall of

partition between us; Having abolished in his flesh the enmity, even the law of commandments contained in ordinances; for to make in himself of twain one new man, so making peace; And that he might reconcile both unto God in one body by the cross, having slain the enmity thereby:

✓ PROPITIATION ... to appease or placate the wrath of God

Christ's sacrifice caused God to look favorably upon us again.

(Romans 3:25) Whom God hath set forth to be a propitiation through faith in his blood, to declare his righteousness for the remission of sins that are past, through the forbearance of God;

(1 John 2:2) And he is the propitiation for our sins: and not for ours only, but also for the sins of the whole world.

(1 John 4:10) Herein is love, not that we loved God, but that he loved us, and sent his Son to be the propitiation for our sins.

"The necessity of appeasing God is something many religions have in common. In ancient pagan religions, as well as in many religions today, the idea is taught that man appeases God by offering various gifts or sacrifices. However, the Bible teaches that God Himself has provided the only means through which His wrath can be appeased and sinful man can be reconciled to Him. In the New Testament, the act of propitiation always refers to the work of God and not the sacrifices or gifts offered by man." GotQuestions.org

✓ REDEMPTION and RANSOM ... both terms signify a release from captivity

Redemption ... To buy back what is rightfully yours. Ransom ... Payment to release another.

Illustration

A boy spent many weeks in his garage crafting a small sail boat from wood, cloth, and string. He carved, sanded, and painted it to perfection. He was very pleased with his creation. On a sunny day he took it down to the river to sail it. Tied to a string, he thought the boat was safe and secure. But along came a wind and the string broke. As the boat sailed out of sight the boy was very sad. One day he was walking in the village and saw his boat in the window of a pawn shop. He ran in to tell the owner of the shop that he had made the boat and that it belonged to him. The shop owner was not very accommodating and told the boy he would have to buy the boat back for $12.00. For weeks the boy did many little jobs and finally earned the money. Rushing back to the pawn shop he bought the boat back. As he walked out of the shop he said to the little boat, "Now you are twice mine".

✓ SUBSTITUTION ... He took our death sentence upon himself and satisfied the justice of God

(2 Corinthians 5:21) *For he hath made him to be sin for us, who knew no sin; that we might be made the righteousness of God in him.*

This is not to say that Christ is a substitute for all people throughout the ages. His substitutionary benefit is only applied when one accepts salvation in Him.

(1 Peter 3:18) *For Christ also hath once suffered for sins, the just for the unjust, that he might bring us to God, being put to death in the flesh, but quickened by the Spirit:*

6.2 The Resurrection of Christ from the Dead

(Matthew 28:5-7) *And the angel answered and said unto the women, Fear not ye: for I know that ye seek Jesus, which was crucified. He is not here: for he is risen, as he said. Come, see the place where the Lord lay. And go quickly, and tell his disciples that he is risen from the dead; and, behold, he goeth before you into Galilee; there shall ye see him: lo, I have told you.*

Christ's resurrection was a literal and bodily one. Christ walked out of that tomb bodily and alive. He was fully recognizable. After the resurrection, he appeared in person to over 500 people. Christ called attention to his own resurrected body.

(Acts 1:3) *To whom also he shewed himself alive after his passion by many infallible proofs, being seen of them forty days, and speaking of the things pertaining to the kingdom of God.*

(John 20:24-29) *But Thomas, one of the twelve, called Didymus, was not with them when Jesus came. The other disciples therefore said unto him, We have seen the Lord. But he said unto them, Except I shall see in his hands the print of the nails, and put my finger into the print of the nails, and thrust my hand into his side, I will not believe. And after eight days again his disciples were within, and Thomas with them: then came Jesus, the doors being shut, and stood in the midst, and said, Peace be unto you. Then saith he to Thomas, Reach hither thy finger, and behold my hands; and reach hither thy hand, and thrust it into my side: and be not faithless, but believing. And Thomas answered and said unto him, My Lord and my God. Jesus saith unto him, Thomas, because thou hast seen me, thou hast believed: blessed are they that have not seen, and yet have believed.*

To deny a physical, bodily resurrection is to be guilty of apostasy.

Who raised Christ from the dead? The Bible says that He was raised by the Father. (Rom 6:4; 10:9) It also says that He was raised by the power of His own might. (Jn 10:18). And it says that He was quickened (made alive) by the Holy Spirit. (1 Pet 3:18; Rom 8:11)

Do we have a contradiction of Bible facts? The obvious conclusion is that Christ was raised from the dead by a coordinated power of the triune Godhead.

As a resurrected God/man he became the perfected man, the prototype of glorified humanity. (1 Cor 15:35-37; Phil 3:20,21) He not only conquered death for us, but He became our own resurrection. (Jn 11:25-26; 2 Tim 1:10) We shall be like him (1 Jn 3:2): a body recognizably the same, (Lk 24:36-43; Jn 20:27), a body not limited to time. (Lk 24:31), a body changed and glorified. (Mt 22:30; 1 Cor 6:13; 15:30-38,51)

The resurrected Christ is now called the judge over the living and the dead. (Acts 10;42; 7:31)

The resurrection of Christ from the dead proved four very important things.

✓ It proved that Old Testament prophecies are true.

These prophecies clearly indicated a resurrected Saviour (Isa 25:8; 53:1-12). The Jews were blind to this truth and were not and are not looking for a crucified and resurrected Saviour.

✓ It proved that the predictions Christ made about Himself were true.

Christ foretold his death and resurrection to the apostles. (Mt 16:21) Christ foretold his death and resurrection to the temple leaders. (Lk 13:32) Christ foretold his death and resurrection to the common people. (Jn 2:19)

✓ It proved that Christ is Deity. (Rom 1:3,4; Acts 2:30-37)

Everyone else in history claiming to be deity is still in their grave. Christ stands alone in raising from the dead. Those who were raised from the dead in the Bible were not raised by their own power. They died only once and were taken up to glory at some unmentioned time. (Heb 9:27) Only two were taken up to Heaven without dying: Elijah and Enoch. These two will return to earth as the "two witnesses" of the Tribulation. They will meet their death then.

✓ It proved that He has the power to grant everlasting life. (Jn 11:25,26; 1 Pet 1:3; 2 Tim 1:10)

What if the resurrection of Christ never happened and Christ still lays in the grave?

Christ would not be God.

The Scriptures would not be true.

Our salvation would not have been accomplished.

Our condemnation would still be intact.

If Christ did not raise from the dead our preaching is in vain and your faith also.

This Week's Memory Verse

For he hath made him to be sin for us, who knew no sin; that we might be made the righteousness of God in him. (2 Corinthians 5:21)

The Doctrine of Christ, The Sacrifice and Resurrection

1. Name the six terms that describe what Christ did for us on the cross AND their definitions

_____

_____

_____

_____

_____

_____

2. The resurrection of Christ from the dead proved four very important things. List them.

_____

_____

_____

_____

_____

Write out this week's Bible verse from memory.

2 Corinthians 5:21

_____

_____

_____

_____

_____

Finish the Phrase

For though he was crucified through weakness, yet he liveth by the _____

Blessed are they whose iniquities are forgiven, and whose sins are _____

Behold, the LORD'S hand is not shortened, that it cannot _____

Herein is love, not that we loved God, but that he loved us, and sent his Son to be the _____

Jesus saith unto him, Thomas, because thou hast seen me, thou hast believed: blessed are they that have not seen, and yet have _____

But your iniquities have separated between you and your God, that he will not _____

As far as the east is from the west, so far hath he removed _____

Extra Credit Chapel Notes

BEST POINT MADE

Proverbs Chapter Six

What were the main themes of this chapter?

_____

_____

_____

_____

What were the instructional points meant to bring you closer to God?

_____

_____

_____

_____

What were the instructional points meant to protect you from spiritual destruction?

_____

_____

_____

_____

What things in your life could use strengthening?

_____

_____

_____

_____

Was there anything in this chapter that was of help in serving the LORD?

_____

_____

_____

_____

Did you learn anything new about the LORD?

_____

_____

_____

_____

Were there any suggestions made whereby you can be a greater blessing to others?

_____

_____

_____

_____

_____

7.1 The Trinity and the Holy Spirit

We have already seen that God is One God, triune in His existence as God the Father, Son, and Holy Spirit. We proved that the Father is recognized as God. We proved that Jesus Christ, God's Son is recognized as God. Now we will examine further Biblical evidence that the Holy Spirit is deity and is the third person in the trinity.

Beware of the religious groups that teach that the Holy Spirit is little more than the energy or power of God. These groups deny that the Holy Spirit is a person of the Godhead or that he is a third person of the Trinity. The material you are about to examine in this chapter will illustrate very well for you the truth of the Holy Spirit's personage.

7.2 Proofs of the Holy Spirit's Divine Personage

The Bible attributes Divine powers and qualities to the Holy Spirit.

Omniscience

(John 14:26) But the Comforter, which is the Holy Ghost, whom the Father will send in my name, he shall teach you all things, and bring all things to your remembrance, whatsoever I have said unto you.

(John 16:12-13) I have yet many things to say unto you, but ye cannot bear them now. howbeit when he, the Spirit of truth, is come, he will guide you into all truth: for he shall not speak of himself; but whatsoever he shall hear, that shall he speak: and he will shew you things to come.

These texts clearly point to the Omniscience of the Holy Spirit. He teaches us all things. He guides us to all truth. In fact, He is the Spirit of truth. Were the Holy Spirit just the outward energy of God the Bible would not refer to Him as "he" nor credit him with this attribute.

Omnipotence

(Luke 1:35) And the angel answered and said unto her, The Holy Ghost shall come upon thee, and the power of the Highest shall overshadow thee: therefore also that holy thing which shall be born of thee shall be called the Son of God.

Language is incapable of expressing the full mystery of this incredible act of God. The conception would be brought about by the Holy Spirit resulting in the child being the Son of God.

Eternity

(Hebrews 9:14) How much more shall the blood of Christ, who through the eternal Spirit offered himself without spot to God, purge your conscience from dead works to serve the living God?

The eternal Holy Spirit empowered the humanity of Jesus Christ to offer Himself without spot to God and in this purged our consciences from dead works.

Holiness

(Ephesians 4:30) And grieve not the holy Spirit of God, whereby ye are sealed unto the day of redemption.

Who is this personage that can be grieved? It is none other than the third part of the Godhead, the Holy Spirit. We, the children of God, are not to grieve him by our unholy actions of the flesh. What is in the Holy Spirit by which He can be grieved? Holiness! It is His holiness that is offended by our carnal words, deeds, and thoughts.

Omnipresence

(Psalm 139:7-8) Whither shall I go from thy spirit? or whither shall I flee from thy presence? If I ascend up into heaven, thou art there: if I make my bed in hell, behold, thou art there.

The Psalmist goes on to say that there is nowhere we can go or hide where we are not in the presence of the Spirit of God. It is His ministry to come along side the work of Christ on earth empowering both the believer and the work of Christ being done by the believer. He dwells in every believer in all places simultaneously. In the next lesson we will examine more of this work.

Absolute Truth (Jn 16:13)

(Psalm 117:2) For his merciful kindness is great toward us: and the truth of the LORD endureth for ever. Praise ye the LORD.

(John 16:13) Howbeit when he, the Spirit of truth, is come, he will guide you into all truth: for he shall not speak of himself; but whatsoever he shall hear, that shall he speak: and he will shew you things to come.

We have learned in previous lessons that God is truth. He is the determiner of all truth and anything contrary to God is untruth.

God's Word is all truth and nothing but the truth. Though the truth of God's Word is hidden from unbelievers, the believer is promised that the Holy Spirit will reveal to him the truth. In the above text the Holy Spirit is revealed as our guide to that truth. It is important that you pray before you read the Word and ask the Holy Spirit to teach you.

Class Discussion Questions

1. Can you think of things that man says is true, but what they say is contrary to the clear teaching of God's Word?

Nothing in the Word of God has ever been shown to be untrue. This lends accreditation to the inspiration and preservation of God's Word. It is amazing that forty men writing over a period of 1500 years never contradict each other. From a humanistic view this is impossible. With God all things are possible.

Life

(Romans 8:2) *For the law of the Spirit of life in Christ Jesus hath made me free from the law of sin and death.*

The Scriptures are the law of the Spirit being that He is the inspiration and writer of its words. By the same Spirit the truth of the written Word is conveyed to our hearts. The Holy Spirit is the Spirit of life in that through Him we discover the way of salvation and life through Christ.

Taking it a step further, no one can know the truth of God's Word without the ministry of the Holy Spirit in them.

What else demonstrates the personage of the Holy Spirit?

The Bible attributes Divine works to the Holy Spirit.

The work of creation is attributed to the Holy Spirit.

(Job 33:4) *The Spirit of God hath made me, and the breath of the Almighty hath given me life.*

(Psalm 104:30) *Thou sendest forth thy spirit, they are created: and thou renewest the face of the earth.*

Creation is clearly a work of the Triune God, all of Him and the three personages of Him.

The work of regeneration is attributed to the Holy Spirit.

(John 3:3-7) *Jesus answered and said unto him, Verily, verily, I say unto thee, Except a man be born again, he cannot see the kingdom of God. Nicodemus saith unto him, How can a man be born when he is old? can he enter the second time into his mother's womb, and be born? Jesus answered, Verily, verily, I say unto thee, Except a man be born of water and of the Spirit, he cannot enter into the kingdom of God.*

That which is born of the flesh is flesh; and that which is born of the Spirit is spirit. Marvel not that I said unto thee, Ye must be born again.

Nicodemus had misunderstood Jesus when Jesus told him that he had to be born again. Knowing it to be impossible to enter into one's mother's womb a second time, Nicodemus was confused. The reference to "water" in this text is not speaking of baptism, but of the water involved in the birth process. Jesus in answering Nicodemus said that one must be born of water (physical) and of the Spirit (spiritual). Were water a reference to baptism, then Jesus would not have answered Nicodemus' question.

(Titus 3:5) Not by works of righteousness which we have done, but according to his mercy he saved us, by the washing of regeneration, and renewing of the Holy Ghost;

What else demonstrates the personage of the Holy Spirit?

The work of resurrecting believers from the dead is attributed to the Holy Spirit.

(Romans 8:11) But if the Spirit of him that raised up Jesus from the dead dwell in you, he that raised up Christ from the dead shall also quicken your mortal bodies by his Spirit that dwelleth in you.

While all dead will be raised to stand before God, this text speaks of Christians who are not only raised from physical death, but they are raised from mortality to immortality.

(1 Corinthians 15:51-54) Behold, I shew you a mystery; We shall not all sleep, but we shall all be changed, In a moment, in the twinkling of an eye, at the last trump: for the trumpet shall sound, and the dead shall be raised incorruptible, and we shall be changed. For this corruptible must put on incorruption, and this mortal must put on immortality. So when this corruptible shall have put on incorruption, and this mortal shall have put on immortality, then shall be brought to pass the saying that is written, Death is swallowed up in victory.

What else demonstrates the personage of the Holy Spirit?

The Holy Spirit has personality.

If the Holy Spirit was the energy of God or the power of God, there would be no personality in Him. Yet, the Bible clearly attributes personality to Him.

✓ He has a will.

(1 Corinthians 12:11) But all these worketh that one and the selfsame Spirit, dividing to every man severally as he will.

The spiritual gifts given to Christians to help carry out the work of God are many. Christians are often asked, "what is your spiritual gift?" No Christian has just one spiritual gift. The Holy Spirit divided the gifts and granted at least two or more of them to every believer. The word "severally" in our verse means more than one. Every believer is a multi-talented servant of the Lord Jesus Christ.

✓ He has a mind.

Romans 8:27 And he that searcheth the hearts knoweth what is the mind of the Spirit, because he maketh intercession for the saints according to the will of God.

Energy has no mind of its own. Only personage does. The mind of the Spirit is always in complete agreement with the mind of He who searches the hearts. Even when we mistakenly pray for the wrong things, the Holy Spirit intercedes for us and speaks for us before the Father correcting our prayers before Him. In other words, the Holy Spirit asks for the right things on our behalf.

One pastor humorously illustrated this truth and suggested that when we pray for a warm coat in freezing weather, the Holy Spirit puts that request before the Father and says, "Father, he prayed for a warm coat, but it is mighty cold down there. He needs a warm hat too." While this illustration is an over simplification, it portrays a right principle.

✓ He has thought, knowledge, and words.

(1 Corinthians 2:10-13) But God hath revealed them unto us by his Spirit: for the Spirit searcheth all things, yea, the deep things of God. For what man knoweth the things of a man, save the spirit of man which is in him? even so the things of God knoweth no man, but the Spirit of God. Now we have received, not the spirit of the world, but the spirit which is of God; that we might know the things that are freely given to us of God. Which things also we speak, not in the words which man's wisdom teacheth, but which the Holy Ghost teacheth; comparing spiritual things with spiritual.

✓ He can be lied to.

(Acts 5:1-3) But a certain man named Ananias, with Sapphira his wife, sold a possession, And kept back part of the price, his wife also being privy to it, and brought a certain part, and laid it at the apostles' feet. But Peter said, Ananias, why hath Satan filled thine heart to lie to the Holy Ghost, and to keep back part of the price of the land?

✓ He can be grieved.

(Ephesians 4:30) And grieve not the

holy Spirit of God, whereby ye are sealed unto the day of redemption.

✓ He can be blasphemed. (Mk 3:29; Lk 12:10)

(Mark 3:29) But he that shall blaspheme against the Holy Ghost hath never forgiveness, but is in danger of eternal damnation:

(Luke 12:10) And whosoever shall speak a word against the Son of man, it shall be forgiven him: but unto him that blasphemeth against the Holy Ghost it shall not be forgiven.

Blasphemy of the Holy Spirit has often been called the "unpardonable sin". What is blasphemy of the Holy Spirit? While there may be numerous ways to blaspheme the Holy Spirit there is one of these described for us in Scripture. Look at the following text. Would you say that this sin is unpardonable?

(Revelation 22:18-19) For I testify unto every man that heareth the words of the prophecy of this book, If any man shall add unto these things, God shall add unto him the plagues that are written in this book: And if any man shall take away from the words of the book of this prophecy, God shall take away his part out of the book of life, and out of the holy city, and from the things which are written in this book.

Why would this sin be blasphemy of

the Holy Spirit? The answer is that the Holy Scriptures are the breath of the Holy Spirit, inspired by Him, and preserved by Him.

One ought to exercise extreme caution in the translation of God's Word taking great care not to add anything, remove anything or change anything. Modern and contemporary translators who profit by new versions are in grave danger.

(2 Peter 1:19-2) We have also a more sure word of prophecy; whereunto ye do well that ye take heed, as unto a light that shineth in a dark place, until the day dawn, and the day star arise in your hearts: Knowing this first, that no prophecy of the scripture is of any private interpretation. For the prophecy came not in old time by the will of man: but holy men of God spake as they were moved by the Holy Ghost.

This Week's Memory Verse

But he that shall blaspheme against the Holy Ghost hath never forgiveness, but is in danger of eternal damnation: (Mark 3:29)

The Doctrine of the Holy Spirit

1. Name the three proofs that the Holy Spirit is personage (a person).

_____

_____

_____

2. Name the six things we listed for the Holy Spirit having personality.

_____

_____

_____

_____

_____

_____

3. What are the three divine works we attributed to the Holy Spirit?

_____

_____

_____

Write out this week's Bible verse from memory.

Mark 3:29

_____

_____

_____

_____

_____

Finish the Phrase

But the Comforter, which is the Holy Ghost, whom the Father will send in my name, he shall teach _____

howbeit when he, the Spirit of truth, is come, he will guide you into all _____

he shall teach you all things, and bring all things to your _____

And grieve not _____

and the truth of the LORD endureth _____

Except a man be born of water and of the Spirit _____

For this corruptible must put on _____

this mortal must put on _____

And he that searcheth the hearts knoweth what is the mind of the _____

If any man shall add unto these things, God shall add unto him the _____

And if any man shall take away from the words of the book of this prophecy, God shall take away his part out of _____

BEST POINT MADE

Proverbs Chapter Seven

What were the main themes of this chapter?

_____

_____

_____

_____

_____

What were the instructional points meant to bring you closer to God?

_____

_____

_____

_____

What were the instructional points meant to protect you from spiritual destruction?

_____

_____

_____

_____

What things in your life could use strengthening?

_____

_____

_____

_____

_____

Was there anything in this chapter that was of help in serving the LORD?

_____

_____

_____

_____

_____

Did you learn anything new about the LORD?

_____

_____

_____

_____

Were there any suggestions made whereby you can be a greater blessing to others?

_____

_____

_____

_____

_____

_____

8.1 The Twofold Ministry of the Holy Spirit on Earth

The Holy Spirit's ministry is primarily twofold on this earth:

✓ To lift up the name and ministry of Jesus Christ, the Son of God, by leading sinners to repentance.

✓ To lift up the name and ministry of Jesus Christ, the Son of God, by ministering to the personal spiritual needs of Christians and empowering their Christian service.

The Holy Spirit never lifts up nor magnifies Himself. This is the error of many charismatic groups. They openly and directly lift up and magnify the Holy Spirit. It is common for these groups to lift up the Holy Spirit in such a way so as to have the effect of giving Jesus Christ a secondary place.

8.2 Ten Ways the Holy Spirit Ministers Through Christians

The Holy Spirit's influence and His ministry in the lives of Christians are abundant and multiple.

The Spirit ministers to Christians in ten primary ways.

1. The Spirit dwells in them and gives them peace of heart.

(Romans 8:11) But if the Spirit of him that raised up Jesus from the dead dwell in you, he that raised up Christ from the dead shall also quicken your mortal bodies by his Spirit that dwelleth in you.

(John 14:27) Peace I leave with you, my peace I give unto you: not as the world giveth, give I unto you. Let not your heart be troubled, neither let it be afraid.

The indwelling of the Spirit is different from the "filling" of the Spirit or the "anointing" of the Spirit.

The indwelling of the Spirit is the residency of the Spirit in your heart and life. He takes up residence in the heart of the believer the moment he or she receives Christ as their personal Saviour.

2. The Spirit teaches them what they need to know and brings it to their memory when it is needed.

(John 14:26) But the Comforter, which is the Holy Ghost, whom the Father will send in my name, he shall teach you all things, and bring all things to your remembrance, whatsoever I have

said unto you.

These are the things we need to know and remember, not only for our lives, but also for our ministries.

3. The Spirit is their source of spiritual power and anoints them to do God's work.

(Acts 1:8) But ye shall receive power, after that the Holy Ghost is come upon you: and ye shall be witnesses unto me both in Jerusalem, and in all Judaea, and in Samaria, and unto the uttermost part of the earth.

(Matthew 10:19) But when they deliver you up, take no thought how or what ye shall speak: for it shall be given you in that same hour what ye shall speak. For it is not ye that speak, but the Spirit of your Father which speaketh in you.

If we attempt to do God's work in the flesh, we reap shallow results. Without the power of the Holy Spirit our work will only look good, sound good, and feel good, but it will not bring forth genuine spiritual fruit.

(Romans 8:8-9) So then they that are in the flesh cannot please God. But ye are not in the flesh, but in the Spirit, if so be that the Spirit of God dwell in you. Now if any man have not the Spirit of Christ, he is none of his.

8.3 The Fruit of the Spirit

In an extended way, the Spirit changes us and manifests Himself through us in a way that does not come natural to us. This is called the fruit of the Spirit.

God cannot use the real you. The real you has so many character flaws that you are useless to God in that state. By nature we are all self-centered. By nature we are all desirous of attention, importance, and recognition. By nature we are always right and never wrong. By nature we think of ourselves more highly than we ought to think. By nature we want power, authority, respect! These are some of the reasons why God cannot use us the way we are. He has to change us from the inside out. When He does the manifestations of these changes are called the fruit of the Spirit.

(Galatians 5:22-23) But the fruit of the Spirit is love, joy, peace, longsuffering, gentleness, goodness, faith, Meekness, temperance: against such there is no law.

LOVE - The Greek word in this text is Agape'. This is a love that is absolutely unconditional, indestructible, and which cannot fade. It means that no matter what someone may do to you by way of insult or injury, your love for that person remains strong and completely intact. It causes you to constantly seek their highest good. In the flesh you cannot love the unlovable.

JOY - Joy is not happiness. Happiness depends largely upon whether things happen to be going your way or not. When you are unhappy, it's because things are not going right for you at that moment. Joy has no base in material things or events, but rises above them. Joy indicates a continuous state of inner well being and absolute confidence and is reflected on and through our entire outer being.

Joy comes from believing that God is on the throne dictating every moment of your life. Joy does not rise and fall upon the circumstances you are in. It rises above them knowing that there is a day coming when circumstances won't be a problem any more.

PEACE - Peace is so similar to joy that people often get the two definitions mixed up. While joy is an inner well being knowing that God is still in control; peace is a sense of relief, rest, and security that comes when something held captive is set free and given life again. Peace is a whole new outlook upon the future. The peace of God comes when your condemned state has been pardoned by the Son of God.

LONGSUFFERING - Longsuffering is a word for great patience. It is God's definition of never-ending PATIENCE. When a person is filled with the Holy Spirit, heavenly waterfalls literally douse the fires of anger. A Holy Spirit-filled person feels no vengeance.

GENTLENESS - It means gracious, tenderhearted, kindness, and easy to be entreated.

GOODNESS - It means totally equipped to carry out good works, and strongly denotes the quality of usefulness. The fruit brings us from a self-centered focus to a focus upon others. Its motivation is NOT found in buying influence and power. Goodness is serving for the sheer pleasure of serving, helping for the sheer joy of helping, and never dreams of making it a debt of loyalty.

(Ephesians 2:10) For we are his workmanship, created in Christ Jesus unto good works, which God hath before ordained that we should walk in them.

FAITH - It means to be faithful and trustworthy. The two biggest words associated directly with this meaning is RELIABILITY and DEPENDABILITY.

(Proverbs 20:6) Most men will proclaim every one his own goodness: but a faithful man who can find?

MEEKNESS - Meekness is a humble spirit manifested toward the needs of others. Meekness is not weakness. It prevents us from speaking in an arrogant manner to anyone else.

TEMPERANCE - To temper something is to make it suitable by mixing into it other qualities. Temperance is the vigorous process whereby all of the previous fruits of the Spirit are mixed in and balanced to achieve a suitable and complete Christian. He has added gentleness, goodness, faith, and meekness.

We said that the Spirit ministers to Christians in ten primary ways.

4. The Spirit assigns all spiritual gifts.

(1 Corinthians 12:1-11)   Now concerning spiritual gifts, brethren, I would not have you ignorant. Ye know that ye were Gentiles, carried away unto these dumb idols, even as ye were led. Wherefore I give you to understand, that no man speaking by the Spirit of God calleth Jesus accursed: and that no man can say that Jesus is the Lord, but by the Holy Ghost. Now there are diversities of gifts, but the same Spirit. And there are differences of administrations, but the same Lord. And there are diversities of operations, but it is the same God which worketh all in all. But the manifestation of the Spirit is given to every man to profit withal. For to one is given by the Spirit the word of wisdom; to another the word of knowledge by the same Spirit; To another faith by the same Spirit; to another the gifts of healing by the same Spirit; To another the working of miracles; to another prophecy; to another discerning of spirits; to another divers kinds of tongues; to another the interpretation of tongues: But all these worketh that one and the selfsame Spirit, dividing to every man severally as he will.

By the word "severally" we see that every Christian has been given more than one gift (talent) by the Spirit.

Class Discussion Questions

1. Since 1 Corinthians chapter 12 gives us only a sampling of spiritual gifts, what other talents can you think of that the Holy Spirit grants in order to better equip Christians to serve?

2. What gifts might be new to our contemporary technologies?

5. The Spirit shows them the sin in their life and then brings them under conviction about it.

(John 16:8) And when he is come, he will reprove the world of sin, and of righteousness, and of judgment:

This assumes that you have a right spirit toward spiritual change.

(Psalm 51:10) Create in me a clean

heart, O God; and renew a right spirit within me.

(Romans 12:1-2) I beseech you therefore, brethren, by the mercies of God, that ye present your bodies a living sacrifice, holy, acceptable unto God, which is your reasonable service. And be not conformed to this world: but be ye transformed by the renewing of your mind, that ye may prove what is that good, and acceptable, and perfect, will of God.

There are four outward avenues the Spirit uses to convict of sin: preaching, teaching, Bible study, and prayer. On occasion the Spirit might use a circumstance that we have observed to speak to our hearts.

6. The Spirit guides them into all truth.

(John 16:13-15) Howbeit when he, the Spirit of truth, is come, he will guide you into all truth: for he shall not speak of himself; but whatsoever he shall hear, that shall he speak: and he will shew you things to come. He shall glorify me: for he shall receive of mine, and shall shew it unto you. All things that the Father hath are mine: therefore said I, that he shall take of mine, and shall shew it unto you.

Truth is hidden from the unbeliever who cannot tap into the help of the Spirit (2 Cor 4:3). This is why the Bible makes sense to the believer, but not the

unbeliever.

Class Discussion Questions

1. By what standard to we measure the truth?

---

7. The Spirit reveals God the Father's "calling" for their life. (Acts 13:2,4)

8. The Spirit both directs and forbids certain courses of action. (Acts 16:6,7)

9. The Spirit makes intercession for them and helps them with and through their infirmities.

(Romans 8:26-27) Likewise the Spirit also helpeth our infirmities: for we know not what we should pray for as we ought: but the Spirit itself maketh intercession for us with groanings which cannot be uttered. And he that searcheth the hearts knoweth what is the mind of the Spirit, because he maketh intercession for the saints according to the will of God.

The above point was discussed thoroughly in Lesson Seven.

10. The Spirit reveals God's will in all matters.

It is important that everything that was discussed in this chapter be held in keeping with our opening statements.

Those statements were:

The Holy Spirit's ministry is primarily twofold on this earth.

✓ To lift up the name and ministry of Jesus Christ, the Son of God, by leading sinners to repentance.

✓ To lift up the name and ministry of Jesus Christ, the Son of God, by ministering to the personal spiritual needs of Christians and empowering their Christian service.

This Week's Memory Verse

Know ye not that ye are the temple of God, and *that* the **Spirit** of God dwelleth in you? (1 Corinthians 3:16)

The Doctrine of the Holy Spirit, His Purpose and Ministry

1. The Holy Spirit's ministry is primarily two-fold on this earth.

   To lift up the name and ministry of Jesus Christ, the Son of God, by

   _____

   To lift up the name and ministry of Jesus Christ, the Son of God, by

   _____
   _____

2. List the 9 fruit of the Spirit.

   _____   _____
   _____   _____
   _____   _____
   _____   _____
   _____

Write out this week's Bible verse from memory.

I Corinthians 3:16

_____
_____
_____
_____
_____

Finish the Phrase

So then they that are in the flesh cannot please _____

But ye shall receive power, after that the Holy Ghost is come upon you: and ye shall be witnesses unto me both in Jerusalem, and in all Judaea, and in Samaria,

_____

Let not your heart be troubled, neither let it be _____

But if the Spirit of him that raised up Jesus from the dead dwell in you, he that raised up Christ from the dead shall also

_____

But the Comforter, which is the Holy Ghost, whom the Father will send in my name, he shall teach you all things, and bring all things to your remembrance,

_____

But the fruit of the Spirit is _____

_____

_____

_____

_____

_____

Create in me a clean heart, O God; and

_____

Likewise the Spirit also helpeth our

_____

I beseech you therefore, brethren, by the mercies of God, that ye present your bodies a living _____

BEST POINT MADE

Proverbs Chapter Eight

What were the main themes of this chapter?

_____

_____

_____

_____

What were the instructional points meant to bring you closer to God?

_____

_____

_____

_____

What were the instructional points meant to protect you from spiritual destruction?

_____

_____

_____

_____

What things in your life could use strengthening?

_____

_____

_____

_____

Was there anything in this chapter that was of help in serving the LORD?

_____

_____

_____

_____

Did you learn anything new about the LORD?

_____

_____

_____

_____

Were there any suggestions made whereby you can be a greater blessing to others?

_____

_____

_____

_____

_____

9.1 The Fullness of the Holy Spirit

We are clearly commanded to be filled with the Holy Spirit.

(Ephesians 5:15-20) See then that ye walk circumspectly, not as fools, but as wise, Redeeming the time, because the days are evil. Wherefore be ye not unwise, but understanding what the will of the Lord is. And be not drunk with wine, wherein is excess; but be filled with the Spirit; Speaking to yourselves in psalms and hymns and spiritual songs, singing and making melody in your heart to the Lord; Giving thanks always for all things unto God and the Father in the name of our Lord Jesus Christ;

Since the Holy Spirit indwells us at the moment of salvation and dwells with us everywhere we go, the indwelling of the Holy Spirit cannot be the same as the filling of the Holy Spirit. The Bible indicates that we must seek for, ask for, and then maintain the filling of the Holy Spirit.

We do not need to seek the gifts of the Holy Spirit because these are divided and given to every Christian. Neither should we seek those gifts which are not assigned to us.

(1 Corinthians 7:20) Let every man abide in the same calling wherein he was called.

(1 Corinthians 12:4-11) Now there are diversities of gifts, but the same Spirit. And there are differences of administrations, but the same Lord. And there are diversities of operations, but it is the same God which worketh all in all. But the manifestation of the Spirit is given to every man to profit withal. For to one is given by the Spirit the word of wisdom; to another the word of knowledge by the same Spirit; To another faith by the same Spirit; to another the gifts of healing by the same Spirit; To another the working of miracles; to another prophecy; to another discerning of spirits; to another divers kinds of tongues; to another the interpretation of tongues: But all these worketh that one and the selfsame Spirit, dividing to every man severally as he will.

This text gives us a sampling of the gifts of the Holy Spirit. The list is not meant to include every gift.

9.2 The Enduing of Power

The filling of the Holy Spirit is a special enduing of power whereby we can please the LORD through greater effectiveness. For example:

✓ Our gifts become more effective. (1 Corinthians 12:4-7)

✓ Our calling becomes more effective. (John 15:1-5)

✓ Our soul-winning becomes more effective. (Acts 1:8)

✓ Our preaching, singing, and serving become more effective. (Colossians 3:16,17)

These gifts are not for our entertainment, nor are they for enhancing our personal greatness. Again, the Holy Spirit's ministry is primarily two-fold on this earth: to lift up the name and ministry of Jesus Christ, the Son of God, by leading sinners to repentance, and to lift up the name and ministry of Jesus Christ, the Son of God, by ministering to the personal, spiritual needs of Christians and empowering their Christian service.

The simple truth is, we neither please God nor bring him pleasure by the works of our own flesh. We cannot be filled with the Holy Spirit until we empty ourselves. We must empty ourselves of sin. We must empty ourselves of pride. We must empty ourselves of personal inspirations, aspirations, and gratifications. In other words, we must empty ourselves of ourselves before we can be filled with the Spirit.

9.3 Quenching the Holy Spirit

We must be careful not to quench the Holy Spirit.

(1 Thessalonians 5:19) Quench not the Spirit.

How can we quench the Holy Spirit's work in us?

✓ By unconfessed sin

(Isaiah 59:2) But your iniquities have separated between you and your God, and your sins have hid his face from you, that he will not hear.

(1 John 1:9) If we confess our sins, he is faithful and just to forgive us our sins, and to cleanse us from all unrighteousness.

If we are going to have the power of the Holy Spirit upon us, we must keep our sins confessed. Your gifts and your talents will be uneffective if carried out in the flesh. Performance may be perfect, but it will bear no fruit if conducted in the flesh. Performance without power amounts to little more than a self-fulfillment. One's preaching is powerless in the flesh. One's singing or instrumentations are powerless in the flesh. One's ministry to others is powerless in the flesh. The list could go on and on. Sadly, there is far too much ministry attempted in the flesh. We must not quench the Spirit by

85

unconfessed sin.

How else might the Spirit be quenched?

✓   By an unsubmissive spirit

(James 4:5-7) Do ye think that the scripture saith in vain, The spirit that dwelleth in us lusteth to envy? But he giveth more grace. Wherefore he saith, God resisteth the proud, but giveth grace unto the humble. Submit yourselves therefore to God. Resist the devil, and he will flee from you.

Submitting ourselves to the will of God must supercede our own plans. Typically, Christians who want to serve God have many ideas of their own. While they may be well intentioned and seem like good ideas, they are not good ideas if they are not ordered by the Holy Spirit. Isaiah points out that our thoughts and our ways are not necessarily the thoughts and ways of God on a given matter.

(Isaiah 55:8-9) For my thoughts are not your thoughts, neither are your ways my ways, saith the LORD. For as the heavens are higher than the earth, so are my ways higher than your ways, and my thoughts than your thoughts.

Therefore it is important that we submit ourselves to the Holy Spirit. He will instruct us and lead us as we do the work of God.

How else might the Spirit be quenched?

✓   By a self-sufficient attitude

While this idea has already been covered in our lesson, it is important that we include this specifically in our list.

How else might the Spirit be quenched?

✓   By carelessly proceeding in anything without His leading

Again, we have discussed this principle already, but choose to specifically include it in our listing. Look again at our text. "Wherefore be ye not unwise, but understanding what the will of the Lord is." (Ephesians 5:17)

When we follow our own way, we will eat the bitter fruit of that way. When we let the Spirit lead, we will dwell safely. (Proverbs 1:30-33)

9.4 The Divine Unity

The Holy Spirit never does anything to contradict God the Father, God the Son, nor the inspired, written WORD. The WORD and the Holy Spirit work in perfect harmony to reveal truth to you and to lead you in the perfect will of God.

"Experiences" which contradict the WORD of God are not of God nor of the Holy Spirit regardless of any claims people make. Just because people say "God led me to do it" does not mean that their claim is legitimate. It is far too easy to let emotions and philosophies direct our path. Many mistakes are made when we do that.

(Proverbs 3:5-7) Trust in the LORD with all thine heart; and lean not unto thine own understanding. In all thy ways acknowledge him, and he shall direct thy paths. Be not wise in thine own eyes: fear the LORD, and depart from evil.

9.5 The Charismatic Error

Throughout the New Testament we read about God's use of tongues in the early church.

The Corinthian church became very enamored with the spectacular and highly visible gifts. They abused both the Holy Spirit and the gifts. To this end the Holy Spirit inspired two scathing letters to the Corinthian congregation. Unfortunately, the Corinthian church became Paul's most carnal church. It became filled with lusts and false doctrine. The record of the Corinthian church is for our warning, not our copying.

Time and space does not allow this book to fully develop a Biblical refutation of today's modern Charismatic movement. Suffice it to say that the movement has many errors. For example:

✓ Is there any place in Scripture that tells us to "seek the baptism of the Holy Spirit?" (answer: no)

✓ Is there any place in Scripture that implies that Christians who do not speak in tongues are somehow defective? (answer: no)

✓ Is there a Biblical record where any woman spoke in tongues in the N.T.? (answer: no)

✓ Does the N.T. allow tongues speaking with no interpreter present? (answer: no. If God forbids it, then by what power are they doing it?)

✓ Is there any record that angels ever spoke in any language other than the languages of men? (answer: no)

✓ Do the writings of the N.T. emphasize the need to speak in tongues or de-emphasize it? (answer: de-emphasize.)

What about the Baptism of the Holy Spirit?

"Every" Christian is baptized by the Holy Spirit at the time they are saved. (1 Corinthians 12:13) By grace, the spiritual gifts are assigned and given by the Holy Spirit to each Christian. "Every" Christian is given at least two gifts. (1 Corinthians 12:11 - "severally") Did all Christians speak in tongues? - No! Look at the coordination between 1 Corinthians 12:12-13, 18, and 28-30. We must conclude that the gifts are NOT a result of earnestly seeking, praying, or crying. No single gift constitutes the baptism of the Holy Spirit.

Contemporary charismatics believe that the baptism of the Holy Spirit was speaking in tongues. They believe that all Christians should seek out speaking in tongues. They further believe that they are not complete until they do speak in tongues.

The tongues of the Bible were not unintelligible jibber-jabber. They were known tongues. Read carefully the following text.

(Acts 2:1-8) And when the day of Pentecost was fully come, they were all with one accord in one place. And suddenly there came a sound from heaven as of a rushing mighty wind, and it filled all the house where they were sitting. And there appeared unto them cloven tongues like as of fire, and it sat upon each of them. And they were all filled with the Holy Ghost, and began to speak with other tongues, as the Spirit gave them utterance. And there were dwelling at Jerusalem Jews, devout men, out of every nation under heaven. Now when this was noised abroad, the multitude came together, and were confounded, because that every man heard them speak in his own language. And they were all amazed and marvelled, saying one to another, Behold, are not all these which speak Galilaeans? And how hear we every man in our own tongue, wherein we were born?

Tongues served a major purpose in the early church in the absence of the written and completed revelation of God known as the New Testament.

Our final consideration will take us to 1 Corinthians chapter thirteen.

(1 Corinthians 13:8-10) Charity never faileth: but whether there be prophecies, they shall fail; whether there be tongues, they shall cease; whether there be knowledge, it shall vanish away. For we know in part, and we prophesy in part. But when that which is perfect is come, then that which is in part shall be done away. When I was a child, I spake as a child, I understood as a child, I thought as a child: but when I became a man, I put away childish things. For now we see through a glass, darkly; but then face to face: now I know in part; but then shall I know even as also I am known. And now abideth faith, hope, charity, these three; but the greatest of these is charity.

Charity (agapé) will never become void of use. It will always be a gift of God for all Christians to serve with. It will always be active through every generation to come. But the revelatory gifts will become void of use. The gift of revelatory prophecies shall fail. They shall fail to speak the yet unwritten Word of God. They shall fail to predict that which was yet future. The gift of tongues will generally cease. Tongues spoke the N.T. Word when there was none yet written. Tongues spoke the praise of Jesus Christ in places He was not yet known. Tongues were *for a sign, not to them that believe, but to them that believe not:* (14:22) The gift of revelatory knowledge shall vanish.

Why would these three "main stays" of the early church eventually fade? Because *that which is perfect* was about to arrive on the scene (vs.10). That which is perfect would take the place of that which was not perfect. The Apostles and early Christians did not have the New Testament Word of God. What they knew, they knew in pieces and parts (vs.9). Early prophecy, tongues, and knowledge were fragmented pieces of the Word of God. What is that which is perfect in our text? There are only two perfect things in the universe: God and God's Word. Which one is referred to in our text? The charismatics say that the text refers to Jesus. Jesus is coming a second time, therefore, they say that tongues are active until the rapture. Biblicists say that the text refers to the Word of God. The revelatory gifts are replaced by the revelatory book. Without the revelatory book, our doctrines and beliefs would be fragmented. We could not be sure what was of God and what was of an evil spirit (1 Jn 4:1). We needed a *more sure word of prophecy;* (2 Pet 1:19) and a completed revelation (Eph 4:11-13; 2 Tim 3:16-17). When that Word was completed, God put a curse upon anyone who would attempt to add to it or take away from it (Rev 22:18-19).

Paul had the right emphasis. *"Yet in the church I had rather speak five words with my understanding, that by my voice I might teach others also, than ten thousand words in an unknown tongue"* (1 Corinthians 14:19).

Do not be persuaded by the Charismatic error.

This Week's Memory Verse

Charity never faileth: but whether there be prophecies, they shall fail; whether there be tongues, they shall cease; whether there be knowledge, it shall vanish away. (1 Corinthians 13:8)

The Doctrine of the Holy Spirit, The Fulness of the Spirit

1. The filling of the Holy Spirit is a special enduing of power whereby we can please the LORD through greater effectiveness. List the four examples.

_____

_____

_____

_____

2. List three ways we can quench the Spirit.

_____

_____

_____

_____

3. Is *that which is perfect* referring to the second coming of Jesus Christ or is it referring to the completed revelation? _____

Write out this week's Bible verse from memory.

1 Corinthians 13:8

_____

_____

_____

_____

_____

Finish the Phrase

See then that ye walk circumspectly, not as fools, but as wise, Redeeming the time, because the _____

Now there are diversities of gifts, but the same _____

Quench not the _____

But your iniquities have separated between you and your God, and your sins have hid his face from you, that he will not _____

Wherefore he saith, God resisteth the _____

Trust in the LORD with all thine heart; and lean not unto _____

In all thy ways acknowledge him, and he shall direct thy _____

Be not wise in thine own eyes: fear the LORD, and _____

Charity never _____

whether there be prophecies, they shall fail; whether there be tongues, they shall _____

But when that which is perfect is come, then that which is in part shall be _____

BEST POINT MADE

Proverbs Chapter Nine

What were the main themes of this chapter?

_____

_____

_____

_____

What were the instructional points meant to bring you closer to God?

_____

_____

_____

What were the instructional points meant to protect you from spiritual destruction?

_____

_____

_____

_____

What things in your life could use strengthening?

_____

_____

_____

_____

_____

Was there anything in this chapter that was of help in serving the LORD?

_____

_____

_____

_____

Did you learn anything new about the LORD?

_____

_____

_____

Were there any suggestions made whereby you can be a greater blessing to others?

_____

_____

_____

_____

_____

10.1 Introduction

The Christian's relationship with God is a very dependent one, not an independent one. While it is true that God equips us, teaches us, and empowers us to serve, He did not equip us to "go it alone."

(Psalm 121:1-2) I will lift up mine eyes unto the hills, from whence cometh my help. My help cometh from the LORD, which made heaven and earth.

(Psalm 18:2) The LORD is my rock, and my fortress, and my deliverer; my God, my strength, in whom I will trust; my buckler, and the horn of my salvation, and my high tower.

Class Discussion Questions

1. When you pray for other people, what are the kinds of things you might ask God on their behalf?

2. When you pray concerning yourself, what are the kinds of things you might ask God?

10.2 The Holy Spirit, Our Prayer Partner

Most Christians know the weakness of their own flesh. They know that they need God's help and God's strength if they are going to live victoriously and serve effectively. In other words, we need God for everything if we are going to do anything. Did you know that you need the Holy Spirit's help when you pray?

Illustration

Johnny was having trouble misbehaving and was sent to his room by his mother to think about it. Ten minutes later he emerged from his room to tell his mother that he had thought about his problem. He even said a prayer about it. His mother asked Johnny, "did you ask God to help you not to misbehave?" He replied, "no, I asked God to help you be able to put up with me."

Like Johnny, we do not always pray for the right things. We need help praying. The Holy Spirit is our prayer partner.

(Romans 8:26-28) Likewise the Spirit also helpeth our infirmities: for we know not what we should pray for as we ought: but the Spirit itself maketh intercession for us with groanings

which cannot be uttered. And he that searcheth the hearts knoweth what is the mind of the Spirit, because he maketh intercession for the saints according to the will of God. And we know that all things work together for good to them that love God, to them who are the called according to his purpose.

The Holy Spirit's interceding for us is different from the interceding of Jesus Christ for us. Examine His intercession for us in the following text:

(Hebrews 7:24-28) But this man, because he continueth ever, hath an unchangeable priesthood. Wherefore he is able also to save them to the uttermost that come unto God by him, seeing he ever liveth to make intercession for them. For such an high priest became us, who is holy, harmless, undefiled, separate from sinners, and made higher than the heavens; Who needeth not daily, as those high priests, to offer up sacrifice, first for his own sins, and then for the people's: for this he did once, when he offered up himself. For the law maketh men high priests which have infirmity; but the word of the oath, which was since the law, maketh the Son, who is consecrated for evermore.

When Christ intercedes for us it is because of our sin. When it says that He makes intercession it means that He speaks to the Father on our behalf and in our defense much as a personal attorney would do.

(1 John 2:1) My little children, these things write I unto you, that ye sin not. And if any man sin, we have an advocate with the Father, Jesus Christ the righteous:

John puts before us God's perfect expectation, "that ye sin not." Because God is perfect, His standard for us cannot be less than perfect. God is holy. He would never say to us, "sin as little as you can." God never approves of sin to any degree. When the Pharisees brought a woman to Jesus who was guilty of adultery, she put herself under a sentence of death by stoning. They attempted to trick Jesus into breaking the law of Moses by publically forgiving her. His response was simple enough. He said to them, "He that is without sin among you, let him first cast a stone at her" (Jn 8:7). One by one her accusers walked away. Jesus then spoke to the woman and said, "Neither do I condemn thee: go, and sin no more." Jesus thus spoke the perfect standard of God.

John writes, "My little children, these things write I unto you, that ye sin not."

God knows that we will not be perfect until we get to Heaven. While God has not given us a license to sin, there is a provision for us in that Christ is our advocate. Christ brings our case back to Calvary where the penalty for our sin was satisfied by His own shed blood and by His death, burial and resurrection.

(Romans 8:34) Who is he that condemneth? It is Christ that died, yea rather, that is risen again, who is even at the right hand of God, who also maketh intercession for us.

This advocacy and intercession of Christ on our behalf because of our sin is NOT the same intercession that the Holy Spirit makes for us.

We were speaking of the Holy Spirit as our prayer partner. This being said we proceed to our next point.

The Holy Spirit intercedes for us and WITH us.

The word "intercession" in Romans 8:26 and 8:27 is not translated from the same word. The first word indicates that the Holy Spirit not only goes "for" us but WITH us to the Father. He goes with us to help plead for our needs.

Why does the Holy Spirit do that? *First*, because we do not always know what to pray for, though we might think so. *Secondly*, because the Holy Spirit knows exactly what needs to happen.

When we pray, this is what should happen:

✓ We should first ask the Holy Spirit to help us to pray for the right things.

✓ As the Holy Spirit impresses upon your heart what you need to pray for, pray it.

✓ The Holy Spirit approaches the Father with you and intercedes for you.

Why does the Holy Spirit go with us to the Father? *Thirdly*, the Holy Spirit goes with us in prayer to help ensure that we ask for the right things. If we ask for the wrong things, we will likely not receive them. It is not that we always ask for the wrong things, but we do not always see things in a spiritual way or from God's perspective. We are fully capable of asking God foolish things for which concession would result in problems. God's will is not only the best plan, it is the only plan whereby God is glorified. Thus, the Holy Spirit goes to the Father with us when we pray.

God promises to meet our needs, but if we please Him and serve Him, He sometimes grants our wants too.

(Psalm 37:4)Delight thyself also in the LORD; and he shall give thee the desires of thine heart.

(John 15:7) If ye abide in me, and my words abide in you, ye shall ask what ye will, and it shall be done unto you.

The Holy Spirit not only intercedes WITH us, but also WITHOUT us

concerning things for which we do not ask.

We said that the word "intercession" in Romans 8:26 and 8:27 is not translated from the same word.

In the second word, the Holy Spirit does not go with us, *but He goes on behalf of us.* He tells the Father about things we did not ask for, did not know about or just plain left out. This is the second way in which the Holy Spirit is our prayer partner.

We ask for sunshine, but the Holy Spirit knows that we need some clouds too. We ask for all successes, but the Holy Spirit knows we need some failures too. We ask for smiles, but the Holy Spirit knows we need some tears too.

This is one reason why verse 28 is added to our Romans 8:27 text. God is reminding us that when our prayers are not answered in the way we wanted, all things are still working for our good and more importantly, for the spiritual good.

It is entirely appropriate to begin prayer by asking the Holy Spirit to help you to pray for the things you ought to pray for while submitting yourself to the outcome, whatever that may be. It is too easy for Christians to become discouraged or even bitter when God does not answer prayer in the way that they want Him to. The world is filled with people who are mad at God. They fail to realize that they are charting a course filled with extra heartache and disappointment.

You need help praying. That help is letting the Holy Spirit be your prayer partner.

This Week's Memory Verse

Likewise the Spirit also helpeth our infirmities: for we know not what we should pray for as we ought: but the Spirit itself maketh intercession for us with groanings which cannot be uttered. (Romans 8:26)

Chapter Ten Quiz & Memory Verse Fill In Study Sheet

The Doctrine of the Holy Spirit, His Intercession

1. When Christ intercedes for us it is because of our _____.

2. John puts before us God's perfect expectation, "_____".

3. Name the three reasons the Holy Spirit goes WITH us to the Father when we pray.

_____

_____

_____

_____

_____

_____

_____

Write out this week's Bible verse from memory.

Romans 8:26

_____

_____

_____

_____

_____

Finish the Phrase

I will lift up mine eyes unto the hills, from whence cometh my help. My help cometh from _____

Likewise the Spirit also helpeth our infirmities: for we know not _____

Spirit itself maketh intercession for us with _____

And we know that all things work together for good to them that

_____

And if any man sin, we have an

_____

Delight thyself also in the LORD; and he shall give thee the _____

(John 15:7) If ye abide in me, and my words abide in you, ye shall ask what ye will, and it shall be _____.

BEST POINT MADE

Proverbs Chapter Ten

What were the main themes of this chapter?

_____

_____

_____

_____

What were the instructional points meant to bring you closer to God?

_____

_____

_____

_____

What were the instructional points meant to protect you from spiritual destruction?

_____

_____

_____

_____

What things in your life could use strengthening?

_____

_____

_____

_____

Was there anything in this chapter that was of help in serving the LORD?

_____

_____

_____

_____

_____

Did you learn anything new about the LORD?

_____

_____

_____

_____

Were there any suggestions made whereby you can be a greater blessing to others?

_____

_____

_____

_____

_____

11.1 The Creation of Man

God created our universe, the earth, and all that is in them in six literal twenty-four hour days. These days were not symbolic of the great time spans that liberals and theistic evolutionists teach.

The Hebrew word for day, *yom*, is used both for a literal, twenty-four hour day and also for an indefinite period of time, such as in the expression "For the day of the Lord is at hand" (Joel 1:15). However, the word, *yom*, always means a twenty-four hour literal day when it is used with a numeral ... day one, day two, first day, second day, etc. There are no exceptions to this rule. In the Genesis Creation account, *yom* is used with a numeral, indicating that it intends the reader to understand that these are literal days of twenty-four hours. Man was created on the sixth day of creation.

Man was given a body, a soul, and a spirit. His body is his material being. God formed man and his DNA code from the dust of the earth. Because of man's eventual sin in the garden, upon death, his body returns to dust.

(Genesis 3:19) In the sweat of thy face shalt thou eat bread, till thou return unto the ground; for out of it wast thou taken: for dust thou art, and unto dust shalt thou return.

(Job 10:9) Remember, I beseech thee, that thou hast made me as the clay; and wilt thou bring me into dust again?

11.2 In His Likeness and Image

(Genesis 1:26-27) And God said, Let us make man in our image, after our likeness: and let them have dominion over the fish of the sea, and over the fowl of the air, and over the cattle, and over all the earth, and over every creeping thing that creepeth upon the earth. So God created man in his own image, in the image of God created he him; male and female created he them.

(Genesis 2:7) And the LORD God formed man of the dust of the ground, and breathed into his nostrils the breath of life; and man became a living soul.

Man was created in the *likeness* and *image* of God. This does not mean that man looked like God, for God is a spirit. These two words are similar in meaning and are linked in this text to add to the emphasis and the intensity of it.

Of no other created thing is it said that it is created in the likeness and image of God. Man stands alone in this.

John Philips writes in his book, *Exploring Genesis*, "Man stands alone. Physically, he alone of all the creatures on the globe walks upright; mentally, he alone has the ability to communicate in a sophisticated manner; spiritually, he alone has the capacity to know the mind and will of God"

Because the contemporary unbeliever denies the origin of man he cannot give man the dignity and worth that God created him with. Thus, man is falsely reduced to that of being a member of the animal kingdom. In this they deny man's dominion over the birds of the air, the beasts of the fields, and the fish of the seas. It is no wonder that the world has gone insane elevating the "rights" of animals above the needs of man. Their premise is a slap in the face to the Creator.

(Genesis 1:26) And God said, Let us make man in our image, after our likeness: and let them have dominion over the fish of the sea, and over the fowl of the air, and over the cattle, and over all the earth, and over every creeping thing that creepeth upon the earth.

Later, God said to Noah,

(Genesis 9:2-3) And the fear of you and the dread of you shall be upon every beast of the earth, and upon every fowl of the air, upon all that moveth upon the earth, and upon all the fishes of the sea; into your hand are they delivered. Every moving thing that liveth shall be meat for you; even as the green herb have I given you all things.

In what way was man created in the likeness and image of God? *GotQuestions.org* puts it in very simple, easy to understand terms. Quote:

> The image of God refers to the immaterial part of man. It sets man apart from the animal world, fits him for the dominion God intended him to have over the earth (Genesis 1:28), and enables him to commune with his Maker. It is a likeness mentally, morally, and socially.
>
> Mentally, man was created as a rational, volitional agent. In other words, man can reason and man can choose. This is a reflection of God's intellect and freedom. Anytime someone invents a machine, writes a book, paints a landscape, enjoys a symphony, calculates a sum, or names a pet, he or she is proclaiming the fact that we are made in God's image.
>
> Morally, man was created in righteousness and perfect innocence, a reflection of God's holiness. God saw all He had

made (mankind included) and called it "very good" (Genesis 1:31). Our conscience or "moral compass" is a vestige of that original state. Whenever someone writes a law, recoils from evil, praises good behavior, or feels guilty, he is confirming the fact that we are made in God's own image.

Socially, man was created for fellowship. This reflects both God's triune nature and His love. In Eden, man's primary relationship was with God (Genesis 3:8 implies fellowship with God), and God made the first woman because "it is not good for the man to be alone" (Genesis 2:18). Every time someone marries, makes a friend, hugs a child, or attends church, he is demonstrating the fact that we are made in the likeness of God.

Part of being made in God's image is that Adam had the capacity to make free choices. Although he was given a righteous nature, Adam made an evil choice to rebel against his Creator. In so doing, Adam marred the image of God within himself, and he passed that damaged likeness on to all his descendants (Romans 5:12). Today, we still bear the image of God (James 3:9), but we also bear the scars of sin. Mentally, morally, socially, and physically, we show the effects of sin.

The good news is that when God redeems an individual, He begins to restore the original image of God, creating a new self, created to be like God in true righteousness and holiness.

(Ephesians 4:24) And that ye put on the new man, which after God is created in righteousness and true holiness.

Redemption is only available by God's grace through faith in Jesus Christ as our Savior from the sin that separates us from God (Ephesians 2:8-9). Through Christ, we are made new creations in the likeness of God.

(2 Corinthians 5:17) Therefore if any man be in Christ, he is a new creature: old things are passed away; behold, all things are become new.

Illustration

Sir Isaac Newton had a replica of the solar system made in miniature. One day a scientist entered Newton's study. Amazed at the miniature solar system, he asked who made the miniature. Newton told him that nobody made it. The scientist replied, "You must think I am a fool. Of course somebody made it and he is a genius." Laying his book aside, Newton placed his hand on the scientist's shoulder and said, "This thing is but a puny imitation of a much grander system whose laws you and I know. I am not able to convince you that this mere toy is without a designer and maker: yet, you profess to believe that the original from which this design is taken has come into being without either designer or maker."

11.3 The Origin of Human Races

The entire human race descended from Adam and Eve. God did not leave the creation of all other people to mere procreation. He still creates every one of us and fashions us as individuals.

(Psalm 139:13-16) For thou hast possessed my reins: thou hast covered me in my mother's womb. I will praise thee; for I am fearfully and wonderfully made: marvellous are thy works; and that my soul knoweth right well. My substance was not hid from thee, when I was made in secret, and curiously wrought in the lowest parts of the earth. Thine eyes did see my substance, yet being unperfect; and in thy book all my members were written, which in continuance were fashioned, when as yet there was none of them.

He creates a purpose for each person and then creates each person for that purpose. Thus, we are not only created with individual design, but an individual purpose.

A question comes to the surface. Where did the human races come from if we all descended from Adam and Eve?

It appears that races and languages are related. Man became divided into races and languages as a result of God's divine judgment at Babel. God's pronounced judgment was swift and permanent. (Read Genesis 11:1-9)

When one studies the origin of languages and the peoples that spoke them, it is easy to see that the division of races and languages coincided. This is the only reasonable explanation for the origins of race.

Intermarriage between the races is a hot topic among Bible believers. Since the Bible does not directly address the question, there is much disagreement about intermarriage. Certainly one can find intermarriage among some rather well know Bible characters.

It is true that the Israelites were forbidden to intermarry with other races by God.

(Deuteronomy 7:3-4) Neither shalt thou make marriages with them; thy daughter thou shalt not give unto his son, nor his daughter shalt thou take unto thy son. For they will turn away thy son from following me, that they may serve other gods: so will the anger of the LORD be kindled against you, and destroy thee suddenly.

The reason for this law is rooted in spiritual reasons rather than racial reasons. Other races of that time were pagan. God was raising up a spiritual people unto Himself. A similar spiritual law is found in the New Testament.

(2 Corinthians 6:14-15) Be ye not unequally yoked together with unbelievers: for what fellowship hath righteousness with unrighteousness? and what communion hath light with darkness? And what concord hath Christ with Belial? or what part hath he that believeth with an infidel?

Some will argue that the Deuteronomy command stands regardless the purpose behind it.

Here are questions some might ask:

Do we have permission to undo the judgement of God at Babel?

Does intermarriage have any adverse effects on the effectiveness of a Christian's witness?

What social problems will the children of such marriages suffer?

Are the individual races beautiful unto God who created all things for his pleasure?

Were there people in the Bible who were interracially married whom God used for His glory?

In Numbers we read that ...Miriam and Aaron spoke against Moses because of the Cushite woman whom he had married, for he had married a Cushite woman (Num 12:1). A Cushite is from Cush, a region south of Ethiopia, where the people are known for their black skin. We know this because of Jeremiah 13:23, "Can the Ethiopian change his skin, or the leopard his spots? Then also you can do good who are accustomed to do evil."

(Numbers 12:1) And Miriam and Aaron spake against Moses because of the Ethiopian woman whom he had married: for he had married an Ethiopian woman.

But God's anger takes aim at Miriam (Moses' sister) not Moses. God struck her with leprosy. (Num 12:10)

Moses went on to be greatly used of God.

Class Discussion Questions

1. Can you think of other Bible characters that were interracially married?

2. Did it turn out good for them, bad for them, or indifferent?

It is important that God alone judges these unanswered questions. There should never be a bias among God's people. On this matter the gospel is color blind. The New Testament Church is color blind. You should be too!

Where and when the races originated is not authoritatively known. But we know these things:

✓ We are all created in the likeness and image of God.

✓ We are all equipped to fellowship and commune with God.

✓ We are all created with the ability to make moral and spiritual choices.

✓ We are all accountable for those choices.

✓ We are all in need of the Saviour.

This Week's Memory Verse

So God created man in his *own* image, in the image of God created he him; male and female created he them. (Genesis 1:27)

The Doctrine Man, Created in His Image

1. The earth was created in six literal, _____ days.

2. Man was created on the _____ day in the _____ and _____ of God.

3. Man was given a body, a _____, and a _____.

4. Physically, he alone of all the creatures on the globe walks _____.

5. Mentally, he alone has the ability to _____ in a sophisticated manner;

6. Spiritually, he alone has the capacity to know the _____ and _____ of God.

7. We are all created with the ability to make _____ and _____ choices.

Write out this week's Bible verse from memory.

Genesis 1:27

_____

_____

_____

_____

_____

Finish the Phrase

And God said, Let us make man in our

_____

And God said, Let us make man in our image, after our likeness: and let them have

_____

for dust thou art, and unto_____

put on the new _____

Therefore if any man be in Christ, he is a _____

Be ye not unequally yoked together with _____

BEST POINT MADE

Proverbs Chapter Eleven

What were the main themes of this chapter?

_____

_____

_____

_____

_____

What were the instructional points meant to bring you closer to God?

_____

_____

_____

_____

What were the instructional points meant to protect you from spiritual destruction?

_____

_____

_____

_____

What things in your life could use strengthening?

_____

_____

_____

_____

_____

Was there anything in this chapter that was of help in serving the LORD?

_____

_____

_____

_____

_____

Did you learn anything new about the LORD?

_____

_____

_____

_____

Were there any suggestions made whereby you can be a greater blessing to others?

_____

_____

_____

_____

_____

_____

12.1 The Garden of Eden

Garden of Eden - (literally, *the garden of delight*) In it grew every tree and vegetation that was beautiful to see or good for food. There were no thorns, weeds, nor thistles. The climate for plant, animal, and man was absolutely perfect. Adam and Eve were commanded to "dress" (arrange it's beauty) the garden. They did not have to fight adverse elements of nature.

What contributed to the garden's perfect environment?

✓ The water canopy

(Genesis 1:6-7) And God said, Let there be a firmament in the midst of the waters, and let it divide the waters from the waters. And God made the firmament, and divided the waters which were under the firmament from the waters which were above the firmament: and it was so.

While modern creationists are moving away from the canopy theory, they are doing so for the wrong reasons. What God did or will do in the future does not have to fit into man's scientific models. Science never trumps Scriptures. The inspired and preserved Word of God is not subject to the whims, changes, and perversions of modern translations.

The truth is, there were waters above and waters below. This had a terrarium effect on the earth which produced a mist instead of rain in an environment of warm temperatures. This made for lush vegetation growth (which dinosaurs and large animals needed) and no need of warm clothing for man.

God never said that Adam and Eve saw the sun, moon, and stars. In fact, such a sight is not mentioned until after the flood. Neither had man ever seen a bow in the sky prior to the collapse.

When did God put His bow in the sky? It was not until after the collapse of the canopy and the flood waters receded.

(Genesis 9:13-16) I do set my bow in the cloud, and it shall be for a token of a covenant between me and the earth. And it shall come to pass, when I bring a cloud over the earth, that the bow shall be seen in the cloud: And I will remember my covenant, which is between me and you and every living creature of all flesh; and the waters shall no more become a flood to destroy all flesh. And the bow shall be in the cloud; and I will look upon it, that I may remember the everlasting covenant between God and every living creature

of all flesh that is upon the earth.

While time and space does not allow for the defense of the Canopy Theory, it is clear that the environment of the Garden was perfect for man, animals, and plants.

Class Discussion Questions

1. What condition did God use to make His bow in the sky?

2. What did this suggest about a prior canopy of water around the earth?

✓ The absence of thorns and thistles

Those would only come later as part of the judgement of God upon Adam's sin.

✓ Peace between man and the animal kingdom

While Genesis does not say that the animals were not carnivorous in the Garden, it is implied that the animals of the Millennial Kingdom will return to being non-carnivorous.

(Isaiah 11:6-7) The wolf also shall dwell with the lamb, and the leopard shall lie down with the kid; and the calf and the young lion and the fatling together; and a little child shall lead them. And the cow and the bear shall feed; their young ones shall lie down together: and the lion shall eat straw like the ox. And the sucking child shall play on the hole of the asp, and the weaned child shall put his hand on the cockatrice' den.

✓ The presence of God and the absence of sin

We have already seen in earlier chapters that man was created with innocence. Such was the state of prefallen man. Imagine a world in which, instead of the presence of sin, we had the presence of God.

(Genesis 3:8) And they heard the voice of the LORD God walking in the garden in the cool of the day: and Adam and his wife hid themselves from the presence of the LORD God amongst the trees of the garden.

12.2 The Tree of Life

The Tree of Life symbolized access to everlasting life. Physically, it appears that consistent eating of its fruit would have sustained life indefinitely for Adam and Eve. After the fall of Adam and Eve into sin God put them out of the garden immediately. Why?

(Genesis 3:22-24) And the LORD God said, Behold, the man is become as one of us, to know good and evil: and now, lest he put forth his hand, and take also of the tree of life, and eat, and live for

ever: Therefore the LORD God sent him forth from the garden of Eden, to till the ground from whence he was taken. So he drove out the man; and he placed at the east of the garden of Eden Cherubims, and a flaming sword which turned every way, to keep the way of the tree of life.

The Tree of Life will again play a role of some sort in heaven.

(Revelation 2:7) He that hath an ear, let him hear what the Spirit saith unto the churches; To him that overcometh will I give to eat of the tree of life, which is in the midst of the paradise of God.

(Revelation 22:1-2) And he shewed me a pure river of water of life, clear as crystal, proceeding out of the throne of God and of the Lamb. In the midst of the street of it, and on either side of the river, was there the tree of life, which bare twelve manner of fruits, and yielded her fruit every month: and the leaves of the tree were for the healing of the nations.

(Revelation 22:14) Blessed are they that do his commandments, that they may have right to the tree of life, and may enter in through the gates into the city.

God has lived forever and will live forever because it is His nature. He cannot cease to exist or be destroyed.

Christians will live forever because it

is God's gift to us in keeping with His promise. But we will never be eternal in the same sense that God is eternal. Some would argue that the Tree of Life has some role in the keeping of the promise to us. Suffice it to say that God has not revealed all Heavenly things to us.

12.3 The Tree of the Knowledge of Good and Evil

Along with all the other fruit trees in the garden was the Tree of the Knowledge of Good and Evil. Eve determined that it was pleasant to the eyes and appeared to be good for food.

Adam and Eve fully understood that the fruit of the tree was forbidden.

(Genesis 2:17) But of the tree of the knowledge of good and evil, thou shalt not eat of it: for in the day that thou eatest thereof thou shalt surely die.

They were permitted to eat of all but the Tree of Knowledge of Good and Evil. Adam and Eve were naked, but they did not seem to be consciously aware of that fact. Conscience requires a knowledge of good and evil. Adam and Eve did not have that knowledge before their fall. They were innocent. Imagine what it must have been like to have no contact with nor knowledge of what sin was!

The tree was used of God to test the

faith of Adam and Eve. Whether or not there was "knowledge" in the fruit itself or just in the test is debated. It is more important to understand that the results of the failed test were real! Upon their disobedience in eating the forbidden fruit the knowledge of good and evil became a permanent part of man's intellectual and spiritual makeup.

Class Discussion Questions

1. Do you think we inherited from Adam a complete knowledge of good and evil or do you think that knowledge grows the longer we live?

2. If our knowledge of good and evil is growing, what is contributing to that factor?

12.4 Death

Adam and Eve's disobedience brought about death and separation.

Death - God had warned Adam that if he ate of the Tree of the Knowledge of Good and Evil he would die.

Separation - It brought about separation from: The Tree of Life; the Garden; and the visible presence of God.

God has never tempted man with evil.

(James 1:13) Let no man say when he is tempted, I am tempted of God: for God cannot be tempted with evil, neither tempteth he any man:

However, God does allow us to be tested. Why? Because everything God wants us to be unto Himself is voluntary in nature.

God could have made us robots and programed obedience into us. The result would be that we would ever only do right.

God loved us and He wants us to love him back. Love is voluntary. God wants us to be loyal to Him. Loyalty is voluntary. God wants us to fellowship with Him. Fellowship is voluntary. God wants us to serve Him. Service is voluntary.

While man is clearly commanded to love the Lord his God with all his heart, and with all his soul, and with all his mind, and with all his strength, God does not force man to do so.

Do you remember what Joshua said to the Israelites?

(Joshua 24:15) And if it seem evil unto you to serve the LORD, choose you this day whom ye will serve; whether the gods which your fathers served that wereon the other side of the flood, or the gods of the Amorites, in whose land ye dwell: but as for me and my house, we will serve the LORD.

This Week's Memory Verse

Let no man say when he is tempted, I am tempted of God: for God cannot be tempted with evil, neither tempteth he any man: (James 1:13)

The Doctrine of Sin, Prefallen Man

1. When did God put His bow in the sky? _____

_____

2. What four things contributed to the garden's perfect environment?

_____

_____

_____

_____

3. **The Tree of Life** - The Tree of Life symbolized _____

_____

4. Why did God put Adam and Eve out of the garden? _____

_____

5. Name the forbidden tree. _____

6. The tree was used of God to test the _____ of Adam and Eve.

Write out this week's Bible verse from memory.

James 1:13

_____

_____

_____

_____

_____

Finish the Phrase

The wolf also shall dwell with the

_____

leopard shall lie the _____

the calf and the young lion and the fatling together; and a little child shall

_____

Behold, the man is become as one of us, to know good and evil: and now, lest he put forth his hand, and take also of the tree of life, and eat, and _____

Blessed are they that do his commandments, that they may have right to the _____

Let no man say when he is tempted, I am _____

*And if it seem evil unto you to serve the LORD, choose you this day*_____

_____

BEST POINT MADE

Proverbs Chapter Twelve

What were the main themes of this chapter?

_____

_____

_____

_____

What were the instructional points meant to bring you closer to God?

_____

_____

_____

_____

What were the instructional points meant to protect you from spiritual destruction?

_____

_____

_____

_____

What things in your life could use strengthening?

_____

_____

_____

_____

_____

Was there anything in this chapter that was of help in serving the LORD?

_____

_____

_____

_____

Did you learn anything new about the LORD?

_____

_____

_____

_____

Were there any suggestions made whereby you can be a greater blessing to others?

_____

_____

_____

_____

_____

13.1 The Origin of Sin

While it was by man sin came into the world, the Scripture clearly establishes the fact that sin did not originate with man. The earliest sin recorded in Scripture is that of Satan. Satan became filled with pride.

(Isaiah 14:12-17) How art thou fallen from heaven, O Lucifer, son of the morning! how art thou cut down to the ground, which didst weaken the nations! For thou hast said in thine heart, I will ascend into heaven, I will exalt my throne above the stars of God: I will sit also upon the mount of the congregation, in the sides of the north: I will ascend above the heights of the clouds; I will be like the most High. Yet thou shalt be brought down to hell, to the sides of the pit. They that see thee shall narrowly look upon thee, and consider thee, saying, Is this the man that made the earth to tremble, that did shake kingdoms; That made the world as a wilderness, and destroyed the cities thereof; that opened not the house of his prisoners?

(Ezekiel 28:12-19) Son of man, take up a lamentation upon the king of Tyrus, and say unto him, Thus saith the Lord GOD; Thou sealest up the sum, full of wisdom, and perfect in beauty. Thou hast been in Eden the garden of God; every precious stone was thy covering, the sardius, topaz, and the diamond, the beryl, the onyx, and the jasper, the sapphire, the emerald, and the carbuncle, and gold: the workmanship of thy tabrets and of thy pipes was prepared in thee in the day that thou wast created. Thou art the anointed cherub that covereth; and I have set thee so: thou wast upon the holy mountain of God; thou hast walked up and down in the midst of the stones of fire. Thou wast perfect in thy ways from the day that thou wast created, till iniquity was found in thee. By the multitude of thy merchandise they have filled the midst of thee with violence, and thou hast sinned: therefore I will cast thee as profane out of the mountain of God: and I will destroy thee, O covering cherub, from the midst of the stones of fire. Thine heart was lifted up because of thy beauty, thou hast corrupted thy wisdom by reason of thy brightness: I will cast thee to the ground, I will lay thee before kings, that they may behold thee. Thou hast defiled thy sanctuaries by the multitude of thine iniquities, by the iniquity of thy traffick; therefore will I bring forth a fire from the midst of thee, it shall devour thee, and I will bring thee to ashes upon the earth in the sight of all them that behold thee. All they that know thee among the people

shall be astonished at thee: thou shalt be a terror, and never shalt thou be any more.

Satan wanted to become his own god. He wanted to compete for God's throne and dominion. Filled with violence, he attempted to fight a holy war with God. In filling God's abodes with "iniquities", he had persuaded legions of angels to follow his rebellion. Satan lost this first holy war. He and his cohorts (fallen angels) were cast down and their future damnation was set.

The time frame of this Holy war is unknown. Some have wondered if part of this war was fought on some previous earth where angels may have dwelled. They cite Jer 4:23-27.

(Jeremiah 4:23-27) I beheld the earth, and, lo, it was without form, and void; and the heavens, and they had no light. I beheld the mountains, and, lo, they trembled, and all the hills moved lightly. I beheld, and, lo, there was no man, and all the birds of the heavens were fled. I beheld, and, lo, the fruitful place was a wilderness, and all the cities thereof were broken down at the presence of the LORD, and by his fierce anger. For thus hath the LORD said, The whole land shall be desolate; yet will I not make a full end.

People who follow this line of thinking mention the fact that God commanded Adam and Eve to "replenish" the earth (Gen 1:28). This is the same command given to Noah when the earth was destroyed by the flood (Gen 9:1). However, Bible scholars are divided on this thinking.

13.2 Descriptive Names and Titles for Satan

The names given to Satan in Scripture indicate the ultimate evil he became. Here are just a few examples:

> **Oral Reading**
>
> Assign the following verses to be read orally to the class as each name or title for Satan is noted.

Abaddon (Rev 9:11)
Accuser of the brethren (Rev 12:10)
Adversary (1 Pet 5:8)
Angel of the bottomless pit. (Rev 9:11)
Apollyon (Rev 9:11)
Beelzebub (Mat 12:24)
Belial (2 Cor 6:15)
Devil (Mat 4:1)
Dragon (Rev 12:9; 20:2)
Enemy (Mat 13:39)
Father of all lies (Jn 8:44)
King of Babylon (Isa 14:4)
Lucifer (Isa 14:12)
Man of sin (2 Thes 2:3)
That old serpent (Rev 12:9; 20:2)
Power of darkness (Col 1:13)
Prince of the power of the air (Eph 2:2)
Prince of this world (Jn 12:31)

Satan (Job 1:6)
Son of perdition (Jn 17:12)
Tempter (Mat 4:3)
Wicked one (Mat 13:19)

13.3 A Second Look at Eve's Temptation

Sin entered the world through four successive doors. Oral Class Reading: Genesis 3:1-13

✓ **Deception** - Eve was deceived.

(1 Timothy 2:14) And Adam was not deceived, but the woman being deceived was in the transgression.

Class Discussion Questions

1. What does "deceived" mean?

✓ **Delight** - Eve was enamored by the possibility of being the god of her own life.

✓ **Disloyalty** - Adam was not deceived, but became more loyal to his wife than to his God.

✓ **Disobedience** - Adam willfully, knowingly, and deliberately sinned.

The perpetual falling of man into sin continues for much the same reasons.

Satan still deceives man. He says to them, did God really say that? How many times have you heard someone say, "show me a chapter and verse" or "prove it to me in the Bible". Christians who are not well-versed in Scriptures are easily deceived by false teachers and carnal Christians. It is vitally important that you "Study to shew thyself approved unto God, a workman that needeth not to be ashamed, rightly dividing the word of truth." (2 Timothy 2:15) Remember, Satan is the author of confusion.

(2 Corinthians 11:3) But I fear, lest by any means, as the serpent beguiled Eve through his subtilty, so your minds should be corrupted from the simplicity that is in Christ.

Man still delights in ruling his own life. He wants to "be his own person". But Christians are not their own people.

(1 Corinthians 6:19-20) What? know ye not that your body is the temple of the Holy Ghost which is in you, which ye have of God, and ye are not your own? For ye are bought with a price: therefore glorify God in your body, and in your spirit, which are God's.

(1 John 2:15-16) Love not the world, neither the things that are in the world. If any man love the world, the love of the Father is not in him. For all that is in the world, the lust of the flesh, and the lust of the eyes, and the pride of life, is not of the Father, but is of the world.

Like Adam, man still has trouble with loyalty to others over loyalty to God.

(Matthew 10:37) He that loveth father or mother more than me is not worthy of me: and he that loveth son or daughter more than me is not worthy of me.

Man still sins willfully, knowingly, and deliberately.

13.4 What is Sin?

Sin is anything that is contrary to the character, will, or pleasure of God. Sin is not only reflected by what we do, but, by what we do not do. Sin is not only reflected by what we are, but what we are not. The opposite of sin is divine perfection. Thus, sin is any aim or shot that falls short of that mark.

(Philippians 3:13-15) Brethren, I count not myself to have apprehended: but this one thing I do, forgetting those things which are behind, and reaching forth unto those things which are before, I press toward the mark for the prize of the high calling of God in Christ Jesus. Let us therefore, as many as be perfect, be thus minded: and if in any thing ye be otherwise minded, God shall reveal even this unto you.

Six things mark this falling short:

✓ Sin is falling short of a complete **obedience** to God's commands. (Rom 6:16) Can you think of an example of this falling short?

✓ Sin is falling short of a complete **submission** to God's will. (Heb 13:20,21; Jas 4:7) Can you think of examples whereby one is not in submission to God's will?

✓ Sin is falling short of a complete **conformity** to God's moral and righteous character. (Rom 12:1,2) Can you think of an example where a Christian is no longer in conformity to God's moral and righteous character.

✓ Sin is falling short of a complete **fellowship** with God. (1 Cor 1:9; 1 Jn 1:3) Can you name the ways Christians fellowship with God?

✓ Sin is falling short of a complete **faith** in God. (Heb 11:6; Rom 8:28; Prov 3:5-7) In what way can a Christian fall short of a complete faith in God?

✓ Sin is falling short of a complete **initiative** to do good. (Jas 4:17; Gal 6:10) Name the last opportunity you had to do good and you did it!

As we come to see the scope of sin, we can then better understand the depth of Romans 3:23, *"For all have sinned, and come short of the glory of God."* Roman Catholicism took it upon itself to label seven sins as deadly. They listed those sins as: avarice/greed, sloth, pride, envy, lust, gluttony, and wrath/anger. The R.C. church made a division between sins which were *venial* and could be forgiven without the need for the sacrament of Confession and those which were *capital* and merited damnation. Capital or Deadly Sins were so called because they could have a fatal effect on an individual's spiritual health according to Catholicism. British wall paintings stressed the connection between committing the Deadly Sins and ending up in Hell. This Catholic doctrine is contrary to the teaching of Scriptures which label all sins as deadly. (Rom 6:23)

Because of sin, our lives are in a constant state of spiritual warfare. We fight against things seen and unseen.

(Ecclesiastes 7:20) For there is not a just man upon earth, that doeth good, and sinneth not.

(1 John 2:16) For all that is in the world, the lust of the flesh, and the lust of the eyes, and the pride of life, is not of the Father, but is of the world.

(Ephesians 6:12) For we wrestle not against flesh and blood, but against principalities, against powers, against the rulers of the darkness of this world, against spiritual wickedness in high places.

(2 Corinthians 10:3-6) For though we walk in the flesh, we do not war after the flesh: (For the weapons of our warfare are not carnal, but mighty through God to the pulling down of strong holds;) Casting down imaginations, and every high thing that exalteth itself against the knowledge of God, and bringing into captivity every thought to the obedience of Christ; And having in a readiness to revenge all disobedience, when your obedience is fulfilled.

Redemption, forgiveness, and victory over sin will be developed in the chapters ahead.

This Week's Memory Verse

Therefore to him that knoweth to do good, and doeth *it* not, to him it is sin. (James 4:17)

The Doctrine Sin, The Origin and Entrance of Sin Into The World

1. The earliest sin recorded in Scripture is that of Satan's. Satan became filled with _____.

2. Satan wanted to become his own god. He wanted to compete for God's _____ and _____.

3. Sin is anything that is contrary to the _____, _____, or _____ of God.

4. Six things mark this falling short:

   Sin is falling short of a complete _____ to God's commands.

   Sin is falling short of a complete _____ to God'swill.

   Sin is falling short of a complete _____ to God's moral and righteous character.

   Sin is falling short of a complete _____ with God.

   Sin is falling short of a complete _____ in God.

   Sin is falling short of a complete _____ to do good.

Write out this week's Bible verse from memory.

James 4:17

_____

_____

_____

_____

_____

Finish the Phrase

*How art thou fallen from heaven, O
Lucifer, son of the* _____

*how art thou cut down to the ground,
which didst weaken the* _____

I will be like the _____

And Adam was not _____

*What? know ye not that your body is the
temple of the* _____

I press toward the _____

*For there is not a just man upon earth,
that doeth good, and* _____

*For we wrestle not against flesh and
blood, but against principalities,
against powers, against the rulers of the
darkness of this world, against* _____

*For though we walk in the flesh, we do
not* _____

BEST POINT MADE

Proverbs Chapter Thirteen

What were the main themes of this chapter?

_____

_____

_____

_____

What were the instructional points meant to bring you closer to God?

_____

_____

_____

What were the instructional points meant to protect you from spiritual destruction?

_____

_____

_____

_____

What things in your life could use strengthening?

_____

_____

_____

_____

Was there anything in this chapter that was of help in serving the LORD?

_____

_____

_____

_____

Did you learn anything new about the LORD?

_____

_____

_____

_____

Were there any suggestions made whereby you can be a greater blessing to others?

_____

_____

_____

_____

_____

_____

14.1 The Consequence of Sin

✓ **Sin brought about a separation.**

(Genesis 3:8-10) And they heard the voice of the LORD God walking in the garden in the cool of the day: and Adam and his wife hid themselves from the presence of the LORD God amongst the trees of the garden. And the LORD God called unto Adam, and said unto him, Where art thou? And he said, I heard thy voice in the garden, and I was afraid, because I was naked; and I hid myself.

Before Adam and Eve fell into sin they were not conscious of their nakedness. It certainly had not previously had any effect on their fellowship with God. But now they knew they were naked and were ashamed to be seen by the eyes of God. So they hid themselves when the voice of God came walking through the garden. How foolish it is to think that anyone could hide from the eyes of God!

(Proverbs 15:3) The eyes of the LORD are in every place, beholding the evil and the good.

Sin now separated Adam and Eve from God. It separated them from the presence of God. He would never walk in the Garden with them again. Their fellowship with God was temporarily broken.

(Isaiah 59:2) But your iniquities have separated between you and your God, and your sins have hid his face from you, that he will not hear.

Thus, sin brought about a twofold separation. It brought about a separation from the presence of God and a separation from fellowship with God.

Have you ever thought about this separation in terms of Hell and eternity? On earth, an unsaved person experiences separation from God only in a limited way. Everywhere he goes he sees and hears God. It is likely that the Holy Spirit still convicts of sin in his heart. He sees the creative hand of God in his surroundings. He sees and hears the work of God through the voice and lives of Christians. While he lives, God remains just a repentant prayer away. Only in Hell will the unsaved experience total separation from both the presence of God and any fellowship with God. In other words, the condemned sinner will be "forever and ever out of the mind of God". It will be a waste of his time to call out to God.

Illustration

There is a bird that sharpens its beak on the rock of mountains. When the birds have completely worn away the mountains, "forever and ever" will not even have experienced its first day.

✓ **Sin brought about a penalty.**

Seven words have been used to summarize this penalty.

1. Death

It is obvious that sin brought about a physical death upon humanity.

(James 2:26) For as the body without the spirit is dead, so faith without works is dead also.

Death is not the cessation of bodily functions or brain waves. Death is the point of no return when the soul and spirit leave the body. All men will die a physical death and they die this death only once, despite the claims of those who say they died and came back to life.

(Hebrews 9:27) And as it is appointed unto men once to die, but after this the judgment:

One might rightly inquire of those who were raised from the dead in the Bible. Did they die again? The answer must be "no". God brought them unto

Himself some other way.

Another death fell upon mankind because of Adam's sin. Every person born is born into sin and sentenced to a spiritual death.

Discussion Questions

1. Name two O.T. saints who are no longer on the earth, but have not died yet?

2. These two will die after they return to earth. Do you know when that is?

(James 1:14-15) But every man is tempted, when he is drawn away of his own lust, and enticed. Then when lust hath conceived, it bringeth forth sin: and sin, when it is finished, bringeth forth death.

2. Loss

Man suffered the loss of paradise and the right to the Tree of Life.

(Genesis 3:22-24) And the LORD God said, Behold, the man is become as one of us, to know good and evil: and now, lest he put forth his hand, and take also of the tree of life, and eat, and live for ever: Therefore the LORD God sent him forth from the garden of Eden, to till the ground from whence he was taken. So he drove out the man; and he

placed at the east of the garden of Eden Cherubims, and a flaming sword which turned every way, to keep the way of the tree of life.

Everything about the garden was perfect for man. With access to the Tree of Life, man would have lived forever.

Man also suffered loss of his relationship to God. Man went from being a child of God to being a child of the Devil. While God is the "Father", He was no longer man's father.

(John 8:44) Ye are of your father the devil, and the lusts of your father ye will do. He was a murderer from the beginning, and abode not in the truth, because there is no truth in him. When he speaketh a lie, he speaketh of his own: for he is a liar, and the father of it.

Man suffered the loss of righteousness and any sense of spiritual direction. He became totally depraved. In other words, he had no natural inclination toward God or his need for God. He had no natural conviction of sin.

(Genesis 6:5) And GOD saw that the wickedness of man was great in the earth, and that every imagination of the thoughts of his heart was only evil continually.

(Isaiah 53:6) All we like sheep have gone astray; we have turned every one to his own way; and the LORD hath laid on him the iniquity of us all.

3. Condemnation

The judgment of God is sure and the sentence of God is sure. While Hell was created for Satan and his cohorts, its jaws were opened now for sinful man. Without the intervention and provision of God, this was man's only destiny.

(Psalm 9:17) The wicked shall be turned into hell, and all the nations that forget God.

(Revelation 21:8) But the fearful, and unbelieving, and the abominable, and murderers, and whoremongers, and sorcerers, and idolaters, and all liars, shall have their part in the lake which burneth with fire and brimstone: which is the second death.

4. Guilt

Man was both guilty and declared guilty of sin. Moving a step farther, man was penalized with the emotion of guilt. Man's conscience would bear the burdens of guilt.

The Psalmist cried, "There is no soundness in my flesh because of thine anger; neither is there any rest in my bones because of my sin. For mine iniquities are gone over mine head: as an heavy burden they are too heavy for me." (Psalm 38:3)

(Psalm 51:3) For I acknowledge my transgressions: and my sin is ever before me.

(Titus 1:15) Unto the pure all things are pure: but unto them that are defiled and unbelieving is nothing pure; but even their mind and conscience is defiled.

The peace and joy that God originally meant for us to have is assaulted by these guilty feelings.

5. Perdition

Perdition signifies a total ruination of those who die in their sin. It means to suffer permanent waste. Judas and the antichrist were both called the "Son of Perdition" by God. Yet, every unsaved person will suffer perdition through eternity.

(2 Peter 3:7) But the heavens and the earth, which are now, by the same word are kept in store, reserved unto fire against the day of judgment and perdition of ungodly men.

6. Punishment

This punishment is the just infliction of eternal torment in a literal fiery Hell. It is a fire so hot the flames are black. Any laborer in a heat treatment facility can tell you about black fire.

Illustration

On Interstate 69 in Michigan a pickup truck exploded into flames. As witnesses looked on in horror they could see the dark figures of people burning alive in the truck's cab. Before their eyes they could see those in the cab shrink as the flames burnt their flesh to a blackened state. One witness commented, "this is what Hell must be like". Another replied to him, "no, this is not even close to what Hell will be like".

(Job 31:2-3) For what portion of God is there from above? and what inheritance of the Almighty from on high? Is not destruction to the wicked? and a strange punishment to the workers of iniquity?

7. Eternal

Eternal indicates an everlasting state of existence without parole, probation, or another chance. It is to be forever and ever out of the mind of God, never again to be remembered.

✓ Sin brought about a separation.
✓ Sin brought about a penalty.

This Week's Memory Verse

The eyes of the LORD are in every place, beholding the evil and the good. (Proverbs 15:3)

The Doctrine Sin, The Consequences

1. We listed a two-fold separation. What were they?

_____

_____

2. Seven words have been used to summarize penalty. What were those words?

_____

_____

_____

_____

_____

_____

_____

3. Death is the point of no return when the soul and _____

_____

Write out this week's Bible verse from memory.

Proverbs 15:3

_____

_____

_____

_____

_____

Finish the Phrase

The eyes of the LORD are in every place, beholding the _____

But your iniquities have separated betweenyou_____

For as the body without the spirit is ___

so faith without works is _____

And as it is appointed unto men _____ but after this the _____

But every man is tempted, when he is drawn away of his own _____

lust hath conceived, it bringeth forth _____

and sin, when it is finished, bringeth forth _____

The wicked shall be turned into hell, and all_____

BEST POINT MADE

Proverbs Chapter Fourteen

What were the main themes of this chapter?

_____

_____

_____

_____

_____

What were the instructional points meant to bring you closer to God?

_____

_____

_____

_____

What were the instructional points meant to protect you from spiritual destruction?

_____

_____

_____

_____

What things in your life could use strengthening?

_____

_____

_____

_____

_____

Was there anything in this chapter that was of help in serving the LORD?

_____

_____

_____

_____

_____

Did you learn anything new about the LORD?

_____

_____

_____

_____

Were there any suggestions made whereby you can be a greater blessing to others?

_____

_____

_____

_____

_____

_____

15.1 Introduction

With the fall of man into sin, God's love reached out to him through a plan of redemption that was in place before the foundation of the world.

(1 Peter 1:18-20) Forasmuch as ye know that ye were not redeemed with corruptible things, as silver and gold, from your vain conversation received by tradition from your fathers; But with the precious blood of Christ, as of a lamb without blemish and without spot: Who verily was foreordained before the foundation of the world, but was manifest in these last times for you,

In an illustration we previously used, we told of a boy who built a small wood boat. One day he took his boat to the river to sail it in the waters. He tied a string to it so as not to lose it. However, the string broke and the boat went down the river. Though he looked for his boat, it was lost. A month later the same boy passed by a pawn shop where he saw his boat in the window. Excited, he went into the shop to claim his boat. The shop keeper told him that the boat may have been his at one time but it was no longer his. If he wanted the boat, he would have to buy it back for five dollars. The boy returned to the shop a few weeks later and bought his boat back for the five dollars. On the way out the boy said, "you are twice mine. I made you. Now I have bought you back again".

Redemption means to buy back. He redeemed his boat.

Though God made us, we became lost because of our sin. We drifted away from God. God had promised Adam that a Redeemer would come.

(Genesis 3:15) And I will put enmity between thee and the woman, and between thy seed and her seed; it shall bruise thy head, and thou shalt bruise his heel.

The serpent, who was the full representation of Satan, who deceived Eve and brought about her fall, was crushed and cursed of God forever through a Saviour to come. God said, "it (that Saviour) shall bruise thy head;"

John Gill wrote,

"The head of a serpent creeping on the ground is easily crushed and bruised, of which it is sensible, and therefore it is careful to hide and cover it. In the mystical sense, "it" or "he" is one of the names of God, (Psalm 102:27) (Isaiah 48:12) and here of the Messiah, the eminent seed of the woman, should bruise the head of the old serpent the devil, that is, destroy him and all his principalities and powers, break and confound all his schemes, and ruin all his works, crush his whole empire, strip him of his authority and sovereignty, and particularly of his power over death, and his tyranny over the bodies and souls of men; all which was done by Christ, when he became incarnate and suffered and died. (Hebrews 2:14 Hebrews 2:15; Colossians 2:15; 1 John 3:8)"

When we understand that God knew the fall of man would happen, for He knows all things past, present, and future; when we understand that God loved man before He even created him; we can then understand the depth of the childhood memory verse.

(John 3:16-17) For God so loved the world, that he gave his only begotten Son, that whosoever believeth in him should not perish, but have everlasting life. For God sent not his Son into the world to condemn the world; but that the world through him might be saved.

15.2 The Sacrificial Lamb

God gave Adam a temporary plan. He commanded that a lamb without blemish or spot be sacrificed for sin until the Redeemer (the Lamb of God) arrived on earth.

Class Discussion Questions

1. What was wrong with Cain's sacrifice in Genesis 4:1-7?

2. Was Cain given another chance?

Eventually that sacrifice would be carried out by the Jewish descendants of Abraham at the tabernacle and later the Temple. We have already discussed this subject and the subject of the two goats in previous chapters. Suffice it to say that Jesus Christ became the Lamb of God who was sacrificed once for our sins. In a previous lesson we looked at the six words that described the work of Christ on the cross.

In review, those words were:

ATONEMENT ... to forgive and cover up so as to remove the condemnation of sin.

RECONCILIATION ... to make equivalent.

PROPITIATION ... to appease or placate the wrath of God.

REDEMPTION ... literally, to buy back what is rightfully yours.

RANSOM ... payment to release another.

SUBSTITUTION ... to take our death sentence upon himself and satisfying the justice of God.

15.3 Man's Failed Attempts at Salvation

Man is obsessed with obtaining a favorable status in the "hereafter" by his own good works.

There are two categories of world religions.

✓ **Autosoterism**: which teaches that salvation is of man (works).

"Henceforth be ye to yourselves your own light, your own refuge, seek no other refuge." Buddha (on his death bed)

✓ **Christianity**: which teaches that salvation is in Christ alone and not by the works of man (by grace through faith).

Autosoterism stands in opposition to Biblical Christianity. Evangelical Christians have always been despised by all other errant religious groups. Evangelical Christians have always been accused of standing in the way of man's progress (humanism).

General William Booth, founder of the Salvation Army made this comment about the 20th century: "I consider that the chief dangers which will confront the twentieth century will be: religion without the Holy Spirit, Christianity without Christ, forgiveness without regeneration, morality without God, and Heaven without Hell."

Some people try to get to Heaven by their own good works. Good works cannot save us because it is not our lack of good works that are keeping us out of Heaven. It is our sin. God specifically omits good works from the plan of salvation.

(Ephesians 2:8-9) For by grace are ye saved through faith; and that not of yourselves: it is the gift of God: Not of works, lest any man should boast.

(Titus 3:5) Not by works of righteousness which we have done, but according to his mercy he saved us, by the washing of regeneration, and renewing of the Holy Ghost;

Other people try to get to Heaven by baptism. Scriptures teach that man is saved apart from water baptism.

The house of Cornelius is a perfect example of this truth.

(Acts 10:34-48) Then Peter opened his mouth, and said, Of a truth I perceive that God is no respecter of persons: But in every nation he that feareth him, and worketh righteousness, is accepted with him. The word which God sent unto the children of Israel, preaching peace by Jesus Christ: (he is Lord of all:)

That word, I say, ye know, which was published throughout all Judaea, and began from Galilee, after the baptism which John preached; How God anointed Jesus of Nazareth with the Holy Ghost and with power: who went about doing good, and healing all that were oppressed of the devil; for God was with him. And we are witnesses of all things which he did both in the land of the Jews, and in Jerusalem; whom they slew and hanged on a tree: Him God raised up the third day, and shewed him openly; Not to all the people, but unto witnesses chosen before of God, even to us, who did eat and drink with him after he rose from the dead. And he commanded us to preach unto the people, and to testify that it is he which was ordained of God to be the Judge of quick and dead. To him give all the prophets witness, that through his name whosoever believeth in him shall receive remission of sins. While Peter yet spake these words, the Holy Ghost fell on all them which heard the word. And they of the circumcision which believed were astonished, as many as came with Peter, because that on the Gentiles also was poured out the gift of the Holy Ghost. For they heard them speak with tongues, and magnify God. Then answered Peter, Can any man forbid water, that these should not be baptized, which have received the Holy Ghost as well as we? And he commanded them to be baptized in the name of the Lord. Then prayed they him to tarry certain days.

What do we see in this account? We see that they were saved before they were water baptized. They were filled with the Holy Ghost before they were water baptized. Only saved people were filled with the Holy Ghost.

The thief on the cross is not an illustration of N.T. salvation (Lk 23:39-43). N.T. salvation requires a belief in the bodily resurrection of Christ (Rom 10:9). The thief was saved by his repentance of sin and faith in Christ as the Messiah. Christ had not yet died and arose from the dead. The thief was saved, but in an Old Testament way.

Other people try to get to Heaven by joining a particular denomination or church. There were no denominations in apostolic times nor in the first few centuries after Christ's death. The Scriptures never say nor imply that salvation is to be found in church membership.

15.4 Salvation in Jesus Christ Alone

Christ was the lamb of God pictured in the Old Testament sacrifices. Salvation is only found in Jesus Christ, the Son of God. Christ is the only Saviour and the only way to Heaven. Through His shed blood, death, burial, and resurrection salvation is offered to sinners.

(Ephesians 1:7) In whom we have redemption through his blood, the forgiveness of sins, according to the

riches of his grace;

(John 14:1-6) Let not your heart be troubled: ye believe in God, believe also in me. In my Father's house are many mansions: if it were not so, I would have told you. I go to prepare a place for you. And if I go and prepare a place for you, I will come again, and receive you unto myself; that where I am, there ye may be also. And whither I go ye know, and the way ye know. Thomas saith unto him, Lord, we know not whither thou goest; and how can we know the way? Jesus saith unto him, I am the way, the truth, and the life: no man cometh unto the Father, but by me.

Christ's resurrection from the dead is proof that He is deity. All other self-proclaimed saviors suffered a natural death and their bodies are in their marked graves today. By this they proved that they were not deity. Examples of these dead who are still in their graves: Mohammed, Buddha, Confucius, and David Koresh. Death proves counterfeit.

(Acts 4:11) This is the stone which was set at nought of you builders, which is become the head of the corner.

15.5 Thoughts on Repentance

There are many aspects to the teachings of repentance in Scripture. If repentance is defined as a "turning away from sin," then it must be noted that no unsaved person can do that. In error, some people say that "if you did not make Him Lord of all, you did not make Him Lord at all."

This unbiblical position is called "Lordship Salvation". Lordship over the Christian life does not come until after salvation and is a life long process of spiritual growing made possible in the strength of Jesus Christ and the power of the Holy Spirit. (1 Pet 2:1-2; 2 Pet 3:18)

(1 Peter 2:1-2) Wherefore laying aside all malice, and all guile, and hypocrisies, and envies, and all evil speakings, As newborn babes, desire the sincere milk of the word, that ye may grow thereby:

(2 Peter 3:18) But grow in grace, and in the knowledge of our Lord and Saviour Jesus Christ. To him be glory both now and for ever. Amen.

15.6 Salvation

Repentance in regard to the salvation decision has a simple Bible definition. Repentance unto salvation is a Godly sorrow for sin.

(2 Corinthians 7:9-10) Now I rejoice, not that ye were made sorry, but that ye sorrowed to repentance: for ye were made sorry after a godly manner, that ye might receive damage by us in nothing. For godly sorrow worketh repentance to salvation not to be repented of: but

the sorrow of the world worketh death.

Simply put, to be saved, a sinner must acknowledge his sinful state and have a regret or sorrow for that fact. The sinner who is coming to Christ is desirous of forgiveness.

(Acts 13:38) Be it known unto you therefore, men and brethren, that through this man is preached unto you the forgiveness of sins:

The Apostles preached repentance. (Acts 2:38; 17:30; 2 Pet 3:9; Rom 2:4; Heb 6:1)

Salvation is a faith decision that causes the sinner to call unto the Lord in prayer for forgiveness and receiving Christ as Saviour.

There are three steps to exercising faith in Christ:

✓ **Faith to believe**

(Romans 10:9-11) That if thou shalt confess with thy mouth the Lord Jesus, and shalt believe in thine heart that God hath raised him from the dead, thou shalt be saved. For with the heart man believeth unto righteousness; and with the mouth confession is made unto salvation. For the scripture saith, Whosoever believeth on him shall not be ashamed.

✓ **Faith to receive**

(Romans 10:13) For whosoever shall call upon the name of the Lord shall be saved.

(John 1:12) But as many as received him, to them gave he power to become the sons of God, even to them that believe on his name:

✓ **Faith to claim**

(1 John 5:11-13) And this is the record, that God hath given to us eternal life, and this life is in his Son. He that hath the Son hath life; and he that hath not the Son of God hath not life. These things have I written unto you that believe on the name of the Son of God; that ye may know that ye have eternal life, and that ye may believe on the name of the Son of God.

In keeping the plan of salvation simple, we must not be careless to make it incomplete.

This Week's Memory Verse

Jesus saith unto him, I am the way, the truth, and the life: no man cometh unto the Father, but by me. (John 14:6)

Chapter Fifteen Quiz & Memory Verse Fill In Study Sheet

The Doctrine Salvation

1. Redemption means to _____.

2. Autosoterism: which teaches that salvation is of _____. (works)

3. Christianity: which teaches that salvation is in _____ alone.

4. Christ's resurrection from the dead is proof that He is _____.

5. There are three steps to exercising faith in Christ.

_____

_____

_____

Write out this week's Bible verse from memory.

John 14:6

_____

_____

_____

_____

_____

Finish the Phrase

Forasmuch as ye know that ye were not redeemed with corruptible things, as silver and gold, from your vain conversation received by tradition from your fathers; But with the _____

For God sent not his Son into the world to condemn the world; but that the world through him _____

Not by works of righteousness which we have done, but according to his mercy he _____

Let not your heart be troubled: ye believe in God, believe also in me. In my _____

And if I go and prepare a place for you, I will come again, and receive you unto myself; that where I am, _____

I am the way, the truth, and the life: no man cometh unto the Father, but by _____

But grow in grace, and in _____

For godly sorrow worketh _____

And this is the record, that God hath given to us _____

BEST POINT MADE

Proverbs Chapter Fifteen

What were the main themes of this chapter?

_____

_____

_____

_____

What were the instructional points meant to bring you closer to God?

_____

_____

_____

What were the instructional points meant to protect you from spiritual destruction?

_____

_____

_____

What things in your life could use strengthening?

_____

_____

_____

_____

Was there anything in this chapter that was of help in serving the LORD?

_____

_____

_____

_____

Did you learn anything new about the LORD?

_____

_____

_____

Were there any suggestions made whereby you can be a greater blessing to others?

_____

_____

_____

_____

_____

16.1 Review of Salvation

Salvation is an absolute offer, whereby we can KNOW that we have eternal life. Scripture is written for this purpose.

(1 John 5:13) These things have I written unto you that believe on the name of the Son of God; that ye may know that ye have eternal life, and that ye may believe on the name of the Son of God.

There are many who believe that Christ is the Son of God who died for us and rose from the dead, yet they do not know if they are going to Heaven. This text clearly corrects the "hope so, maybe so" or "no one can know" crowd.

We can put the salvation decision into three categorical steps.

✓ **Acknowledge your lost and sinful condition.**

Every person that ever lived was and is a hopeless sinner.

(Romans 3:10) As it is written, There is none righteous, no, not one:

(Romans 3:23) For all have sinned, and come short of the glory of God;

(Ecclesiastes 7:20) For there is not a just man upon earth, that doeth good, and sinneth not.

Each person inherited this sinful condition from Adam. (Rom 5:12; Psa 51:5)

(Romans 5:12) Wherefore, as by one man sin entered into the world, and death by sin; and so death passed upon all men, for that all have sinned:

Good works are not good enough to get you to Heaven because a lack of good works is not standing in the way of you going to Heaven. It is your sin problem that stands between you and God, between you and Heaven, between you and salvation.

It is the goodness of God that leads a person to repentance. Repentance is manifested by a sorrow for sin.

(2 Corinthians 7:9-10) Now I rejoice, not that ye were made sorry, but that ye sorrowed to repentance: for ye were made sorry after a godly manner, that ye might receive damage by us in nothing. For godly sorrow worketh repentance to salvation not to be repented of: but the sorrow of the world worketh death.

It is this sorrow that causes us to

genuinely seek forgiveness. The books of Hebrews and Second Peter tie repentance to the very foundation of salvation (Heb 6:1; 2 Pet 3:9). It would be pointless to ask forgiveness if one were not sorry for the offense.

✓ **Believe that Christ paid sin's price for you and took the penalty of your death upon Himself.**

The penalty for sin is both physical death and eternal damnation.

(Romans 6:23) For the wages of sin is death; but the gift of God is eternal life through Jesus Christ our Lord.

(Revelation 20:10-15) And the devil that deceived them was cast into the lake of fire and brimstone, where the beast and the false prophet are, and shall be tormented day and night for ever and ever. And I saw a great white throne, and him that sat on it, from whose face the earth and the heaven fled away; and there was found no place for them. And I saw the dead, small and great, stand before God; and the books were opened: and another book was opened, which is the book of life: and the dead were judged out of those things which were written in the books, according to their works. And the sea gave up the dead which were in it; and death and hell delivered up the dead which were in them: and they were judged every man according to their works. And death and hell were cast into the lake of fire. This is the second death. And whosoever was not found written in the book of life was cast into the lake of fire.

God's demanded payment for sin is the shed blood of a perfect lamb, without sin. Christ was that lamb who shed His blood for you. Without the shed blood of Christ no person could ever be saved. It was not the death of Christ that washed away our sin, it was His shed blood. However, when Christ died, he took your death penalty upon Himself and died in your place. It was for your sin He died.

(Romans 5:8-9) But God commendeth his love toward us, in that, while we were yet sinners, Christ died for us. Much more then, being now justified by his blood, we shall be saved from wrath through him.

✓ **Call upon Jesus Christ.**

Confess that Christ was and is the Son of God. Confess that you know Christ died for you and rose again from the grave.

(Romans 10:9-13) That if thou shalt confess with thy mouth the Lord Jesus, and shalt believe in thine heart that God hath raised him from the dead, thou shalt be saved. For with the heart man believeth unto righteousness; and with the mouth confession is made unto salvation. For the scripture saith, Whosoever believeth on him shall not be ashamed. For there is no difference

between the Jew and the Greek: for the same Lord over all is rich unto all that call upon him. For whosoever shall call upon the name of the Lord shall be saved.

Ask the LORD to forgive you for your sin and to come into your life to be your personal Saviour.

Sample Prayer

Dear Jesus, I know that I have sinned against you. I believe you are the Son of God who died for me and rose from the dead. Please forgive me for my sins and come into my life to be my Saviour. I put my trust in you alone. Thank you for saving me and giving to me eternal life. Amen

16.2 All Things New

(2 Corinthians 5:17) Therefore if any man be in Christ, he is a new creature: old things are passed away; behold, all things are become new.

Real salvation produces four things that are new for us.

✓ Salvation produces a **NEW DESIRE.**

(1 Peter 2:1-2) Wherefore laying aside all malice, and all guile, and hypocrisies, and envies, and all evil speakings, As newborn babes, desire the sincere milk of the word, that ye may grow thereby:

People who genuinely get saved will develop new spiritual desires not previously had. These desires will include things like a hunger:

for the WORD (Mt 5:6)
for PRAYER (Jude 1:20,21)
for FELLOWSHIP (1 Jn 1:3)
for GROWTH (1 Pet 2:2)
for PREACHING (Col 1:25-28)
for RIGHTEOUSNESS (Rev 19:8)

✓ Salvation produces a **NEW DIRECTION.**

(Ephesians 4:17-24) This I say therefore, and testify in the Lord, that ye henceforth walk not as other Gentiles walk, in the vanity of their mind, Having the understanding darkened, being alienated from the life of God through the ignorance that is in them, because of the blindness of their heart: Who being past feeling have given themselves over unto lasciviousness, to work all uncleanness with greediness. But ye have not so learned Christ; If so be that ye have heard him, and have been taught by him, as the truth is in Jesus: That ye put off concerning the former conversation the old man, which is corrupt according to the deceitful lusts; And be renewed in the spirit of your mind; And that ye put on the new man, which after God is created in righteousness and true holiness.

(Ephesians 5:15-17) See then that ye walk circumspectly, not as fools, but

as wise, Redeeming the time, because the days are evil. Wherefore be ye not unwise, but understanding what the will of the Lord is.

Of course, we are on a new path toward eternity, but our point here is broader than that. Our old paths were self-serving, self-focused, and self-directed. Salvation changes the entire direction of our lives, our aspirations, and our pursuits. While everyone participates in things that have no eternal consequence, Christians are mindful of the fact that these things are secondary to all spiritual activities. Salvation gives a serving heart. We serve the LORD with gladness and we serve others with pleasure.

(Psalm 100:1-5) Make a joyful noise unto the LORD, all ye lands. Serve the LORD with gladness: come before his presence with singing. Know ye that the LORD he is God: it is he that hath made us, and not we ourselves; we are his people, and the sheep of his pasture. Enter into his gates with thanksgiving, and into his courts with praise: be thankful unto him, and bless his name. For the LORD is good; his mercy is everlasting; and his truth endureth to all generations.

(Galatians 5:13) For, brethren, ye have been called unto liberty; only use not liberty for an occasion to the flesh, but by love serve one another.

Because we are no longer our own, for we are bought with a price, the will of God for us is to submit ourselves to HIS will in all things. One quickly discovers that the will of God is always good and fills us not only with joy, but the peace of God that passes all understanding. Outside of the will of God, a Christian might have short lived fun, but he will not find peace and fulfillment. Sadly, Christians die every day who have done nothing of any eternal consequence. Their works will burn up at the Bema seat judgement. (1 Corinthians 3:11-15)

✓ Salvation produces a **NEW STRENGTH.**

Serving the LORD and doing good unto others can be a very tiring experience once the newness of it all wears off. In this somewhat weakened state we become more vulnerable to discouragement and temptation. Yet, the Lord's strength is readily available and easily renewed on a daily basis.

(Isaiah 40:31) But they that wait upon the LORD shall renew their strength; they shall mount up with wings as eagles; they shall run, and not be weary; and they shall walk, and not faint.

(2 Corinthians 12:9) And he said unto me, My grace is sufficient for thee: for my strength is made perfect in weakness. Most gladly therefore will I rather glory in my infirmities, that the power of

Christ may rest upon me.

✓ Salvation produces a **NEW VICTORY.**

(1 Corinthians 15:56-59) The sting of death is sin; and the strength of sin is the law. But thanks be to God, which giveth us the victory through our Lord Jesus Christ. Therefore, my beloved brethren, be ye stedfast, unmoveable, always abounding in the work of the Lord, forasmuch as ye know that your labour is not in vain in the Lord.

Victory belongs to the LORD who gives us the victory over temptation. The stronger we become in our prayer life and in our Bible reading, the stronger we will become in overcoming the temptation to sin or err from the truth. Before salvation, man is almost helpless in resisting Satan's devices. But in Christ, he can be victorious. Greater is He that is in us than anyone or anything in the world.

(1 Corinthians 10:13) There hath no temptation taken you but such as is common to man: but God is faithful, who will not suffer you to be tempted above that ye are able; but will with the temptation also make a way to escape, that ye may be able to bear it.

15.3 Five Evidences of Salvation

✓ The evidence of a loving life (1 Jn 2:9-10)

✓ The evidence of a chastened life (Heb 12:5-8)

✓ The evidence of a changed life (2 Cor 5:17; 6:17)

✓ The evidence of a devotional life (Pro 8:17; Psa 1:2-3)

✓ The evidence of a soul-winning life (Jn 4:35; Jude 1:21-23)

Write down the evidence of your own genuine salvation.

The evidence of a chastened life:

_____

_____

_____

The evidence of a changed life:

_____

_____

_____

The evidence of a devotional life:

_____

_____

_____

The evidence of a soul-winning life:

_____

_____

_____

This Week's Memory Verse

Therefore if any man be in Christ, he is a new creature: old things are passed away; behold, all things are become new. (2 Corinthians 5:17)

The Doctrine Salvation, New Life in Christ

1. List the five evidences of genuine salvation.

_____

_____

_____

_____

_____

2. List the four new things salvation produces.

_____

_____

_____

_____

Write out this week's Bible verse from memory.

2 Corinthians 5:17

_____

_____

_____

_____

_____

Finish the Phrase

These things have I written unto you that believe on the name of the Son of God; that ye may

_____

For there is not a just man upon earth, that doeth good, and _____

For godly sorrow worketh _____

See then that ye walk circumspectly, not as fools, but as wise, Redeeming the time, because

_____

But they that wait upon the LORD shall renew their _____

My grace is sufficient for thee: for my strength is made perfect _____

Therefore, my beloved brethren, be ye stedfast, unmoveable, always abounding in _____

Extra Credit Chapel Notes

_____   _____
_____   _____
_____   _____
_____   _____
_____   _____
_____   _____
_____   _____
_____   _____
_____   _____
_____   _____
_____   _____
_____   _____
_____   _____
_____   _____
_____   _____
_____   _____
_____
_____   **BEST POINT MADE**
_____
_____   _____
_____   _____
_____   _____
_____   _____
_____   _____
_____   _____
_____   _____
_____   _____

Proverbs Chapter Sixteen

What were the main themes of this chapter?

_____

_____

_____

_____

_____

What were the instructional points meant to bring you closer to God?

_____

_____

_____

_____

What were the instructional points meant to protect you from spiritual destruction?

_____

_____

_____

_____

What things in your life could use strengthening?

_____

_____

_____

_____

_____

Was there anything in this chapter that was of help in serving the LORD?

_____

_____

_____

_____

Did you learn anything new about the LORD?

_____

_____

_____

_____

Were there any suggestions made whereby you can be a greater blessing to others?

_____

_____

_____

_____

_____

17.1 The Term

The term "eternal security" is used to describe the permanent and eternal assets of salvation. The phrase "once saved always saved" refers to the fact that if a person is truly saved, he cannot lose that salvation. He is eternally secure in Christ.

This flies in the face of logic until you come to an understanding of what the Bible says about God's intent, God's purpose, and God's plan.

(Ephesians 1:3-7) Blessed be the God and Father of our Lord Jesus Christ, who hath blessed us with all spiritual blessings in heavenly places in Christ: According as he hath chosen us in him before the foundation of the world, that we should be holy and without blame before him in love: Having predestinated us unto the adoption of children by Jesus Christ to himself, according to the good pleasure of his will, To the praise of the glory of his grace, wherein he hath made us accepted in the beloved. In whom we have redemption through his blood, the forgiveness of sins, according to the riches of his grace;

17.2 The Effects of Christ's Sacrifice

We have already established that Christ shed his blood on the cross for our sins and without that shed blood there would be no remission of sins.

The effects of the sacrifice and shed blood of Jesus Christ are both permanent and all encompassing. It is very important that you read and understand the following Bible texts.

(Hebrews 9:11-28) But Christ being come an high priest of good things to come, by a greater and more perfect tabernacle, not made with hands, that is to say, not of this building; Neither by the blood of goats and calves, but by his own blood he entered in once into the holy place, having obtained eternal redemption for us. For if the blood of bulls and of goats, and the ashes of an heifer sprinkling the unclean, sanctifieth to the purifying of the flesh: How much more shall the blood of Christ, who through the eternal Spirit offered himself without spot to God, purge your conscience from dead works to serve the living God? And for this cause he is the mediator of the new testament, that by means of death, for the redemption of the transgressions that were under the first testament, they which are called might receive the promise of eternal inheritance. For where a testament is, there must also of necessity be the death of the testator. For a testament is of force

after men are dead: otherwise it is of no strength at all while the testator liveth. Whereupon neither the first testament was dedicated without blood. For when Moses had spoken every precept to all the people according to the law, he took the blood of calves and of goats, with water, and scarlet wool, and hyssop, and sprinkled both the book, and all the people, Saying, This is the blood of the testament which God hath enjoined unto you. Moreover he sprinkled with blood both the tabernacle, and all the vessels of the ministry. And almost all things are by the law purged with blood; and without shedding of blood is no remission. It was therefore necessary that the patterns of things in the heavens should be purified with these; but the heavenly things themselves with better sacrifices than these. For Christ is not entered into the holy places made with hands, which are the figures of the true; but into heaven itself, now to appear in the presence of God for us: Nor yet that he should offer himself often, as the high priest entereth into the holy place every year with blood of others; For then must he often have suffered since the foundation of the world: but now once in the end of the world hath he appeared to put away sin by the sacrifice of himself. And as it is appointed unto men once to die, but after this the judgment: So Christ was once offered to bear the sins of many; and unto them that look for him shall he appear the second time without sin unto salvation.

(1 Timothy 2:5-6) For there is one God, and one mediator between God and men, the man Christ Jesus; Who gave himself a ransom for all, to be testified in due time.

(Hebrews 10:17-19) And their sins and iniquities will I remember no more. Now where remission of these is, there is no more offering for sin. Having therefore, brethren, boldness to enter into the holiest by the blood of Jesus,

✓ All of our sins (past, present, and future) are atoned for.

✓ All of our sins (past, present, and future) are paid for.

✓ All of our sins (past, present, and future) are remitted.

✓ All of our sins (past, present, and future) are already judged.

17.3 The Benefits of Christ's Sacrifice

Not only are the effects of the sacrifice and shed blood of Jesus Christ permanent and all-encompassing, but the benefits of the sacrifice and shed blood of Jesus Christ are permanent and all-encompassing.

✓ Our condemnation is removed forever.

(John 5:24) Verily, verily, I say unto you, He that heareth my word, and

believeth on him that sent me, hath everlasting life, and shall not come into condemnation; but is passed from death unto life.

✓ Our everlasting life is secured forever.

(John 4:14) But whosoever drinketh of the water that I shall give him shall never thirst; but the water that I shall give him shall be in him a well of water springing up into everlasting life.

(John 10:27-29) My sheep hear my voice, and I know them, and they follow me: And I give unto them eternal life; and they shall never perish, neither shall any man pluck them out of my hand. My Father, which gave them me, is greater than all; and no man is able to pluck them out of my Father's hand.

(1 John 5:12-13) He that hath the Son hath life; and he that hath not the Son of God hath not life. These things have I written unto you that believe on the name of the Son of God; that ye may know that ye have eternal life, and that ye may believe on the name of the Son of God.

✓ Our relationship to God is sealed (tamper proofed) forever.

(Ephesians 4:30) And grieve not the holy Spirit of God, whereby ye are sealed unto the day of redemption.

(Hebrews 13:5-6) Let your conversation be without covetousness; and be content with such things as ye have: for he hath said, I will never leave thee, nor forsake thee. So that we may boldly say, The Lord is my helper, and I will not fear what man shall do unto me.

✓ Our sanctification is declared forever.

(Hebrews 10:10) By the which will we are sanctified through the offering of the body of Jesus Christ once for all.

✓ Our adoption is settled forever.

(Galatians 4:4-7) But when the fulness of the time was come, God sent forth his Son, made of a woman, made under the law, To redeem them that were under the law, that we might receive the adoption of sons. And because ye are sons, God hath sent forth the Spirit of his Son into your hearts, crying, Abba, Father. Wherefore thou art no more a servant, but a son; and if a son, then an heir of God through Christ.

(1 John 3:1-2) Behold, what manner of love the Father hath bestowed upon us, that we should be called the sons of God: therefore the world knoweth us not, because it knew him not. Beloved, now are we the sons of God, and it doth not yet appear what we shall be: but we know that, when he shall appear, we shall be like him; for we shall see him as he is.

Once a person is saved, he will not and cannot be cast out.

(John 6:37) All that the Father giveth me shall come to me; and him that cometh to me I will in no wise cast out.

17.4 Answering Opposing Arguments

Some people argue against the doctrine of eternal security. They say that while Christ will never leave you, you can leave Christ. They overlook the obvious. Christ is inside the believer. The believer is not inside of Christ. One might better ask where did you take Christ this past week, what did you make Him watch, what did you make Him listen to or what did you make Him be a part of? Christ, who never leaves us, goes with us wherever we go. He never leaves us.

Some would say that if you deny Christ, He will deny you. They base this premise on a Luke text.

(Luke 12:8-9) Also I say unto you, Whosoever shall confess me before men, him shall the Son of man also confess before the angels of God: But he that denieth me before men shall be denied before the angels of God.

Again, some obvious things are overlooked. Peter denied Christ (Lk 22:31-34). Thomas denied Christ (Jn 20:24-28). The disciples on the road to Emmaus denied Christ (Lk 24:13-32).

Protestant reformer Martin Luther stated "Fear God and you will have nothing else to fear". Chapter twelve of Luke begins the subject of Christ's words at hand. *"Beware ye of the leaven of the Pharisees, which is hypocrisy"* (vs.1) The Pharisees denied Christ not out of fear, but out of disbelief. They refused to put their trust in Christ because they refused His identity as the Son of God. The text is their rebuke and the rebuke of all others of the same unbelief. The Pharisees were not men who once believed in Christ then decided later they did not believe in Christ. They never believed in Christ and thus denied Him.

Others who oppose the doctrine of eternal security will point to the following text in Hebrews.

(Hebrews 6:4-6) For it is impossible for those who were once enlightened, and have tasted of the heavenly gift, and were made partakers of the Holy Ghost, And have tasted the good word of God, and the powers of the world to come, If they shall fall away, to renew them again unto repentance; seeing they crucify to themselves the Son of God afresh, and put him to an open shame.

Our answer stands upon the obvious. If this text teaches that a Christian can lose his salvation, then it also teaches that salvation can never be regained. However, this text is not about the repentance of salvation, but the repentance that brings the wayward Christian back to God again. The warning is in the fact that some Christians say "no" to God once too often and are put on a spiritual shelf, never to be renewed again in their spiritual desire. Imagine being so worldly as to sear the conscience with a hot iron. It is a good insert here to remind every Christian that it is the goodness of God that leads us to repentance. But be warned, don't test the limits of the Almighty!

What about Christians who deny that Christ is the Son of God? To this we answer that it is impossible to deny a Christ who truly lives within. And why is this? Because of the witness of the Holy Spirit inside every Christian.

(Romans 8:16) The Spirit itself beareth witness with our spirit, that we are the children of God:

17.5 A License to Sin?

Because we cannot lose our salvation can we live the way we want to?

Other denominations do not know what to think of Baptists. On the one hand they accuse us of believing that we can live any way we want to without fear of losing our salvation. On the other hand they accuse us of being legalists because we take a stand against everything. Logic tells us that we cannot be guilty of both at the same time. In truth, we do not believe that the Christian can live any way he wants to. God's chastisement is sure.

(Hebrews 12:6-8) For whom the Lord loveth he chasteneth, and scourgeth every son whom he receiveth. If ye endure chastening, God dealeth with you as with sons; for what son is he whom the father chasteneth not? But if ye be without chastisement, whereof all are partakers, then are ye bastards, and not sons.

Can Christians live any way they want to? The answer is "no". We would ask, "why would a true Christian want to live any way they want to?".

We put forth the question Paul asked.

(Romans 6:1-2) What shall we say then? Shall we continue in sin, that grace may abound? God forbid. How shall we, that are dead to sin, live any longer therein?

One Final Thought

Satan wants all saved people to think they are lost and all lost people to think they are saved.

This Week's Memory Verse

For by one offering he hath perfected for ever them that are sanctified. (Hebrews 10:14)

Chapter Seventeen Quiz & Memory Verse Fill In Study Sheet

The Doctrine Salvation, Eternal Security

1. List the four benefits of Christ's sacrifice.

      All of our sins (past, present, and future) are _____

      All of our sins (past, present, and future) are _____

      All of our sins (past, present, and future) are _____

      All of our sins (past, present, and future) are _____

2. List the five benefits of Christ's sacrifice.

      Our _____

      Our _____

      Our _____

      Our _____

      Our _____

Write out this week's Bible verse from memory.

Hebrews 10:14

_____

_____

_____

_____

_____

Finish the Phrase

Neither by the blood of goats and calves, but by his own blood he entered in once into the _____

For Christ is not entered into the holy places made with hands, which are the figures of the true; but into heaven itself, now to appear in the presence of God for us: Nor yet that he should offer himself

_____

And their sins and iniquities will I remember no more _____

Nowwhereremissionoftheseis,thereisno more _____

Verily, verily, I say unto you, He that heareth my word, and believeth on him that sent me, hath everlasting life, and shall not _____

My Father, which gave them me, is greater than all; and no man is able to

_____

Let your conversation be without covetousness; and be content with such things as ye have: for he hath said, I will never

_____

All that the Father giveth me shall come to me; and him that cometh to me I will in no wise _____

The Spirit itself beareth witness with our spirit, that we are the _____

BEST POINT MADE

Proverbs Chapter Seventeen

What were the main themes of this chapter?

_____

_____

_____

_____

What were the instructional points meant to bring you closer to God?

_____

_____

_____

_____

What were the instructional points meant to protect you from spiritual destruction?

_____

_____

_____

_____

What things in your life could use strengthening?

_____

_____

_____

_____

Was there anything in this chapter that was of help in serving the LORD?

_____

_____

_____

_____

_____

Did you learn anything new about the LORD?

_____

_____

_____

_____

Were there any suggestions made whereby you can be a greater blessing to others?

_____

_____

_____

_____

_____

_____

18.1 Introduction

Scripture clearly declares that all men will stand before God after they die. This judgement will take place after death.

(Hebrews 9:27) And as it is appointed unto men once to die, but after this the judgment:

The judgement of God has always been sure, it is sure, and will always be sure. Divine judgment is spoken of in both the Old and New Testaments.

(Psalm 96:13) Before the LORD: for he cometh, for he cometh to judge the earth: he shall judge the world with righteousness, and the people with his truth.

18.2 All Judgement Given to Christ

God the Father has chosen not to be the judge of man. The Bible teaches that God the Father has committed all judgment over to His Son.

(John 5:22) For the Father judgeth no man, but hath committed all judgment unto the Son:

While this may seem to be an oddity to men, we accept the authority of Scripture. They are inspired without error, preserved without loss, and continue to express the absolute truth of God. What God says is so whether it seems so or not.

The Son of God is man's judge.

✓ To Israel, Christ will judge them as Messiah.

✓ To New Testament Christians, He will judge them as the Saviour of the World.

✓ To the lost, He will judge them as the King of Kings and Lord of Lords.

Judgment is not an option with God.

(Romans 14:11-12) For it is written, As I live, saith the Lord, every knee shall bow to me, and every tongue shall confess to God. So then every one of us shall give account of himself to God.

(2 Corinthians 5:10-11) For we must all appear before the judgment seat of Christ; that every one may receive the things done in his body, according to that he hath done, whether it be good or bad. Knowing therefore the terror of the Lord, we persuade men; but we are made manifest unto God; and I trust also are made manifest in your

consciences.

The lost will suffer retribution while Christians shall gain reward (Gal 6:7-8). The lost will appear before God at the Great White Throne. Christians will appear before God at the Bema Seat.

18.3 Judgement Terms

✓ MERCY: When God withholds from Christians the punishment they deserve.

✓ GRACE: When God blesses Christians in a way that they do not deserve.

✓ DAMNATION: When God eternally punishes the unsaved for their sins and their rejection of Christ.

The human brain contains over 12 billion memory cells. Everything we have ever seen, heard, observed, done, or said is permanently recorded by these cells and is capable of being recalled under the right stimulation or circumstances. When unsaved man stands before God, his life will be played back in its entirety and in minute detail.

For the unsaved, there will be no disputation of the facts of their sin or corresponding guilt. They will stand before God without excuse or refute.

For the saved, there will be no disputation concerning the spiritual worth of their works or lack thereof.

The God who sees all, knows all, and remembers all will have no difficulty recalling all.

(Hebrews 2:3) How shall we escape, if we neglect so great salvation; which at the first began to be spoken by the Lord, and was confirmed unto us by them that heard him;

Four things demand judgement:

✓ The justice of God demands judgment. (Job 37:23; Jer 23:5,6; Heb 2:1-3)

✓ Man's sin demands judgment. (Rom 6:23)

✓ Heaven demands judgment. (Rev 21:27)

✓ Man's judgment against his fellow man demands judgment. (Mt 7:1-5)

18.4 Judgement in Relation to Justification

If the justice of God demands that all sin be punished, then how can God be just by not punishing the sins of Christians? The fact of the matter is, the sins of every Christian were punished. Christ took our punishment upon the cross dying in our place. The actual word "justification" appears only in the New Testament.

JUSTIFICATION is the judicial declaration of God whereby the sinner is declared to be righteous and thus able to have a relationship and fellowship with God again.

(Acts 13:38-39) Be it known unto you therefore, men and brethren, that through this man is preached unto you the forgiveness of sins: And by him all that believe are justified from all things, from which ye could not be justified by the law of Moses.

(Romans 3:23-26) For all have sinned, and come short of the glory of God; Being justified freely by his grace through the redemption that is in Christ Jesus: Whom God hath set forth to be a propitiation through faith in his blood, to declare his righteousness for the remission of sins that are past, through the forbearance of God; To declare, I say, at this time his righteousness: that he might be just, and the justifier of him which believeth in Jesus.

Through Christ's meritorious work of redemption on the cross, God declares justice to have been carried out and the Christian absolved of his sin. Because the sins of Christians are under the blood of Christ, God looks at Christians as righteous. Paul expounds upon this.

(Romans 5:12-21) Wherefore, as by one man sin entered into the world, and death by sin; and so death passed upon all men, for that all have sinned: (For until the law sin was in the world: but sin is not imputed when there is no law. Nevertheless death reigned from Adam to Moses, even over them that had not sinned after the similitude of Adam's transgression, who is the figure of him that was to come. But not as the offence, so also is the free gift. For if through the offence of one many be dead, much more the grace of God, and the gift by grace, which is by one man, Jesus Christ, hath abounded unto many. And not as it was by one that sinned, so is the gift: for the judgment was by one to condemnation, but the free gift is of many offences unto justification. For if by one man's offence death reigned by one; much more they which receive abundance of grace and of the gift of righteousness shall reign in life by one, Jesus Christ.) Therefore as by the offence of one judgment came upon all men to condemnation; even so by the righteousness of one the free gift came upon all men unto justification of life. For as by one man's disobedience many were made sinners, so by the obedience of one shall many be made righteous. Moreover the law entered, that the offence might abound. But where sin abounded, grace did much more abound: That as sin hath reigned unto death, even so might grace reign through righteousness unto eternal life by Jesus Christ our Lord.

As a reversal of God's attitude toward the repentant sinner justification is:

✓ *Declarative*: The sinner's punishment is declared satisfied in Christ and the Christian is set free.

(Romans 4:6-8) Even as David also describeth the blessedness of the man, unto whom God imputeth righteousness without works, Saying, Blessed are they whose iniquities are forgiven, and whose sins are covered. Blessed is the man to whom the Lord will not impute sin.

(2 Corinthians 5:19-21) To wit, that God was in Christ, reconciling the world unto himself, not imputing their trespasses unto them; and hath committed unto us the word of reconciliation. Now then we are ambassadors for Christ, as though God did beseech you by us: we pray you in Christ's stead, be ye reconciled to God. For he hath made him to be sin for us, who knew no sin; that we might be made the righteousness of God in him.

Not only does God not impute our iniquity to us, He imputes His righteousness to us and credits it to our account.

(Romans 4:5-8) But to him that worketh not, but believeth on him that justifieth the ungodly, his faith is counted for righteousness. Even as David also describeth the blessedness of the man, unto whom God imputeth righteousness without works, Saying, Blessed are they whose iniquities are forgiven, and whose sins are covered. Blessed is the man to whom the Lord will not impute sin.

✓ *Judicial*: Christ is accepted as a proper substitute in fulfillment of O.T. law.

(Galatians 3:13) Christ hath redeemed us from the curse of the law, being made a curse for us: for it is written, Cursed is every one that hangeth on a tree:

(2 Corinthians 5:21) For he hath made him to be sin for us, who knew no sin; that we might be made the righteousness of God in him.

✓ *Remissive*: Man's sins are remitted and forgiven.

(Ephesians 1:7) In whom we have redemption through his blood, the forgiveness of sins, according to the riches of his grace;

✓ *Restorative*: The repentant sinner's relationship is restored with God.

The major emphasis of justification is that it is a judicial declaration. READ Romans 4:1-25

God's righteousness was imputed (credited) to Abraham. Through faith in God's Son, righteousness is imputed (credited) to Christians.

This Week's Memory Verse

For we must all appear before the judgment seat of Christ; that every one may receive the things done in his body, according to that he hath done, whether it be good or bad. (2 Corinthians 5:10)

The Doctrine of Judgement

1. Four things demand judgement:

_____

_____

_____

_____

2. As a reversal of God's attitude toward the repentant sinner justification is:
(Four words)

_____

_____

_____

_____

Write out this week's Bible verse from memory.

2 Corinthians 5:10

_____

_____

_____

_____

_____

Finish the Phrase

And as it is appointed unto men once to die, but after this the _____

For the Father judgeth no man, but hath committed all judgment unto the _____

So then every one of us shall give account of _____

Blessed are they whose iniquities are forgiven, and whose sins are _____

Blessed is the man to whom the Lord will not impute _____

For he hath made him to be _____

For we must all appear before the judgment _____

BEST POINT MADE

Proverbs Chapter Eighteen

What were the main themes of this chapter?

_____

_____

_____

_____

What were the instructional points meant to bring you closer to God?

_____

_____

_____

_____

What were the instructional points meant to protect you from spiritual destruction?

_____

_____

_____

_____

What things in your life could use strengthening?

_____

_____

_____

_____

Was there anything in this chapter that was of help in serving the LORD?

_____

_____

_____

_____

_____

Did you learn anything new about the LORD?

_____

_____

_____

_____

Were there any suggestions made whereby you can be a greater blessing to others?

_____

_____

_____

_____

_____

19.1 The Seat

Christians will stand before a "Bema" seat judgment shortly after the Rapture. The word *Bema* is translated "judgment" in 2 Corinthians 5:10 and Romans 14:10. It indicates the sort of judgment seat that Christians will stand before in Heaven.

(1 Corinthians 5:10) For we must all appear before the judgment seat of Christ; that every one may receive the things done in his body, according to that he hath done, whether it be good or bad.

(Romans 14:10) But why dost thou judge thy brother? or why dost thou set at nought thy brother? for we shall all stand before the judgment seat of Christ.

The ruins of an old bema judgment seat can still be found in ancient Corinth. A bema was a judgment seat where a person's deeds were judged, but not in matters of life and death.

God's Bema Seat is not a judgment whereby the sins of Christians are judged or punished. This is because the sins of Christians were already judged at the cross.

At the cross, we were all judged guilty of our sins and condemned to death. It was there that Christ took upon Himself the sins, the guilt, and the death sentence of all who would accept His sacrifice and gift through salvation. (1 Pet 2:21-24)

(1 Peter 2:21-24) For even hereunto were ye called: because Christ also suffered for us, leaving us an example, that ye should follow his steps: Who did no sin, neither was guile found in his mouth: Who, when he was reviled, reviled not again; when he suffered, he threatened not; but committed himself to him that judgeth righteously: Who his own self bare our sins in his own body on the tree, that we, being dead to sins, should live unto righteousness: by whose stripes ye were healed.

Class Discussion Questions

1. Have you ever heard a preacher or another Christian say to someone who is saved, "you're going to answer to God for that"?

2. Why is this accusation not a true statement?

The so called "blood on the hands"

theory for not soul-winning is incorrect. The theory is based heavily on an O.T. text (Ezek 33:7-8). However, we cannot take God's warning to Jewish prophet watchmen and apply it to N.T. soul-winners on the other side of Calvary. We readily acknowledge that all Christians are commanded to be soul-winners.

For Christians, the matter of sin will not be taken up again at the Bema Seat.

The Bema Seat is not a judgment whereby eternal life or death is determined. In salvation, Jesus Christ already granted eternal life. (Jn 10:27,28) There simply is no condemnation left for Christians. (Jn 3:18)

The Bema Seat Judgment will test by fire the rewardable value (if any) of our works.

(1 Corinthians 3:11-15) For other foundation can no man lay than that is laid, which is Jesus Christ. Now if any man build upon this foundation gold, silver, precious stones, wood, hay, stubble; Every man's work shall be made manifest: for the day shall declare it, because it shall be revealed by fire; and the fire shall try every man's work of what sort it is. If any man's work abide which he hath built thereupon, he shall receive a reward. If any man's work shall be burned, he shall suffer loss: but he himself shall be saved; yet so as by fire.

Works equated with wood, hay and stubble will burn up. These include works which were not wrong, but they were of no spiritual value. Our life is full of works which have nothing to do with right or wrong. They represent the activities which fill our lives through employment, relaxation, social interests, recreation, etc.

Wood, hay, and stubble will also include spiritual works which were not done with the right motives. God sees the heart and discerns our motives and intents.

(Hebrews 4:12-13) For the word of God is quick, and powerful, and sharper than any twoedged sword, piercing even to the dividing asunder of soul and spirit, and of the joints and marrow, and is a discerner of the thoughts and intents of the heart. Neither is there any creature that is not manifest in his sight: but all things are naked and opened unto the eyes of him with whom we have to do.

Wrong motives would include works which we did because we felt we had little choice in the matter (1 Cor 9:16-18), works which we did hoping to get praise from peers (Mt 6:2,5,16), or maybe works we may have done just to keep people "off our backs".

Works equated with gold, silver, and precious stones will not burn up and will be the basis upon which rewards are granted. There are many works listed in the Bible that we are commanded to do. Are these the only works that are of consequence at the Bema Seat? Not at all. There might be any number of good works of eternal consequence that are not listed, but may qualify as gold, silver, and precious stones.

Salvation is guaranteed to every Christian regardless the outcome of the test of fire. Imagine a Christian so carnal that he or she does not earn a single reward throughout their Christian lifetime. It is sad to think that there are Christians so ungrateful for their salvation. Yet, if they are saved, they are eternally saved.

In 1 Corinthians 3:15 we see another verse indicating eternal security.

(1 Corinthians 3:15) If any man's work shall be burned, he shall suffer loss: but he himself shall be saved; yet so as by fire.

The Bema Seat ought to be looked forward to rather than feared. The hymn writer said it well. *"It will be worth it all when we see Jesus!"* Many Christians serve in thankless positions. They go unrecognized for their work. But our Heavenly reward is far greater than the praise of men.

19.2 Rewards

Christians sometimes wonder what is really important to God and how to sort these things out from those which are merely emphasized by men. While no one has all of the answers to this question, a safe place to begin is with the things that God specifically said that He would reward. It might be far better to cast your efforts into things listed by God rather than things not listed. It would be a sad thing to give your life to something that has no rewardable value.

The rewards named in our Bible are easy enough to find. Here they are:

✓ For enduring persecution

(Luke 6:22-23) Blessed are ye, when men shall hate you, and when they shall separate you from their company, and shall reproach you, and cast out your name as evil, for the Son of man's sake. Rejoice ye in that day, and leap for joy: for, behold, your reward is great in heaven: for in the like manner did their fathers unto the prophets.

✓ For secrecy (giving in secret, praying in secret, and fasting in secret. - Mt 6:4,6,18)

✓ For meeting the needs of preachers (Mt 10:41)

✓ For loving your enemies (Lk 6:35)

✓ For planting and watering the gospel seed (1 Cor 3:8)

(1 Corinthians 3:7-9) So then neither is he that planteth any thing, neither he that watereth; but God that giveth the increase. Now he that planteth and he that watereth are one: and every man shall receive his own reward according to his own labour. For we are labourers together with God: ye are God's husbandry, ye are God's building.

✓ For preaching the gospel and winning souls (1 Cor 9:16)

✓ For faithfully seeking after God (Heb 11:6)

19.3 Crowns

The specific and nonspecific crowns listed in our Bible are these:

✓ An Incorruptible Crown - for running the Christian race and not quitting on God.

(1 Corinthians 9:24-27) Know ye not that they which run in a race run all, but one receiveth the prize? So run, that ye may obtain. And every man that striveth for the mastery is temperate in all things. Now they do it to obtain a corruptible crown; but we an incorruptible. I therefore so run, not as uncertainly; so fight I, not as one that beateth the air: But I keep under my body, and bring it into subjection: lest that by any means, when I have preached to others, I myself should be a castaway.

✓ A Soul-Winner's Crown - for bringing the lost to salvation

(Philippians 4:1) Therefore, my brethren dearly beloved and longed for, my joy and crown, so stand fast in the Lord, my dearly beloved.

✓ A Crown of Rejoicing - for those in Heaven because of your witness

(1 Thessalonians 2:19) For what is our hope, or joy, or crown of rejoicing? Are not even ye in the presence of our Lord Jesus Christ at his coming?

✓ A Crown of Righteousness - for those who lived righteously and thus will love Christ's appearing

(2 Timothy 4:8) Henceforth there is laid up for me a crown of righteousness, which the Lord, the righteous judge, shall give me at that day: and not to me only, but unto all them also that love his appearing.

✓ A Crown of Life - for those who "love" Christ enough to endure temptation

(James 1:12) Blessed is the man that endureth temptation: for when he is tried, he shall receive the crown of life, which the Lord hath promised to them that love him.

✓ A Crown of Glory - for those pastors who fed their flock faithfully

(1 Peter 5:2-4) Feed the flock of God which is among you, taking the oversight thereof, not by constraint, but willingly; not for filthy lucre, but of a ready mind; Neither as being lords over God's heritage, but being ensamples to the flock. And when the chief Shepherd shall appear, ye shall receive a crown of glory that fadeth not away.

There will come an awesome realization at the Bema Seat that it was not we who did well, but Christ that lived and worked in us.

(Galatians 2:20) I am crucified with Christ: nevertheless I live; yet not I, but Christ liveth in me: and the life which I now live in the flesh I live by the faith of the Son of God, who loved me, and gave himself for me.

This realization indicates the absence of all previous pride. (1 John 2:16) We will fully know that it was God who won every soul. (1 Cor 3:4-9) We will fully know that it was God who built His work. (Psa 127:1) This realization will cause us to give our crowns back to Christ.

(Revelation 4:10-11) The four and twenty elders fall down before him that sat on the throne, and worship him that liveth for ever and ever, and cast their crowns before the throne, saying, Thou art worthy, O Lord, to receive glory and honour and power: for thou hast created all things, and for thy pleasure they are and were created.

Class Discussion Questions

1. Why do you think that the four and twenty elders cast their crowns before the throne of Christ?

2. Do you think all the saints will do this? Why or why not?

One thing is certain. In that day, we will no longer take the credit for what Christ has done, nor shall we give it to someone else. We will give God all the glory that we failed to give him on earth.

This Week's Memory Verse

And, behold, I come quickly; and my reward is with me, to give every man according as his work shall be. (Revelation 22:12)

The Doctrine of Judgment, The Bema Seat, Rewards and Crowns

1. List the six crowns mentioned in the Bible and what they are given for.

_____

_____

_____

_____

_____

_____

Write out this week's Bible verse from memory.

Revelation 22:12

_____

_____

_____

_____

_____

Finish the Phrase

For we must all appear before the

_____

If any man's work abide which he hath built thereupon, he shall receive

_____

If any man's work shall be burned, he shall suffer loss: but he himself

_____

So then neither is he that planteth any thing, neither he that watereth; but God that giveth

_____

Blessed is the man that endureth temptation: for when he is tried, he shall receive the crown _____

BEST POINT MADE

Proverbs Chapter Nineteen

What were the main themes of this chapter?

_____

_____

_____

_____

What were the instructional points meant to bring you closer to God?

_____

_____

_____

_____

What were the instructional points meant to protect you from spiritual destruction?

_____

_____

_____

_____

What things in your life could use strengthening?

_____

_____

_____

_____

_____

Was there anything in this chapter that was of help in serving the LORD?

_____

_____

_____

_____

_____

Did you learn anything new about the LORD?

_____

_____

_____

_____

Were there any suggestions made whereby you can be a greater blessing to others?

_____

_____

_____

_____

_____

_____

20.1 A Body and A Robe

(Revelation 19:6-9) And I heard as it were the voice of a great multitude, and as the voice of many waters, and as the voice of mighty thunderings, saying, Alleluia: for the Lord God omnipotent reigneth. Let us be glad and rejoice, and give honour to him: for the marriage of the Lamb is come, and his wife hath made herself ready. And to her was granted that she should be arrayed in fine linen, clean and white: for the fine linen is the righteousness of saints. And he saith unto me, Write, Blessed are they which are called unto the marriage supper of the Lamb. And he saith unto me, These are the true sayings of God.

In Heaven, Christians will be given a new body. This new body will NOT be like the earthly one. It will not be a reconstructed body from the old materials. It will not be a body of flesh and blood in the same manner that the old one was.

(1 Corinthians 15:50-54) Now this I say, brethren, that flesh and blood cannot inherit the kingdom of God; neither doth corruption inherit incorruption. Behold, I shew you a mystery; We shall not all sleep, but we shall all be changed, In a moment, in the twinkling of an eye, at the last trump: for the trumpet shall sound, and the dead shall be raised incorruptible, and we shall be changed. For this corruptible must put on incorruption, and this mortal must put on immortality. So when this corruptible shall have put on incorruption, and this mortal shall have put on immortality, then shall be brought to pass the saying that is written, Death is swallowed up in victory.

Illustration – Humor

Speaking of old bodies, someone once said that you know you're getting old when you go up stairs at home only to forget half way up what you were going to do. You then have to try to decide if you want to continue going up (hoping you will remember what you wanted to do) or just forget it and go back down. So you sit on the step to contemplate your situation only to forget whether you were upstairs or downstairs.

The new body of the Christian will be a glorious one.

✓   It will be a body bestowed upon us by a creative act of God.

(1 Corinthians 15:35-38) But some man will say, How are the dead raised up? and with what body do they come?

Thou fool, that which thou sowest is not quickened, except it die: And that which thou sowest, thou sowest not that body that shall be, but bare grain, it may chance of wheat, or of some other grain: But God giveth it a body as it hath pleased him, and to every seed his own body.

✓ It will be a body which will, in looks, be different from the other saints.

(1 Corinthians 15:41-42) There is one glory of the sun, and another glory of the moon, and another glory of the stars: for one star differeth from another star in glory. So also is the resurrection of the dead. It is sown in corruption; it is raised in incorruption:

✓ It will be a body which will be fashioned after Christ's own glorious body.

(1 John 3:2) Beloved, now are we the sons of God, and it doth not yet appear what we shall be: but we know that, when he shall appear, we shall be like him; for we shall see him as he is.

(Philippians 3:21) Who shall change our vile body, that it may be fashioned like unto his glorious body, according to the working whereby he is able even to subdue all things unto himself.

✓ It will be a body which is immortal and will neither disintegrate nor corrupt. (1 Corinthians 15:52-54)

✓ It will be a body not subject to former weaknesses and limitations. (Rev 7:16,17; 21:3-5)

(Revelation 7:16-17) They shall hunger no more, neither thirst any more; neither shall the sun light on them, nor any heat. For the Lamb which is in the midst of the throne shall feed them, and shall lead them unto living fountains of waters: and God shall wipe away all tears from their eyes.

(Revelation 21:3-5) And I heard a great voice out of heaven saying, Behold, the tabernacle of God is with men, and he will dwell with them, and they shall be his people, and God himself shall be with them, and be their God. and God shall wipe away all tears from their eyes; and there shall be no more death, neither sorrow, nor crying, neither shall there be any more pain: for the former things are passed away. And he that sat upon the throne said, Behold, I make all things new. And he said unto me, Write:

for these words are true and faithful.

Class Discussion Questions

1. Based on the implications of 2 Corinthians 5:10, do you think we will receive our new body before our works are judged or after our works are judged?

2. After reading 1 Corinthians 13:12, do you think Christians will know each other in Heaven?

The new body will be clothed in beautiful new raiment. This raiment will be gloriously fashioned.

✓ They shall be robes of pure white.

(Revelation 7:9-10) After this I beheld, and, lo, a great multitude, which no man could number, of all nations, and kindreds, and people, and tongues, stood before the throne, and before the Lamb, clothed with white robes, and palms in their hands; And cried with a loud voice, saying, Salvation to our God which sitteth upon the throne, and unto the Lamb.

✓ They shall be robes of fine linen material, fit for a wedding.

(Revelation 19:7-8) Let us be glad and rejoice, and give honour to him: for the marriage of the Lamb is come, and his wife hath made herself ready. And to her was granted that she should be arrayed in fine linen, clean and white: for the fine linen is the righteousness of saints.

✓ They shall be robes characterized by righteousness. (*Rev 19:8 ... for the fine linen is the righteousness of saints.*)

Wouldn't it be wonderful if our present raiment reflected righteousness? Godly Christians should give much thought and prayer to this subject. Our earthly raiment is a public statement. It states what crowd we identify with the most. It states what we believe about modesty. It states what we believe about ourselves. There is a difference between being beautiful and being attractive. "Beauty" is God calling attention to His own creative hand. "Attractive" is the deliberate act of calling attention to one's own self. Whatever we are trying to say about ourselves, our clothes tend to say it for us.

20.2 The Marriage Supper of the Lamb

The reunion of Christ with His saints in Heaven is a celestial marriage. Scripture describes the beauty of this relationship of Christ to His church and speaks of a great marriage supper in Heaven. All the saints of all the ages will be there. While it is clear that the bride is the church, some suggest that the remaining saints are the guests.

(Luke 14:15-24) And when one of them

187

that sat at meat with him heard these things, he said unto him, Blessed is he that shall eat bread in the kingdom of God. Then said he unto him, A certain man made a great supper, and bade many: And sent his servant at supper time to say to them that were bidden, Come; for all things are now ready. And they all with one consent began to make excuse. The first said unto him, I have bought a piece of ground, and I must needs go and see it: I pray thee have me excused. And another said, I have bought five yoke of oxen, and I go to prove them: I pray thee have me excused. And another said, I have married a wife, and therefore I cannot come. So that servant came, and shewed his lord these things. Then the master of the house being angry said to his servant, Go out quickly into the streets and lanes of the city, and bring in hither the poor, and the maimed, and the halt, and the blind. And the servant said, Lord, it is done as thou hast commanded, and yet there is room. And the lord said unto the servant, Go out into the highways and hedges, and compel them to come in, that my house may be filled. For I say unto you, That none of those men which were bidden shall taste of my supper.

(Revelation 19:9) And he saith unto me, Write, Blessed are they which are called unto the marriage supper of the Lamb. And he saith unto me, These are the true sayings of God.

(John 3:29) He that hath the bride is the bridegroom: but the friend of the bridegroom, which standeth and heareth him, rejoiceth greatly because of the bridegroom's voice: this my joy therefore is fulfilled.

Christ is the Groom and the raptured believers of the church constitute His bride. When Christ first returns to earth at the rapture, it is to get His bride. The marriage supper will follow the Bema Seat Judgment and the receiving of our white robes.

Though our new bodies will have the capacity to eat (and we will eat), nothing is said about eating being necessary to maintain the quality of eternal life. It appears that we enjoy this marriage banquet for the sheer celebration and pleasure of it.

The Tree of Life

When God created the Tree of Life, he gave it both healing and life-giving power. Man's access to the tree was prevented after the fall of man in the garden *lest he put forth his hand, and take also of the tree of life, and eat, and live for ever (Gen 3:6).*

Access to the Tree of Life is restored to the saints in Glory. Carefully read and compare the information God gives to us in the following Scripture texts.

(Revelation 2:7) He that hath an ear, let

him hear what the Spirit saith unto the churches; To him that overcometh will I give to eat of the tree of life, which is in the midst of the paradise of God.

(Revelation 22:2) In the midst of the street of it, and on either side of the river, was there the tree of life, which bare twelve manner of fruits, and yielded her fruit every month: and the leaves of the tree were for the healing of the nations. (14) Blessed are they that do his commandments, that they may have right to the tree of life, and may enter in through the gates into the city.

(Genesis 3:22-24) And the LORD God said, Behold, the man is become as one of us, to know good and evil: and now, lest he put forth his hand, and take also of the tree of life, and eat, and live for ever: Therefore the LORD God sent him forth from the garden of Eden, to till the ground from whence he was taken. So he drove out the man; and he placed at the east of the garden of Eden Cherubims, and a flaming sword which turned every way, to keep the way of the tree of life.

(Ezekiel 47:12) And by the river upon the bank thereof, on this side and on that side, shall grow all trees for meat, whose leaf shall not fade, neither shall the fruit thereof be consumed: it shall bring forth new fruit according to his months, because their waters they issued out of the sanctuary: and the fruit thereof shall be for meat, and the leaf thereof for medicine.

It is important to understand that we have eternal life because it is promised to us, not because we will have access to the tree. How God will maintain our glorious body in an eternal state is not yet revealed to us. The Tree of Life might be or might not be the means by which we live forever. God is eternal because it is His nature. We will live forever because God ordained it and chooses to keep us by His power.

This Week's Memory Verse

Beloved, now are we the sons of God, and it doth not yet appear what we shall be: but we know that, when he shall appear, we shall be like him; for we shall see him as he is. (1 John 3:2)

The Doctrine of Judgment, A Body, A Robe, and A Supper

1. Our new body will be a glorious one.

   It will be a body _____
   It will be a body _____
   It will be a body _____
   It will be a body _____

2. When Christ first returns to earth at the rapture, it is to get His _____

3. It is important to understand that we have eternal life because it is
   _____, not because we will have access to the tree.

Write out this week's Bible verse from memory.

I John 3:2

_____
_____
_____
_____
_____

Finish the Phrase

Now this I say, brethren, that flesh and blood cannot _____

Behold, I shew you a mystery; We shall not all sleep, but we shall all be _____

but we know that, when he shall appear, we shall be _____

Who shall change our vile body, that it may be fashioned like unto his _____

Go out into the highways and hedges, and compel them to come in, that _____

Blessed are they that do his commandments, that they may have right to the _____

_____   _____
_____   _____
_____   _____
_____   _____
_____   _____
_____   _____
_____   _____
_____   _____
_____   _____
_____   _____
_____   _____
_____   _____
_____   _____
_____   _____
_____   _____
_____   _____
_____   _____
_____   _____

BEST POINT MADE

_____
_____   _____
_____   _____
_____   _____
_____   _____
_____   _____
_____   _____
_____   _____
_____   _____
_____   _____

Proverbs Chapter Twenty

What were the main themes of this chapter?

_____

_____

_____

_____

What were the instructional points meant to bring you closer to God?

_____

_____

_____

_____

What were the instructional points meant to protect you from spiritual destruction?

_____

_____

_____

_____

What things in your life could use strengthening?

_____

_____

_____

_____

Was there anything in this chapter that was of help in serving the LORD?

_____

_____

_____

_____

_____

Did you learn anything new about the LORD?

_____

_____

_____

_____

Were there any suggestions made whereby you can be a greater blessing to others?

_____

_____

_____

_____

_____

21.1 Great White Throne Judgment

(Revelation 20:11-15) And I saw a great white throne, and him that sat on it, from whose face the earth and the heaven fled away; and there was found no place for them. And I saw the dead, small and great, stand before God; and the books were opened: and another book was opened, which is the book of life: and the dead were judged out of those things which were written in the books, according to their works. And the sea gave up the dead which were in it; and death and hell delivered up the dead which were in them: and they were judged every man according to their works. And death and hell were cast into the lake of fire. This is the second death. And whosoever was not found written in the book of life was cast into the lake of fire.

It is called "great" because of the one who sits upon it. He is the Word which became flesh, who is the King of Kings and Lord of Lords. He is the judge of the whole world and will judge on that great and dreadful day of the Lord.

(Malachi 4:5) Behold, I will send you Elijah the prophet before the coming of the great and dreadful day of the LORD:

(Jude 1:6) And the angels which kept not their first estate, but left their own habitation, he hath reserved in everlasting chains under darkness unto the judgment of the great day.

This throne is also said to be a "white" one. Surely this is indicative of the absolute righteousness of the one sitting upon it and the purity of justice with which judgement will be meted out.

We read that from His face *the earth and the heaven fled away; and there was found no place for them.* This indicates that the White Throne Judgment takes place in eternity after the destruction of this present creation. This is after the Battle of Gog and Magog. It is after the final defeat of Satan. It is befitting that Satan and his legions are cast into Hell first.

(2 Peter 3:10) But the day of the Lord will come as a thief in the night; in the which the heavens shall pass away with a great noise, and the elements shall melt with fervent heat, the earth also and the works that are therein shall be burned up.

The unsaved from all the ages will be bodily resurrected at the end of time to stand before God Almighty at the Great White Throne judgment seat. The terror of this holy place is so awesome that the heavens and earth react to it. Some have speculated that this is the moment that the earth and heaven are destroyed.

There are two important points to remember about the resurrection of the unsaved dead.

✓ The souls and spirits of these damned have already been suffering in Hell.

(Luke 16:19-31) There was a certain rich man, which was clothed in purple and fine linen, and fared sumptuously every day: And there was a certain beggar named Lazarus, which was laid at his gate, full of sores, And desiring to be fed with the crumbs which fell from the rich man's table: moreover the dogs came and licked his sores. And it came to pass, that the beggar died, and was carried by the angels into Abraham's bosom: the rich man also died, and was buried; And in hell he lift up his eyes, being in torments, and seeth Abraham afar off, and Lazarus in his bosom. And he cried and said, Father Abraham, have mercy on me, and send Lazarus, that he may dip the tip of his finger in water, and cool my tongue; for I am tormented in this flame. But Abraham said, Son, remember that thou in thy lifetime receivedst thy good things, and likewise Lazarus evil things: but now he is comforted, and thou art tormented. And beside all this, between us and you

there is a great gulf fixed: so that they which would pass from hence to you cannot; neither can they pass to us, that would come from thence. Then he said, I pray thee therefore, father, that thou wouldest send him to my father's house: For I have five brethren; that he may testify unto them, lest they also come into this place of torment. Abraham saith unto him, They have Moses and the prophets; let them hear them. And he said, Nay, father Abraham: but if one went unto them from the dead, they will repent. And he said unto him, If they hear not Moses and the prophets, neither will they be persuaded, though one rose from the dead.

Class Discussion Questions

1. Is the story of the rich man and Lazarus a parable or a real event?

2. What word precedes parables that help us to identify them?

✓ Their bodies have been in the grave awaiting this frightful day.

(John 5:26-29) For as the Father hath life in himself; so hath he given to the Son to have life in himself; And hath given him authority to execute judgment also, because he is the Son of man. Marvel not at this: for the hour is coming, in the which all that are in

the graves shall hear his voice, And shall come forth; they that have done good, unto the resurrection of life; and they that have done evil, unto the resurrection of damnation.

At the Great White Throne there will be no defense and no hope.

The record books will be opened. The books of works have every evil deed recorded and stand as proof of guilt. From these books the damned face their judgments. Their names have been *"blotted out"* of the Lamb's Book of Life thereby sealing their eternal sentence of damnation.

Imagine the horror of those who tried to enter Heaven some other way. Imagine those who thought they were saved, many of whom had trusted in their good works, their baptism, or denomination.

(Matthew 7:21-23) Not every one that saith unto me, Lord, Lord, shall enter into the kingdom of heaven; but he that doeth the will of my Father which is in heaven. Many will say to me in that day, Lord, Lord, have we not prophesied in thy name? and in thy name have cast out devils? and in thy name done many wonderful works? And then will I profess unto them, I never knew you: depart from me, ye that work iniquity.

No one will be at the Great White Throne who was once saved, but somehow lost their salvation. Notice that the LORD will declare that He *"never knew"* them.

They face only the second death, which is the everlasting curse of Hell.

21.2 A Literal Hell

Hell is both a real place and a literal existence. The Old Testament (Heb. *Sheol* translated "Hell") places Hell in the depths of the earth.

(Psalm 55:15) Let death seize upon them, and let them go down quick into hell: for wickedness is in their dwellings, and among them.

(Proverbs 9:18) But he knoweth not that the dead are there; and that her guests are in the depths of hell.

(Amos 9:2) Though they dig into hell, thence shall mine hand take them; though they climb up to heaven, thence will I bring them down:

What kind of place is Hell?

✓ It is a place of great sorrow (Psa 18:5; 116:3) and destruction. (Pro 15:11; 27:20)

✓ It is a place of affliction. (Jonah 2:2)

✓ It is a place of the dead (Pro 9:18 cf. Rev 20:14,15) and inescapable bars.

196

(Job 7:16)

✓ It is a place of no bottom. (Isa 14:15; Isa 38:18; cf. Rev 9:1,2; 20:1-3)

Class Discussion Questions

1. If Hell is in the center of the earth, why does it have no bottom?

In the New Testament we have the Greek words *Gehenna, Hades, tartaroo* which are translated "Hell". These give us further insight into this terrible place.

✓ It is a place into which the body and soul are cast. (Mt 5:29,30; 10:28)

✓ It is a place of literal, unquenchable fire. (Mt 18:9; Mk 9:43-48; Rev 20:14)

✓ It is a place of outer darkness, weeping, and gnashing of teeth. (Mt 8:12; 13:42)

Class Discussion Questions

1. If there is literal fire in Hell, why is there only darkness?

Anyone who has worked in a corporate heat treatment facility can tell you what black fire is. Find the answer to this so that you will know why Hell is dark.

✓ It is a place of physical torments (Lk 16:23) and damnation. (Mt 23:33)

Five reasons why Satan does not want you to believe in a literal, fiery Hell.

1. So you will not consider the matter of salvation to be **important**.

2. So you will not consider the matter of soul-winning to be **urgent**.

3. So you will not consider the matter of Bible authority to be **final**.

4. So you will not consider the matter of Bible preaching and teaching to be **educated**.

5. So you will not consider the matter of serving God to be **essential**.

Five more reasons why we believe in a literal, fiery Hell.

1. Because we believe in a verbally inspired, supernaturally preserved WORD of GOD.

2. Because Hell was created for Satan, whose crimes are so heinous that a literal Hell is justified.

3. Because the price God paid to keep us from going there is too great if Hell were merely a symbolic place.

4. Because God cannot let anything or anyone into Heaven that defileth.

5. Because, in spite of the desperately high cost of salvation, God still offers it FREELY without cost to you.

Popular Misconceptions

✓ No one will see friends in Hell because of the outer darkness.

✓ No one will move about at will because the pit has no floor or bottom.

✓ No one will party because of the excruciating pain and suffering.

✓ No one will ever get out of Hell because of the great gulf that cannot be crossed.

✓ No one will be annihilated because their bodies will live forever.
What does eternal separation from God mean? It means to be forever and ever out of the mind of God!

Will Christian mothers in Heaven remember their lost children in Hell? The answer is no. There is no one in Heaven that will remember anyone in Hell.

(Revelation 21:4) And God shall wipe away all tears from their eyes; and there shall be no more death, neither sorrow, nor crying, neither shall there be any more pain: for the former things are passed away.

This Week's Memory Verse

Many will say to me in that day, Lord, Lord, have we not prophesied in thy name? and in thy name have cast out devils? and in thy name done many wonderful works? And then will I profess unto them, I never knew you: depart from me, ye that work iniquity. (Matthew 7:22-23)

The Doctrine of Judgment, The Great White Throne and Hell

1. Name 5 reasons Satan does not want you to believe in a literal Hell.

_____

_____

_____

_____

_____

_____

_____

2. Name 5 reasons we do believe in a literal Hell.

_____

_____

_____

_____

_____

_____

_____

Write out this week's Bible verse from memory.

Matthew 7:22-23

_____

_____

_____

_____

Finish the Phrase

And I saw a great white throne, and him that sat on it, from whose face the earth and the heaven _____

And whosoever was not found written in the book of life was _____

But the day of the Lord will come as a

_____

Many will say to me in that day, Lord, Lord, have we not prophesied in thy name? and in thy name have cast out devils? and in thy name done many wonderful works? And then will I profess unto them, _____

BEST POINT MADE

Proverbs Chapter Twenty-One

What were the main themes of this chapter?

_____

_____

_____

_____

What were the instructional points meant to bring you closer to God?

_____

_____

_____

_____

What were the instructional points meant to protect you from spiritual destruction?

_____

_____

_____

_____

What things in your life could use strengthening?

_____

_____

_____

_____

Was there anything in this chapter that was of help in serving the LORD?

_____

_____

_____

_____

Did you learn anything new about the LORD?

_____

_____

_____

_____

Were there any suggestions made whereby you can be a greater blessing to others?

_____

_____

_____

_____

_____

22.1 Methods for Interpreting Prophetic Scriptures

There are two methods used to interpret prophecies. The *Allegorical Method* and the *Literal Method*. The two methods are incompatible. Therefore, the outcomes of these two methods are irreconcilable. They cannot be blended.

Who believes which method?

Premillennialists, including pre-tribulation rapturists emphasize the literal interpretation of the Bible.

Amillennialists, including mid-tribulation and post tribulation rapturists, are "allegorizers" and "spiritualizers".

Fundamentalists are always literalists. They take what the Bible states at face value.

✓ The Allegorical Method

Allegorism is a method of interpreting the Bible that treats the text of the Bible as a mere vehicle for which spiritual and more profound messages are hidden beneath its words. When applied to Scripture, every event is made an allegory of some kind. However, this method makes man the judge of the Bible rather than the Bible the judge of man. By their disregarding what is clearly stated, the door is open to fanciful invention and personal interpretation. Authority is then placed in the mind of the interpreter rather than in the divine Author. Conclusions proposed by the allegorical system cannot be tested for truth, accuracy, or Divine authority. The opinions of men form the ground upon which disagreement flourishes. An allegorist, at best, can only offer his own private interpretation.

(2 Peter 1:19-21) We have also a more sure word of prophecy; whereunto ye do well that ye take heed, as unto a light that shineth in a dark place, until the day dawn, and the day star arise in your hearts: Knowing this first, that no prophecy of the scripture is of any private interpretation. For the prophecy came not in old time by the will of man: but holy men of God spake as they were moved by the Holy Ghost.

✓ The Literal Method

Literalism is the method of interpreting that gives each word of the text the same basic meaning that it would have in normal, customary, or historic usage.

Consider the logic and the necessity of literalism.

1. The literal meaning of sentences is the first and normal approach in all languages.

2. Understanding parables begins with accepting the normal usage of its words.

3. The majority of Bible texts make perfect sense when interpreted literally.

4. Literalism does not ignore the use of parables or allegories in the Bible.

5. Literalism is objective rather than subjective and is the only method in harmony with the idea of verbally inspired, supernaturally preserved Bible.

6. Literalism emphasizes that which is clearly stated as truth and then takes that which is obscure and interprets it by that which is clear.

God likes plain words and uses plain words to communicate exactly what He wants us to know.

(1 Corinthians 14:9) So likewise ye, except ye utter by the tongue words easy to be understood, how shall it be known what is spoken? for ye shall speak into the air.

(2 Corinthians 3:12) Seeing then that we have such hope, we use great plainness of speech:

22.2 Important Terms

Millennium – While not in the Bible, it is a word taken from Latin meaning "one-thousand" and used to refer to the time period spoken of in the book of Revelation.

(Revelation 20:1-7) And I saw an angel come down from heaven, having the key of the bottomless pit and a great chain in his hand. And he laid hold on the dragon, that old serpent, which is the Devil, and Satan, and bound him a thousand years, And cast him into the bottomless pit, and shut him up, and set a seal upon him, that he should deceive the nations no more, till the thousand years should be fulfilled: and after that he must be loosed a little season. And I saw thrones, and they sat upon them, and judgment was given unto them: and I saw the souls of them that were beheaded for the witness of Jesus, and for the word of God, and which had not worshipped the beast, neither his image, neither had received his mark upon their foreheads, or in their hands; and they lived and reigned with Christ a thousand years. But the rest of the dead lived not again until the thousand years were finished. This is the first resurrection. Blessed and holy is he that hath part in the first resurrection: on such the second death hath no power, but they shall be priests of God and of Christ, and shall reign with him a

thousand years. And when the thousand years are expired, Satan shall be loosed out of his prison,

The meaning of the "thousand years" and its relationship to Christ's return to earth has given rise to various millennial views. Evangelical Christians teach Christ's return in the context of one of three main views: Postmillenialism, Amillennialism, and Premillennialism,

Postmillennialism. The term teaches that the growth of the church and the power of the gospel will cause the world to get better and better until the present order blends into the millennial period during which the righteous will be in charge on earth. Evil will be practically nonexistent. Christ will return only at the end of the millennium at a time when Satan reasserts his power. The final victory of Christ will occur at that time with final judgment and the resurrection of the dead to inaugurate the Eternal Age. (This false doctrine is represented in the song *"The King Is Coming"* by Bill Gaither.)

Amillennialism. The term suggests that there is no literal thousand year period, but is merely a symbolic expression related to spiritual blessing of present Christianity in which Satan is a defeated enemy and believers reign in life by Christ Jesus. Therefore, this view does not look for a literal, future thousand year reign of Christ on the earth during which Satan is bound. Amillennialists also deny that Israel has any future and they see the church as a new Israel.

Premillennialism. The term means "before the millennium or thousand years." Such a view positions the return of Christ prior to a millennial period. There are two broad types of premillennialism.

In *Dispensational premillennialism,* we take the thousand years to be literal both as to fact and number. The millennium follows the seven-year tribulation period. At the beginning of the tribulation, believers are taken out of the world in an event called the Rapture. The rapture is the first phase of the second coming of Christ. During the millennium, Christ will reign on the earth with His saints while Satan is bound in the bottomless pit. The Jews as a nation are seen to have a major place in the events of the Tribulation and the Millennium. This view correctly believes that God has two plans which must be kept separate: an earthly national plan for Israel and a spiritual redemptive plan for the church. We call this Rapture a *pretrib rapture.*

Classical premillennialism holds to a literal, future reign of Christ on earth, during which Satan is bound a thousand years and the saints reign with Christ. They teach that the reign of Christ will be literal, but the length of the reign may or may not be exactly

1,000 years. They do not divide the second coming into two phases. They put the rapture between the Tribulation and Millennium, thus we have the term *posttrib* rapture. The view teaches that the Kingdom of God has to do primarily with redemption. They say that the kingdom was offered to Israel, but when it was rejected, its blessings were given to "another nation" (Mt 21:43) - the church. *Classical premillennialism* is an incorrect position.

22.3 The Rapture

(1 Thessalonians 4:13-17) But I would not have you to be ignorant, brethren, concerning them which are asleep, that ye sorrow not, even as others which have no hope. For if we believe that Jesus died and rose again, even so them also which sleep in Jesus will God bring with him. For this we say unto you by the word of the Lord, that we which are alive and remain unto the coming of the Lord shall not prevent them which are asleep. For the Lord himself shall descend from heaven with a shout, with the voice of the archangel, and with the trump of God: and the dead in Christ shall rise first: Then we which are alive and remain shall be caught up together with them in the clouds, to meet the Lord in the air: and so shall we ever be with the Lord.

Christ's return is staged in two phases: the Rapture and the Second Advent or second coming. The Rapture ushers in the seven year Tribulation period while the Second Advent ushers in the Millennium which immediately follows the Tribulation.

The Rapture is no secret to students of the Bible. The word RAPTURE is a descriptive term used for the catching up of believers by Christ at the time Christ first returns in the sky. Although the term rapture appears nowhere in the English Bible, the word came into use by way of the Latin word *rapio* used to translate the Greek term of 1 Th 4:17.

From our Greek text, *harpage-sometha* is translated "caught up". Living believers are literally "caught up" to meet the Lord at His coming. We have come to use the term "Rapture" because it is an easy one-word description. At the rapture all believers both alive at the time and those deceased are bodily resurrected to stand before the Bema Seat of Christ.

Three things signal the announced moment: (1 Th 4:16)

✓ The descending of Jesus Christ from Heaven with a shout

And what is that shout?

(Revelation 4:1) After this I looked, and, behold, a door was opened in heaven: and the first voice which I heard was as it were of a trumpet talking with

me; which said, Come up hither, and I will show thee things which must be hereafter.

The same voice repeats itself as the Two Witnesses of the Tribulation are murdered (Rev 11:8-12). We will speak of them later.

✓ The voice of the archangel

✓ The trump of God

(1 Corinthians 15:51-54) Behold, I shew you a mystery; We shall not all sleep, but we shall all be changed, In a moment, in the twinkling of an eye, at the last trump: for the trumpet shall sound, and the dead shall be raised incorruptible, and we shall be changed. For this corruptible must put on incorruption, and this mortal must put on immortality. So when this corruptible shall have put on incorruption, and this mortal shall have put on immortality, then shall be brought to pass the saying that is written, Death is swallowed up in victory.

(Luke 12:39-40) And this know, that if the goodman of the house had known what hour the thief would come, he would have watched, and not have suffered his house to be broken through. Be ye therefore ready also: for the Son of man cometh at an hour when ye think not.

Imagine the split moment that comes without warning when suddenly from the skies a shout, the voice of an archangel, a trumpet, and the appearance of Christ in the clouds as He says to the saints both dead and alive at the time, "come up hither".

Do you remember what the disciples were told when the resurrected Christ was taken up into Heaven?

(Acts 1:8-11) But ye shall receive power, after that the Holy Ghost is come upon you: and ye shall be witnesses unto me both in Jerusalem, and in all Judaea, and in Samaria, and unto the uttermost part of the earth. And when he had spoken these things, while they beheld, he was taken up; and a cloud received him out of their sight. And while they looked stedfastly toward heaven as he went up, behold, two men stood by them in white apparel; Which also said, Ye men of Galilee, why stand ye gazing up into heaven? this same Jesus, which is taken up from you into heaven, shall so come in like manner as ye have seen him go into heaven.

Imagine the chaos the world is suddenly thrust into as they realize graves are empty and millions of Christians have disappeared from the earth!

22.4 Differences Between the Rapture and the Second Advent

1. The Rapture entails the removal of all believers from the earth. The Second

Advent brings them back to the earth.

2. The Rapture sees Christ coming FOR His Bride. The Second Advent sees Christ coming WITH His bride.

3. The Rapture removes the Saints from harms way. The Second Advent sets the Saints to rule in the aftermath.

4. The Rapture ushers in the Seven-year Tribulation. The Second Advent ushers in the 1,000-year Millennial Reign of Christ.

5. The Rapture is imminent. The Second Advent is set on a seven-year time clock.

6. The Rapture brings rejoicing. The Second Advent brings Armageddon.

7. The Rapture brings only the appearing of Christ in the skies. The Second Advent brings Christ to earth again.

8. The Rapture brings no announcement and reveals few signs of the times. The Second Advent comes 84 months after the disappearance of the Saints.

Class Discussion Questions

As your imagination is allowed to run wild, what chaos and tragedy will suddenly unfold on the earth as Christians are taken without warning in the middle of whatever they are doing at the time.

1. What about pilots in the air?

2. What about drivers at 70 mph?

3. What about commuter trains operated by Christians?

4. What other scenarios can you think of that would bring instant trouble or tragedy?

5. Are you praying for people you know that would be left behind on earth if the Rapture were to take place today?

This Week's Memory Verse

Therefore be ye also ready: for in such an hour as ye think not the Son of man cometh. (Matthew 24:44)

The Doctrine of End Times, Interpretations and Millennialism

1. Fundamentalists are always _____.

2. Amillennialists, including mid-tribulation and post tribulation rapturists, are "_____" and "_____".

3. Christ's return is staged in two phases: the _____ and the _____ Advent.

4. The Rapture ushers in the seven year _____ period while the Second Advent ushers in the _____ which immediately follows the Tribulation.

5. The Rapture entails the removal of all believers from the earth. The Second <u>Advent</u> brings them _____.

6. The Rapture sees Christ coming _____ His Bride. The Second <u>Advent</u> sees Christ coming _____ His bride.

7. The Rapture brings only the appearing of Christ in the skies. The Second <u>Advent</u> brings Christ to _____.

Write out this week's Bible verse from memory.

Matthew 24:44

_____

_____

_____

_____

_____

Finish the Phrase

We have also a more sure word of _____

Knowing this first, that no prophecy of the scripture is of any _____

For the prophecy came not in old time by the will of man: but holy men of God spake as they were moved by _____

Seeing then that we have such hope, we use great plainness _____

And I saw an angel come down from heaven, having the key of the _____

For if we believe that Jesus died and rose again, even so them also which sleep in Jesus will God _____

Behold, I shew you a mystery; We shall not all _____

then shall be brought to pass the saying that is written, Death is swallowed up in _____

Be ye therefore ready also: for the Son of man cometh at an _____

BEST POINT MADE

Proverbs Chapter Twenty-Two

What were the main themes of this chapter?

_____

_____

_____

_____

What were the instructional points meant to bring you closer to God?

_____

_____

_____

_____

What were the instructional points meant to protect you from spiritual destruction?

_____

_____

_____

_____

What things in your life could use strengthening?

_____

_____

_____

_____

Was there anything in this chapter that was of help in serving the LORD?

_____

_____

_____

_____

_____

Did you learn anything new about the LORD?

_____

_____

_____

_____

Were there any suggestions made whereby you can be a greater blessing to others?

_____

_____

_____

_____

_____

Scripture is clear. For those who heard the gospel prior to the Rapture, there will be no second chance at salvation after the Rapture. Their doom is absolute, even though they have not died yet. God will ensure that they are each made to believe the lie of the Antichrist. (2 Th 2:11)

REVIEW 1 Thessalonians 4:16 thru 5:9 and 2 Thessalonians 2:1-12

23.1 Daniel's Seventieth Week

Daniel spoke of these seven terrible years 332 years before the birth of Christ. In his prophetic calendar, Daniel called it the 70th week.

The six prophetic books of the Bible characterize this period in plain words: Wrath (Revelation, 1 Thessalonians, and Zephaniah), Judgment (Revelation), Indignation and Punishment (Isaiah), Hour of Trouble (Jeremiah), Hour of Trial (Revelation), Destruction and Darkness (Joel, Zephaniah, and Amos)

The main purpose of the Tribulation is to bring Israel to her knees in acceptance of Jesus as Messiah. The period ends with the Battle of Armageddon, but not before the Son of God showers judgments down upon the earth and its inhabitants.

23.2 The Book of Wrath

READ Revelation 5:1-14

We read of a book with seven seals, but no one is worthy to open it. However, one comes forward who is worthy. He is called: the Lion of the Tribe of Judah and the Root of David. He is also the Slain Lamb of God. As He opens the Book, judgments pour out.

The Seal Judgments

✓ Seal One - The release of the Anti-Christ

(Revelation 6:1-2) And I saw when the Lamb opened one of the seals, and I heard, as it were the noise of thunder, one of the four beasts saying, Come and see. And I saw, and behold a white horse: and he that sat on him had a bow; and a crown was given unto him: and he went forth conquering, and to conquer.

Notice his bow has no arrows. He comes proclaiming peace. He comes proclaiming allegiance to Israel. (It's a lie!) Notice his white horse. He comes presenting himself as the true saviour of the world. He comes with a crown, but it is a stolen crown. He comes as an imposter. In Revelation 19:11 Christ's

Horse comes out of Heaven; Satan's horse out of Hell. In Revelation 19:12 Christ comes with many Crowns; Satan comes with only one. In Revelation 19:15 Christ's weapon is a sword; Satan's is a bow without arrows.

✓ Seal Two - Seven solid years of war

(Revelation 6:3-4) And when he had opened the second seal, I heard the second beast say, Come and see. And there went out another horse that was red: and power was given to him that sat thereon to take peace from the earth, and that they should kill one another: and there was given unto him a great sword.

This horse is RED. It is the Bear of the North (Russia) and the king's of the East.

✓ Seal Three - A devastating famine in countries near unto Israel

(Revelation 6:5-6) And when he had opened the third seal, I heard the third beast say, Come and see. And I beheld, and lo a black horse; and he that sat on him had a pair of balances in his hand. And I heard a voice in the midst of the four beasts say, A measure of wheat for a penny, and three measures of barley for a penny; and see thou hurt not the oil and the wine.

The black horse indicates famine. The ravages of war have left serious food shortages. One loaf of barley bread will require a day's wages of an average man. Notice that the oil and wine are left unhurt. The rich will get richer while the poor get poorer.

Africa, Russia, and Iraq are hit the hardest. As the seven years unfold, the eyes of these three nations eventually rise up to fall prey upon the resources of Israel. Under pressure from its own citizens, it appears that the USA will have pulled out of Iraq paving way for radical Islamic rule once again. By this time during the Tribulation it is likely that the USA has either been obliterated or rendered completely helpless. We will comment on this further before the end of the chapter.

✓ Seal Four - Death

(Revelation 6:7-8) And when he had opened the fourth seal, I heard the voice of the fourth beast say, Come and see. And I looked, and behold a pale horse: and his name that sat on him was Death, and Hell followed with him. And power was given unto them over the fourth part of the earth, to kill with sword, and with hunger, and with death, and with the beasts of the earth.

One-fourth of the world's population dies. One-fourth of the beasts of the earth dies either by war or by starvation. This is just the Grim Reaper's first pass. Later, death will rain down upon one third of the remaining population of the earth.

Keep in mind that the Antichrist will annihilate three world powers to secure his position as supreme ruler. Where does one get one fourth and one third of the population? Not the Bear of the North, God destroys it later. Not the Kings to the South, Christ destroys them in the battle of Armageddon. Not the Kings of the East, They are destroyed in the Valley of Meggido.

It is believed by many that the three destroyed world powers are part of the one fourth and one third population death tolls. These likely are part of the Western Alliance. Could this be why the United States is totally absent during the tribulation? It makes sense considering that with the rapture of millions of Christians in the USA renders it easy prey amid its chaos.

✓ Seal Five - The slaughter of new Christians

(Revelation 6:9-11) And when he had opened the fifth seal, I saw under the altar the souls of them that were slain for the word of God, and for the testimony which they held: And they cried with a loud voice, saying, How long, O Lord, holy and true, dost thou not judge and avenge our blood on them that dwell on the earth? And white robes were given unto every one of them; and it was said unto them, that they should rest yet for

a little season, until their fellowservants also and their brethren, that should be killed as they were, should be fulfilled.

Tens of thousands who had never previously heard the gospel in a clear presentation will be saved in the first evangelistic wave. However, these new Christians are beheaded for their faith nearly as fast as they come to Christ. See Revelation 20:4. Beheading is and always will be the preferred mode of execution among Islamic forces of the Middle East.

During the Tribulation, those who rejected the gospel before the rapture are all made to believe the lie of the Antichrist. They are doomed who had previously rejected Christ.

(2 Thessalonians 2:8-11) And then shall that Wicked be revealed, whom the Lord shall consume with the spirit of his mouth, and shall destroy with the brightness of his coming: Even him, whose coming is after the working of Satan with all power and signs and lying wonders, And with all deceivableness of unrighteousness in them that perish; because they received not the love of the truth, that they might be saved. And for this cause God shall send them strong delusion, that they should believe a lie: Those who are saved during the Tribulation will be beheaded.

✓　Seal Six - Destruction

(Revelation 6:12-17) And I beheld when he had opened the sixth seal, and, lo, there was a great earthquake; and the sun became black as sackcloth of hair, and the moon became as blood; And the stars of heaven fell unto the earth, even as a fig tree casteth her untimely figs, when she is shaken of a mighty wind. And the heaven departed as a scroll when it is rolled together; and every mountain and island were moved out of their places. And the kings of the earth, and the great men, and the rich men, and the chief captains, and the mighty men, and every bondman, and every free man, hid themselves in the dens and in the rocks of the mountains; And said to the mountains and rocks, Fall on us, and hide us from the face of him that sitteth on the throne, and from the wrath of the Lamb: For the great day of his wrath is come; and who shall be able to stand?

A record earth quake will shake every mountain on the earth and every island in the sea. The Sun will become blackened, as it did at Calvary. The moon will appear blood red, possibly from the hydrogen explosions of war in the earth's atmosphere. Meteor showers that have been predicted for decades will come to pass. Men's fear in all these things will utterly destroy the peace and security of his heart and soul.

(Revelation 8:1-2) And when he had opened the seventh seal, there was silence in heaven about the space of half an hour. And I saw the seven angels which stood before God; and to them were given seven trumpets.

The Trumpet Judgments

✓　Trumpet One - Hail mingled with fire

(Revelation 8:7) The first angel sounded, and there followed hail and fire mingled with blood, and they were cast upon the earth: and the third part of trees was burnt up, and all green grass was burnt up.

One third of the earth's vegetation burns. The fire is mixed with the blood of men and animals. This is the second time God has used this judgment upon the earth.　See Exodus 9:24-25.

✓　Trumpet Two - A mountain of fire erupts in the sea

(Revelation 8:8-9) And the second angel sounded, and as it were a great mountain burning with fire was cast into the sea: and the third part of the sea became blood; And the third part of the creatures which were in the sea, and had life, died; and the third part of the ships were destroyed.

The volcanic explosion erupts in an unnamed sea. Two-thirds of the ships on that sea and one-third of the life in that sea are destroyed. The sea water flows red with the blood of its dead.

✓ Trumpet Three - A large burning star

(Revelation 8:10-11) And the third angel sounded, and there fell a great star from heaven, burning as it were a lamp, and it fell upon the third part of the rivers, and upon the fountains of waters; And the name of the star is called Wormwood: and the third part of the waters became wormwood; and many men died of the waters, because they were made bitter.

The star is not identified. Whatever it is, it appears to be radioactive. One-third of all the fresh water on earth is poisoned. Many die of drinking it.

✓ Trumpet Four - One-third of the light from the Heavens is kept from reaching the earth

(Revelation 8:12) And the fourth angel sounded, and the third part of the sun was smitten, and the third part of the moon, and the third part of the stars; so as the third part of them was darkened, and the day shone not for a third part of it, and the night likewise.

One might conclude that the earth's atmosphere is so polluted from explosions that the light cannot cut through the radioactive dust. Every

superpower knows perfectly well what will happen to the earth if the unthinkable buttons are pushed. Presently, smaller, rogue nations with nuclear weapons seem to be so radicalized that their hatred overrides common sense.

✓ Trumpet Five - The release of killer locusts ("Woe" Rev 8:13 and 9:1-11)

(Revelation 8:13) And I beheld, and heard an angel flying through the midst of heaven, saying with a loud voice, Woe, woe, woe, to the inhabiters of the earth by reason of the other voices of the trumpet of the three angels, which are yet to sound!

The judgements that follow are often called the "Woe Judgments".

(Revelation 9:1-12) And the fifth angel sounded, and I saw a star fall from heaven unto the earth: and to him was given the key of the bottomless pit. And he opened the bottomless pit; and there arose a smoke out of the pit, as the smoke of a great furnace; and the sun and the air were darkened by reason of the smoke of the pit. And there came out of the smoke locusts upon the earth: and unto them was given power, as the scorpions of the earth have power. And it was commanded them that they should not hurt the grass of the earth, neither any green thing, neither any tree; but only those men which have not the seal of God in their foreheads. And to them

it was given that they should not kill them, but that they should be tormented five months: and their torment was as the torment of a scorpion, when he striketh a man. And in those days shall men seek death, and shall not find it; and shall desire to die, and death shall flee from them. And the shapes of the locusts were like unto horses prepared unto battle; and on their heads were as it were crowns like gold, and their faces were as the faces of men. And they had hair as the hair of women, and their teeth were as the teeth of lions. And they had breastplates, as it were breastplates of iron; and the sound of their wings was as the sound of chariots of many horses running to battle. And they had tails like unto scorpions, and there were stings in their tails: and their power was to hurt men five months. And they had a king over them, which is the angel of the bottomless pit, whose name in the Hebrew tongue is Abaddon, but in the Greek tongue hath his name Apollyon. One woe is past; and, behold, there come two woes more hereafter.

Killer locusts, which swarm and deliberately kill, are but a small picture of that which is to come. These killer locusts will sting like scorpions resulting in a five month, tormentive illness.

✓ Trumpet Six - 200 million soldiers begin their march toward Israel

(Revelation 9:13-21) And the sixth angel sounded, and I heard a voice from the four horns of the golden altar which is before God, Saying to the sixth angel which had the trumpet, Loose the four angels which are bound in the great river Euphrates. And the four angels were loosed, which were prepared for an hour, and a day, and a month, and a year, for to slay the third part of men. And the number of the army of the horsemen were two hundred thousand thousand: and I heard the number of them. And thus I saw the horses in the vision, and them that sat on them, having breastplates of fire, and of jacinth, and brimstone: and the heads of the horses were as the heads of lions; and out of their mouths issued fire and smoke and brimstone. By these three was the third part of men killed, by the fire, and by the smoke, and by the brimstone, which issued out of their mouths. For their power is in their mouth, and in their tails: for their tails were like unto serpents, and had heads, and with them they do hurt. And the rest of the men which were not killed by these plagues yet repented not of the works of their hands, that they should not worship devils, and idols of gold, and silver, and brass, and stone, and of wood: which neither can see, nor hear, nor walk: Neither repented they of their murders, nor of their sorceries, nor of their fornication, nor of their thefts.

Before the Seventh Trumpet Sounds, two witnesses come forth preaching.

This Week's Memory Verse

Brethren, my heart's desire and prayer to God for Israel is, that they might be saved. (Romans 10:1)

ESCHATOLOGY, Tribulation Judgments

1. Identify the following:

Seal One   _____

Seal Two   _____

Seal Three   _____

Seal Four   _____

Seal Five   _____

Seal Six   _____

2. Identify the following:

Trumpet One   _____

Trumpet Two   _____

Trumpet Three   _____

Trumpet Four   _____

Trumpet Five   _____

Trumpet Six   _____

Write out this week's Bible verse from memory.

Romans 10:1

_____

_____

_____

_____

_____

Finish the Phrase

For the Lord himself shall descend from heaven with a _____

dead in Christ shall rise _____

And then shall that Wicked be revealed, whom the Lord shall consume with the spirit of _____

And for this cause God shall send them strong delusion, that they should believe

_____

And the third angel sounded, and there fell a great star from heaven, burning as it were a lamp, and it fell upon the third part of the rivers, and upon the fountains of waters; And the name of the star is called _____

And when he had opened the seventh seal, there was silence in heaven about the space of _____

BEST POINT MADE

Proverbs Chapter Twenty-Three

What were the main themes of this chapter?

_____

_____

_____

_____

What were the instructional points meant to bring you closer to God?

_____

_____

_____

_____

What were the instructional points meant to protect you from spiritual destruction?

_____

_____

_____

_____

What things in your life could use strengthening?

_____

_____

_____

_____

Was there anything in this chapter that was of help in serving the LORD?

_____

_____

_____

_____

Did you learn anything new about the LORD?

_____

_____

_____

_____

Were there any suggestions made whereby you can be a greater blessing to others?

_____

_____

_____

_____

_____

After the rapture, 144,000 Jews begin testifying of Christ. They are 12,000 from each tribe of Israel. (Rev 7:1-8) When and where these come from is not clear.

24.1 The Two Witnesses

Before the Seventh Trumpet Sounds, two witnesses come forth preaching.

In the midst of Tribulation chaos, destruction, torment, and death arise two ancient O.T. prophets. Sent down from Heaven by the LORD Himself, their message is repentance. These two witnesses are accompanied by signs and wonders.

They have divinely granted powers to shut up the heavens and stop the rains, turn water to blood, and to smite the earth with plagues.

For 1,260 days they preach under God's intervening hand of protection. The Scriptures refer to these men as candlesticks.

(Revelation 11:4) These are the two olive trees, and the two candlesticks standing before the God of the earth.

Clothed in sack cloth, they seek no honor for themselves. Sack cloth was a humble garment of animal hair. Scripture equates sack cloth with national mourning and repentance.

Their ministry to Israel compares to that of Elijah and John the Baptist who were sent to Israel in times of apostasy to call Israel to repentance. The two witnesses of the Tribulation are preaching the same message that John did: *Repent, for the King of Israel will arrive shortly.*

Though they preach the *Gospel of the Kingdom* found in Matt 24, they do not neglect the preaching of the *Cross*.

All the preaching of Daniel's 70th week is accompanied by the preaching of the Cross.

(Revelation 7:14) And I said unto him, Sir, thou knowest. And he said to me, These are they which came out of great tribulation, and have washed their robes, and made them white in the blood of the Lamb.

(Zechariah 13:8-9) And it shall come to pass, that in all the land, saith the LORD, two parts therein shall be cut off and die; but the third shall be left therein. and I will bring the third part through the fire, and will refine them as silver is refined, and will try them

as gold is tried: they shall call on my name, and I will hear them: I will say, It is my people: and they shall say, The LORD is my God.

Remember, no message is committed to the New Testament church during the Tribulation because the church is gone. It has been previously raptured.

At the end of the 1,260 days, the Beast of the Antichrist ascends from Hell and murders the two witnesses in the streets of Jerusalem.

(Revelation 11:7) And when they shall have finished their testimony, the beast that ascendeth out of the bottomless pit shall make war against them, and shall overcome them, and kill them.

Their bodies lie there in the street for three-and-a-half days. News media outlets and the powers of world government rejoice in their death. A holiday is called causing the people of the world to make merry and send one another gifts because the two men that had tormented the earth are dead! The two had converted untold thousands to Christ.

At the end of three-and-a-half days the hand of God moves and the power of the Almighty over-shadows the two dead bodies. As the Spirit of God breathes life into them they stand up on their feet. They are alive! Resurrected from the dead!

Shock sets in, first in Jerusalem, and then the nations of the earth. The voice of God thunders out of Heaven "Come up hither"! (Rev 11:12) In sight of those whose eyes are upon them, the witnesses ascend up into Heaven in a cloud!

Within an hour an earthquake flattens a tenth of Jerusalem and 7,000 residents lose their lives

Who are these two witnesses who, in ancient times, walked the earth preaching before?

The first witness is surely Elijah! It is predicted in Malachi that Elijah would come before the Second Advent preparing the way for Messiah.

(Malachi 3:1-3) Behold, I will send my messenger, and he shall prepare the way before me: and the Lord, whom ye seek, shall suddenly come to his temple, even the messenger of the covenant, whom ye delight in: behold, he shall come, saith the LORD of hosts. But who may abide the day of his coming? and who shall stand when he appeareth? for he is like a refiner's fire, and like fullers' soap: And he shall sit as a refiner and purifier of silver: and he shall purify the sons of Levi, and purge them as gold and silver, that they may offer unto the LORD an offering in righteousness.

(Malachi 4:5-6) Behold, I will send you Elijah the prophet before the coming

of the great and dreadful day of the LORD: And he shall turn the heart of the fathers to the children, and the heart of the children to their fathers, lest I come and smite the earth with a curse.

Remember, Elijah has not yet died the first time (*see* 2 Kgs 2:9-12) Scripture is clear. Man dies only once! (Heb 9:27)

(Hebrews 9:27) And as it is appointed unto men once to die, but after this the judgment:

The Book of 1 Kings relates how Elijah was given power over the rain (1 Kgs 17). The period of the drought in those days was of the same duration as the time and ministry of the two witnesses.

What is the identity of the second witness?

Some name Moses, reasoning that Moses was with Elijah at the transfiguration. (Mt 17:3) They also reason that Moses had turned the Egyptian waters to blood. (Ex 7:19-20) They further point out that no one ever found the body of Moses. But Moses is dead. He died already.

There is yet one more O.T. prophet to be considered. He is a prophet so spiritual, so Godly, so close to God that he walked into the presence of God without ever seeing death!

Enoch has not yet died. He is a prophet of judgment as was Elijah. (Gen 5:23-24; Heb 11:5; Jude 1:14-15)

Elijah and Enoch are the two witnesses of the Tribulation. They will meet their death in the streets of Jerusalem.

24.2 The Vial Judgments

✓ Vial One - An incurable sore

(Revelation 16:1-2) And I heard a great voice out of the temple saying to the seven angels, Go your ways, and pour out the vials of the wrath of God upon the earth. And the first went, and poured out his vial upon the earth; and there fell a noisome and grievous sore upon the men which had the mark of the beast, and upon them which worshipped his image.

An incurable sore falls upon those who received the Mark of the Beast. There has been much speculation concerning just what the mark of the beast is.

(Revelation 13:16-18) And he causeth all, both small and great, rich and poor, free and bond, to receive a mark in their right hand, or in their foreheads: And that no man might buy or sell, save he that had the mark, or the name of the beast, or the number of his name. Here is wisdom. Let him that hath understanding count the number of the beast: for it is the number of a man; and his number is Six hundred threescore

and six.

We do know that it is a mark which is put on the hand or forehead. Without this mark, no person in the world will be able to function. Without this international identification mark a person will be unable to buy anything or sell anything, go anywhere or travel anywhere, get medical treatments or use banks. What brings the world to this necessity? Three things:

* Massive problems with identity theft
* Terrorism
* An obsession to eradicate the world of Christians

Amazingly, this technology is in place and being used right now! With a small implanted computer "chip", you can now be identified from a considerable distance. The Federal Reserve is using this technology now. Livestock breeders have been using a chip like this in hogs for a number of years. GPS (Global Positioning System) is now a part of all digital cell phones.

The sore falls upon those which were made to believe that infamous lie of the Antichrist. (2 Th 2:5-12)

In receiving the mark of the beast implanted in their hand or forehead people seal their eternal damnation forever and ever.

(Revelation 19:20) And the beast was taken, and with him the false prophet that wrought miracles before him, with which he deceived them that had received the mark of the beast, and them that worshipped his image. These both were cast alive into a lake of fire burning with brimstone.

✓ Vial Two - God smites yet another sea upon the earth

(Revelation 16:3-7) And the second angel poured out his vial upon the sea; and it became as the blood of a dead man: and every living soul died in the sea. And the third angel poured out his vial upon the rivers and fountains of waters; and they became blood. And I heard the angel of the waters say, Thou art righteous, O Lord, which art, and wast, and shalt be, because thou hast judged thus. For they have shed the blood of saints and prophets, and thou hast given them blood to drink; for they are worthy. And I heard another out of the altar say, Even so, Lord God Almighty, true and righteous are thy judgments.

The sea is mingled with death. Every living thing in and on the sea at that time dies.

✓ Vial Three - The rivers and fountains become a sea of blood

(Revelation 16:4-7) And the third angel poured out his vial upon the rivers and fountains of waters; and they became

blood. And I heard the angel of the waters say, Thou art righteous, O Lord, which art, and wast, and shalt be, because thou hast judged thus. For they have shed the blood of saints and prophets, and thou hast given them blood to drink; for they are worthy. And I heard another out of the altar say, Even so, Lord God Almighty, true and righteous are thy judgments.

This is a direct and divine retaliation for the beheading of Tribulation Christians. God Almighty declared that vengeance is His!

✓　Vial Four - Record blistering heat temperatures

(Revelation 16:8-9) And the fourth angel poured out his vial upon the sun; and power was given unto him to scorch men with fire. And men were scorched with great heat, and blasphemed the name of God, which hath power over these plagues: and they repented not to give him glory.

The Sun becomes so hot that the earth scorches with fires burning out of control. So scorched are men that they blaspheme God and refuse to repent.

✓　Vial Five - Sores fall upon officers of the Beast and his government

(Revelation 16:10-11) And the fifth angel poured out his vial upon the seat of the beast; and his kingdom was full of darkness; and they gnawed their tongues for pain, And blasphemed the God of heaven because of their pains and their sores, and repented not of their deeds.

They join in the blaspheming of God. Remember, that before the end of the Tribulation, the surviving governments of the world will unite to fight against the Son of God coming down from glory.

✓　Vial Six - The Euphrates River dries up

(Revelation 16:12-16) And the sixth angel poured out his vial upon the great river Euphrates; and the water thereof was dried up, that the way of the kings of the east might be prepared. And I saw three unclean spirits like frogs come out of the mouth of the dragon, and out of the mouth of the beast, and out of the mouth of the false prophet. For they are the spirits of devils, working miracles, which go forth unto the kings of the earth and of the whole world, to gather them to the battle of that great day of God Almighty. Behold, I come as a thief. Blessed is he that watcheth, and keepeth his garments, lest he walk naked, and they see his shame. And he gathered them together into a place called in the Hebrew tongue Armageddon.

The way is now paved to Armageddon. With the Euphrates dried up, 200 million soldiers of the King's of the

East can now march upon Jerusalem.

✓ Vile Seven - The final two-fold plague befalls the earth before Armageddon begins

(Revelation 16:17-21) And the seventh angel poured out his vial into the air; and there came a great voice out of the temple of heaven, from the throne, saying, It is done. And there were voices, and thunders, and lightnings; and there was a great earthquake, such as was not since men were upon the earth, so mighty an earthquake, and so great. And the great city was divided into three parts, and the cities of the nations fell: and great Babylon came in remembrance before God, to give unto her the cup of the wine of the fierceness of his wrath. And every island fled away, and the mountains were not found. And there fell upon men a great hail out of heaven, every stone about the weight of a talent: and men blasphemed God because of the plague of the hail; for the plague thereof was exceeding great.

Catastrophic events of this plague are accompanied by a loud voice out of the temple of Heaven. There is thundering and lightning. Other voices are also heard. The fierceness of God's wrath pours out upon the earth.

The judgment is two-fold.

First, the severest earthquake in the history of the earth strikes. As the time of man's self-rule enters its closing chapter, the entire earth goes into convulsions. The damage is severe. The Great City is split into three parts. (The identity of this city is not clear)

Jerusalem? (Rev 11:8, cf. Zech 14:4)

A rebuilt Babylon? (Rev 16:19)

Rome? (considered to be a spiritual Babylon)

It is clear that every city on earth will have serious damage. The earth's topography is greatly changed.

Secondly, there are great hail stones weighing about a talent that hit the earth. A *talent* = 100 lbs. (silver) or 200 lbs. (gold). No doubt, great loss of life and property is the result. Rather than repent, men blaspheme God because of the hail. (vs.21)

This time on earth will be so terrible no Christian ought to want anyone to go through it. The horror of the seven year Tribulation ought to motivate every believer to be a soul-winner. They ought to pray day and night for their lost loved ones and friends that they will soon accept Christ as their personal Saviour.

(Jude 1:22-23) And of some have compassion, making a difference: And others save with fear, pulling them out of the fire; hating even the garment

spotted by the flesh.

This Week's Memory Verse

For God hath not appointed us to
wrath, but to obtain salvation by our
Lord Jesus Christ,
(1 Thessalonians 5:9)

ESCHATOLOGY, Two Witnesses and Vial Judgements

1. Identify the following:

Vial One   _____

Vial Two   _____

Vial Three   _____

Vial Four   _____

Vial Five   _____

Vial Six   _____

2. What are the two judgments of Vial Seven?

_____

_____

3. Name the Two Witnesses:

_____

_____

Write out this week's Bible verse from memory.

1 Thessalonians 5:9

_____

_____

_____

_____

_____

Finish the Phrase

Behold, I will send you Elijah the prophet before the coming of the great and _____

And as it is appointed unto men once to die, but after this the _____

And they sing the song of Moses the servant of God, and the song of the Lamb, saying, Great and marvellous are thy _____

And of some have compassion, making a _____

_____   _____
_____   _____
_____   _____
_____   _____
_____   _____
_____   _____
_____   _____
_____   _____
_____   _____
_____   _____
_____   _____
_____   _____
_____   _____
_____   _____
_____   _____
_____   _____
_____   _____
_____   _____

BEST POINT MADE

_____   _____
_____   _____
_____   _____
_____   _____
_____   _____
_____   _____
_____   _____
_____   _____
_____   _____

Proverbs Chapter Twenty-Four

What were the main themes of this chapter?

_____

_____

_____

_____

What were the instructional points meant to bring you closer to God?

_____

_____

_____

_____

What were the instructional points meant to protect you from spiritual destruction?

_____

_____

_____

_____

What things in your life could use strengthening?

_____

_____

_____

_____

Was there anything in this chapter that was of help in serving the LORD?

_____

_____

_____

_____

_____

Did you learn anything new about the LORD?

_____

_____

_____

_____

Were there any suggestions made whereby you can be a greater blessing to others?

_____

_____

_____

_____

_____

_____

25.1 Introduction

(Revelation 13:1) And I stood upon the sand of the sea, and saw a beast rise up out of the sea, having seven heads and ten horns, and upon his horns ten crowns, and upon his heads the name of blasphemy. And the beast which I saw was like unto a leopard, and his feet were as the feet of a bear, and his mouth as the mouth of a lion: and the dragon gave him his power, and his seat, and great authority. And I saw one of his heads as it were wounded to death; and his deadly wound was healed: and all the world wondered after the beast. And they worshipped the dragon which gave power unto the beast: and they worshipped the beast, saying, Who is like unto the beast? who is able to make war with him? And there was given unto him a mouth speaking great things and blasphemies; and power was given unto him to continue forty and two months. And he opened his mouth in blasphemy against God, to blaspheme his name, and his tabernacle, and them that dwell in heaven. And it was given unto him to make war with the saints, and to overcome them: and power was given him over all kindreds, and tongues, and nations. And all that dwell upon the earth shall worship him, whose names are not written in the book of life of the Lamb slain from the foundation of the world.

The word "Antichrist" is composed of two parts, "anti" and "Christ". His name does not render a denial of Christ's existence, but rather a total rejection of Christ's position and authority. The word is found in the Bible four times.

(1 John 2:18) Little children, it is the last time: and as ye have heard that antichrist shall come, even now are there many antichrists; whereby we know that it is the last time.

(1 John 4:3) And every spirit that confesseth not that Jesus Christ is come in the flesh is not of God: and this is that spirit of antichrist, whereof ye have heard that it should come; and even now already is it in the world.

(2 John 1:7) For many deceivers are entered into the world, who confess not that Jesus Christ is come in the flesh. This is a deceiver and an antichrist.

(1 John 2:22) Who is a liar but he that denieth that Jesus is the Christ? He is antichrist, that denieth the Father and the Son.

"Antichrist" represents both a person and a system. The person of the

Antichrist and the beast are so closely connected, that they appear to many to be one in the same person.

From time to time, some have asked about a New World Order president being the Antichrist. This was brought up under the rule of Bill Clinton, and really heated up under Barack Obama. The answer is always "no". While they manifested some of the trademarks of the Antichrist, their rise to power was not timed correctly and neither of them enjoyed overwhelming love and loyalty in the European Economic Community. There are other reasons why they could not be the Antichrist.

25.2 The person of the Antichrist

The basics of the Antichrist's life

✓ He will exalt himself through worldly wisdom and riches. (Ezek 28:1-10)

✓ He will speak great things to the world. (Dan 7:7-8, 20-26)

✓ He will persecute true believers. (Dan 8:23-25)

✓ He will institute his own religion by uniting all churches. This is the harlot church and the final product of the ecumenical movement. (Dan 9:26-27; 11:36-45)

When will the Antichrist appear?

He will appear in the "latter time" (Dan 8:23). The "latter time" will be when the day of Christ has begun.

(2 Thessalonians 2:1-2) Now we beseech you, brethren, by the coming of our Lord Jesus Christ, and by our gathering together unto him, That ye be not soon shaken in mind, or be troubled, neither by spirit, nor by word, nor by letter as from us, as that the day of Christ is at hand.

The day of Christ will be preceded by a departure - Rapture. His appearing and his influence are presently restricted by the Holy Spirit.

(2 Thessalonians 2:6-10) And now ye know what withholdeth that he might be revealed in his time. For the mystery of iniquity doth already work: only he who now letteth will let, until he be taken out of the way. And then shall that Wicked be revealed, whom the Lord shall consume with the spirit of his mouth, and shall destroy with the brightness of his coming: Even him, whose coming is after the working of Satan with all power and signs and lying wonders, And with all deceivableness of unrighteousness in them that perish; because they received not the love of the truth, that they might be saved.

Where will the person of the Antichrist come from?

It is presently debated whether he is a Jew or a Gentile. However, he is likely neither because he arises up out of the sea. In other words, he has no birth certificate. Some have suggested that the sea represents Gentile nations (Rev 17:15). This suggestion seems weak in that the Antichrist is an ultimate evil being whose origin is surely the bottomless pit. He does however, rule the last form of Gentile domination over the world. (He will have power over the lion, the bear, and the leopard of Daniel 7.)

The Antichrist's rise to power

He uses his "harlot" church to help him rise to power. (Rev 17-18) We just pointed out that the harlot church is the final product of the present day Ecumenical Movement. This present apostate movement is dedicated to uniting all churches.

He also uses a political platform of "world peace" (Dan 8:25; 11:21). In rising, he must eliminate three world powers to gain power. (Dan 7:8,24) The USA is likely one of those powers eliminated. This makes sense when comparing Tribulation death numbers to the present national populations. Remember, the USA is put into extreme chaos and rendered weak from the Rapture having taken so many of its citizens. The Western alliance might well comprise the three world powers eliminated.

Eventually, another alliance rises up against the Antichrist (Ezek 28:7; Dan 11:40-45). This causes him to take direct control of Palestine. In taking control of Palestine, he moves his headquarters from Rome to Jerusalem. His ecumenical headquarters had been the Vatican described as the seven hilled city whose colors are purple and scarlet. Pope Benedict XVI stated that the Antichrist would be a future apostate pope.

The extent of the Antichrist's power

His immediate power comes directly from Satan (Rev 13:1-8). It is clear that his influence is world wide, except over the kings of the East and the Bear of the North. The seven heads and ten horns of the old Roman Empire are under his control. The seven heads are seven nations. The ten horns are ten kings. This alliance and rule are by their consent. Through deceit he forms a covenant alliance with Israel (Dan 9) and then breaks it.

His authority in these alliances is so absolute (Dan 11:36) that he is able to change both laws and customs (Dan 7:25). The acceptance of homosexuality will flourish under his rule. He himself has no natural desire for women.

His ability to perform miracles will be accepted by the world as divine (2 Th 2:9-10) while his ultimate duplication will be the resurrection from the dead.

(Revelation 13:3) And I saw one of his heads as it were wounded to death; and his deadly wound was healed: and all the world wondered after the beast.

Satan has long been known as a replicator of Divine miracles in order to confuse. We saw this in the magicians which stood before Pharaoh with Moses. We saw this in the church at Corinth in reference to speaking in tongues. We see this today in the "hocus pocus", mystical practice of Christianity in some circles of charismatic influence.

After he destroys his own "harlot" system he introduces a type of idolatry (Dan 9:27). Setting himself up as a deity, he will be accepted as Deity by many (Dan 11:36-37; 2 Th 2:4,11). But Israel turns against him when he commits the abomination of desolation in the rebuilt temple.

(Matthew 24:15-22) When ye therefore shall see the abomination of desolation, spoken of by Daniel the prophet, stand in the holy place, (whoso readeth, let him understand:) Then let them which be in Judaea flee into the mountains: Let him which is on the housetop not come down to take any thing out of his house: Neither let him which is in the field return back to take his clothes. And woe unto them that are with child, and to them that give suck in those days! But pray ye that your flight be not in the winter, neither on the sabbath day: For then shall be great tribulation, such as was not since the beginning of the world to this time, no, nor ever shall be. And except those days should be shortened, there should no flesh be saved: but for the elect's sake those days shall be shortened.

This is referring to Daniel 9:27, "And he shall confirm the covenant with many for one week: and in the midst of the week he shall cause the sacrifice and the oblation to cease, and for the overspreading of abominations he shall make it desolate, even until the consummation, and that determined shall be poured upon the desolate."

In 167 B.C. a Greek ruler by the name of Antiochus Epiphanies set up an altar to Zeus over the altar of burnt offerings in the Jewish temple in Jerusalem. He also sacrificed a pig on the altar in the Temple in Jerusalem. This event is known as the abomination of desolation. Whatever the Antichrist does to constitute the latter abomination of desolation, we know that he does declare himself to be deity.

His rule will be terminated by a direct act of God. (Dan 7:22,26; 8:25) God will cast him into the lake of fire at Christ's own second advent.

(Revelation 19:20) And the beast was taken, and with him the false prophet that wrought miracles before him, with which he deceived them that had received the mark of the beast, and them that worshipped his image. These both were cast alive into a lake of fire burning with brimstone.

25.3 The False Prophet

(Revelation 13:11-17) And I beheld another beast coming up out of the earth; and he had two horns like a lamb, and he spake as a dragon. And he exerciseth all the power of the first beast before him, and causeth the earth and them which dwell therein to worship the first beast, whose deadly wound was healed. And he doeth great wonders, so that he maketh fire come down from heaven on the earth in the sight of men, And deceiveth them that dwell on the earth by the means of those miracles which he had power to do in the sight of the beast; saying to them that dwell on the earth, that they should make an image to the beast, which had the wound by a sword, and did live. And he had power to give life unto the image of the beast, that the image of the beast should both speak, and cause that as many as would not worship the image of the beast should be killed. And he causeth all, both small and great, rich and poor, free and bond, to receive a mark in their right hand, or in their foreheads: And that no man might buy or sell, save he that had the mark, or the name of the beast, or the number of his name.

The False Prophet is the second beast. He is a Jew out of Palestine and deals with religious affairs. He too is motivated directly by Satan, but he will be granted power by the first beast.

The False Prophet compels people to worship the first beast. Working miracles is a major part of his deception. It appears that he has at least some economic powers in that he requires every person to bear the mark of the beast in order to buy or sell anything. His final destination is the lake of fire.

An unholy trinity is clear: the Dragon (a type of god), the Beast (a type of Christ), the False Prophet (a type of Holy Spirit).

This Week's Memory Verse

Little children, it is the last time: and as ye have heard that antichrist shall come, even now are there many antichrists; whereby we know that it is the last time. (1 John 2:18)

ESCHATOLOGY, The Antichrist and the False Prophet

1. He will speak _____ to the world.

2. He will _____true believers.

3. He will institute his own religion by uniting all _____.

4. The harlot church is the final product of the _____.

5. He will exalt himself through worldly _____ and _____.

6. The False Prophet is the _____ beast.

7. The False Prophet compels people to worship the _____ beast.

Write out this week's Bible verse from memory.

1 John 2:18

_____
_____
_____
_____
_____

Finish the Phrase

*And I stood upon the sand of the sea,
and saw a beast rise up out of _____*

*And I saw one of his heads as it were
wounded to death; and his deadly wound
was _____*

*And they worshipped the dragon which
gave power_____*

*And he opened his mouth in blasphemy
against God, to blaspheme his name, and*

_____

*He is antichrist, that denieth the Father
and_____*

*And all that dwell upon the earth shall
worship him, whose names are not*

_____

BEST POINT MADE

Proverbs Chapter Twenty-Five

What were the main themes of this chapter?

_____

_____

_____

_____

What were the instructional points meant to bring you closer to God?

_____

_____

_____

_____

What were the instructional points meant to protect you from spiritual destruction?

_____

_____

_____

_____

What things in your life could use strengthening?

_____

_____

_____

_____

Was there anything in this chapter that was of help in serving the LORD?

_____

_____

_____

_____

_____

Did you learn anything new about the LORD?

_____

_____

_____

_____

Were there any suggestions made whereby you can be a greater blessing to others?

_____

_____

_____

_____

_____

26.1 Introduction

(Revelation 16:12-16) And the sixth angel poured out his vial upon the great river Euphrates; and the water thereof was dried up, that the way of the kings of the east might be prepared. And I saw three unclean spirits like frogs come out of the mouth of the dragon, and out of the mouth of the beast, and out of the mouth of the false prophet. For they are the spirits of devils, working miracles, which go forth unto the kings of the earth and of the whole world, to gather them to the battle of that great day of God Almighty. Behold, I come as a thief. Blessed is he that watcheth, and keepeth his garments, lest he walk naked, and they see his shame. And he gathered them together into a place called in the Hebrew tongue Armageddon.

Saddam Hussein had been preparing himself since the day he rose to power to fight what Islam calls the Mother of All Battles. The Arab world longs for it, prays for it, and prepares for it daily. Do not be foolish in thinking that Islam will ever get off the collision course with Israel and her allies. Islamic Terrorism is growing at a fierce rate. Shiite Muslims will never accept anything short of Islamic rule. The Koran calls it "Holy War". Russian president Vladimir Putin called it World War III. The Bible calls it Armageddon.

Herbert W. Bush consulted Billy Graham before he invaded Iraq the first time. Some believe that this consultation greatly scaled back the invasion plans of the then President. It does seem that the Mother of All Battles was put on hold.

When President Bill Clinton invaded again, the United Nations scrambled to avert a world crises. Yeltzen insisted that an unstoppable sequence of invasions would begin if we continued. They reminded the U.S. that they are solidly allied with the Arab world. Arab missiles strike Israel weekly. At the time this book is being written, Iran is working feverishly on a nuclear weapon while the USA is doing little to stop them. Israel is promising a preemptive strike on Iran if they are not stopped soon. The U.S. presently stands in the way of a United Arab attack, but will be a none-existent force in the Tribulation. However, the U.S. is on the opposite side of Russia and China in this conflict. The Israeli government has been telling its citizens that Iraq was never the main threat. Iran is! Israeli citizens are being told to prepare for the worst.

26.2 Armageddon is a series of battles.

Armageddon is actually a series of battles that take place in the second three and one half years of the Tribulation Period.

These battles involve:

- ✓ 10 federations under the Antichrist
- ✓ The Northern Alliance (Russia, Iran, Turkey, Libya, and Ethiopia)
- ✓ One king to the South
- ✓ The kings of the East
- ✓ The King of Kings

The beginning of Armageddon

War begins with an invasion of Israel by an alliance of nations near unto Israel (Dan 11:40).

Ezekiel 38:1 to 39:24 gives us this summary:

Russia is seen to make an alliance with what we call Iran, Ethiopia, Libya, Germany, and Turkey.

The group invades Israel for its spoil and land, and to recover Arab Holy sites, especially the temple mount.

Israel protests, but the New World Order ignores her.

The success of this invasion fails.

Russian troops are destroyed by natural disaster on the mountain tops to the north. But, Jerusalem is heavily damaged in the attack. It takes seven months for them to find and dispose of their dead. (Ezek 39:12)

This is not the final force of the Armageddon campaign. The first invasion involves definite allies. The second invasion involves the united remaining military powers of the earth.

We must remember that the Antichrist destroys three world superpowers to gain power. One-third of the population is killed. There is a reason that the USA is never mentioned in prophecy. She has already been obliterated by that time. The chaos of the Rapture left the USA weak and vulnerable.

The invasion of Russia alarms the Antichrist who is attempting to set up his own world government.(Dan 11) His federation moves into Israel under the pretense of friendship. A new coalition is established. As we mentioned earlier in this book, the Antichrist's headquarters is then moved from Rome to Jerusalem. (Dan 11:41,42) While there, the Antichrist receives another alarming report. (Dan 11:44) This report says that the King's of the East are on the march toward Jerusalem with 200 million soldiers. This force involves China and Muslim allies. Now that Russia and the USA are out of the way, the Kings of the East are challenging the authority and power of the Antichrist and his revived Roman Empire (European Economic Community).

The Antichrist fortifies his positions (Dan 11:45). Revelation 16:12 suggests that God clears the way for the ground troop invasion by drying up the River Euphrates.

With the two great armies drawn up against each other at the Valley of Megiddo, something happens in the heavens (Mt 24:30). Whatever they see, it is so terrifying that the armies of the Antichrist and the Kings of the East unite against Christ. (Rev 19:11-21; 16:14; 17:14)

They are no match for the King of Kings coming with devastating power. The slaughter is great. The blood runs so deep in the Valley of Megiddo that it touches the leather tack on the horses. A brief internet search will show you many photos of this area.

The conclusion to Armageddon

The beast and false prophet are cast into the Bottomless Pit. Satan is bound for a thousand years. Unbelievers are purged out of Israel. As these are cast into the Bottomless Pit, the thousand-year reign of Christ on earth begins. This thousand-year period is called the Millennium.

Where does that put us today?

It places us with the solemn reminder that the Rapture takes place seven years before Armageddon is ever fought and finished. God held back Bill Clinton and George W. Bush. God stopped Saddam Hussein. But the situation in the Arab world is hotter than Chinese fireworks. A democratic government will not be successfully installed in Iraq. Islamic terrorists will not permit it.

Israel is surrounded by grave danger and is receiving inadequate support from her "allies". As prophetic scripture unfolds things will "wax worse and worse". America believes that to knock out terrorism is to establish peace and safety. Do not be deceived by American peace efforts. God's prophetic clock is a ticking time bomb.

(1 Thessalonians 5:3) For when they shall say, Peace and safety; then sudden destruction cometh upon them, as travail upon a woman with child; and they shall not escape.

26.3 The Reign of Christ on Earth

The end of the Tribulation marks the beginning of the thousand-year reign of Christ upon the earth. (millennial means "thousand")

Satan and his forces are bound and cast into the Bottomless Pit during this thousand-year period.

(Revelation 20:3) And cast him into the bottomless pit, and shut him up, and set a seal upon him, that he should deceive the nations no more, till the thousand years should be fulfilled: and after that he must be loosed a little season.

Without Satan's evil workings, life upon the earth will change drastically as Christ rules with a rod of iron (Rev 19:15) along with the saints from the N.T. church and those saved out of the Tribulation. (2 Tim 2:12; Rev 20:4-6)

During the thousand-year reign of Christ the earth will experience drastic changes.

The earth will experience PHYSICAL CHANGES.

Sickness will be absent from the earth while comfort reigns. (Isa 65:20; 33:24)

The animal kingdom will no longer be carnivorous. (Isa 11:6-10)

Garden of Eden type conditions will be restored. (Psa 67:6; Isa 51:3; Ezek 34:26; 36:30; 47:9-12: Rom 8:9-23)

The earth will experience SOCIOLOGICAL CHANGES.

There will be no war or social strife. (Isa 2:4)

Truth will characterize the period. (Isa 16:5)

Justice will be accomplished in all walks of life.

The earth will experience SPIRITUAL CHANGES.

The millennium will be characterized by: Righteousness (Isa 51:5; Psa 72:7), by Obedience. (Jer 31:33-34; Psa 22:27), by Holiness. (Joel 3:17; Zech 14:20), and by the Fullness of the Holy Spirit. (Ezek 36:27)

The earth will experience GOVERNMENTAL CHANGES.

Christ will theocratically rule with a "rod of iron". (Rev 19:15) Israel will submit joyfully. The kings of the earth will submit begrudgingly. The saints of the previous ages will rule with Christ in every village and town.

26.4 The Last Battle

Satan is loosed for a season at the end of this thousand-year reign of Christ.

(Revelation 20:7-10) And when the thousand years are expired, Satan shall be loosed out of his prison, And shall go out to deceive the nations which are in the four quarters of the earth, Gog and Magog, to gather them together to battle: the number of whom is as the sand of the sea. And they went up on

the breadth of the earth, and compassed the camp of the saints about, and the beloved city: and fire came down from God out of heaven, and devoured them. And the devil that deceived them was cast into the lake of fire and brimstone, where the beast and the false prophet are, and shall be tormented day and night for ever and ever.

At the end of the thousand-year period, Satan will be loosed for a short season to tempt the world and lure the nations away from the reign of Christ. The battle is short and Christ's victory is absolute. Satan and all who followed him will be cast into the Lake of Fire forever.

This Week's Memory Verse

And death and Hell were cast into the lake of fire. This is the second death. And whosoever was not found written in the book of life was cast into the lake of fire. (Revelation 20:14-15)

ESCHATOLOGY, Armageddon and the Reign of Christ On Earth

1. Armageddon is actually a series of battles that take place in the second three and one half years of the Tribulation Period.

These battles involve:

_____

_____

_____

_____

_____

2. The Antichrist moves his headquarters from Rome to _____.

3. The Antichrist destroys _____ world superpowers to gain power.

4. During the thousand-year reign of Christ the earth will experience drastic changes.

_____ changes

_____ changes

_____ changes

_____ changes

Write out this week's Bible verse from memory.

Revelation 20:14-15

_____

_____

_____

_____

_____

Finish the Phrase

And I saw three unclean spirits like frogs come out of the mouth of the _____

Behold, I come as a _____

And he gathered them together into a place called in the Hebrew tongue _____

For when they shall say, Peace and safety; then sudden destruction cometh upon them, as travail upon a woman with child; and they shall _____

And when the thousand years are expired, Satan shall be loosed out of his _____

And shall go out to deceive the nations which are in the four quarters of the earth, Gog and _____

And the devil that deceived them was cast into the lake of fire and _____

Extra Credit Chapel Notes

_____   _____
_____   _____
_____   _____
_____   _____
_____   _____
_____   _____
_____   _____
_____   _____
_____   _____
_____   _____
_____   _____
_____   _____
_____   _____
_____   _____
_____   _____
_____   _____
_____
_____   **BEST POINT MADE**
_____
_____   _____
_____   _____
_____   _____
_____   _____
_____   _____
_____   _____
_____   _____
_____   _____

Proverbs Chapter Twenty-Six

What were the main themes of this chapter?

_____

_____

_____

_____

What were the instructional points meant to bring you closer to God?

_____

_____

_____

_____

What were the instructional points meant to protect you from spiritual destruction?

_____

_____

_____

_____

What things in your life could use strengthening?

_____

_____

_____

_____

Was there anything in this chapter that was of help in serving the LORD?

_____

_____

_____

_____

_____

Did you learn anything new about the LORD?

_____

_____

_____

_____

Were there any suggestions made whereby you can be a greater blessing to others?

_____

_____

_____

_____

_____

_____

27.1 Introduction

(John 14:1-3) Let not your heart be troubled: ye believe in God, believe also in me. In my Father's house are many mansions: if it were not so, I would have told you. I go to prepare a place for you. And if I go and prepare a place for you, I will come again, and receive you unto myself; that where I am, there ye may be also.

There is probably no subject in the Bible as universally accepted among the religions of Christianity and those who associate themselves with such than the existence of heaven. People who do not believe in Hell often believe in heaven. People who believe little about the Bible often believe in heaven. Even secular politicians find it politically expedient to espouse a belief in Heaven.

Illustrations

Following a campaign speech, a young man rushed up to Senator Everett Dirksen and said, "Senator, I wouldn't vote for you if you were St. Peter!" Dirksen eyed the young man for a moment, then said, "Son, if I were St. Peter, you couldn't vote for me, because you wouldn't be in my district."

A little girl was taking an evening walk with her father. In awe, she looked up at the stars and exclaimed, "Oh, Daddy, if the wrong side of heaven is so beautiful, what must the right side be?"

Russian Cosmonauts have flown in and out of outer space and reported that there is no Heaven. Astronomers have looked through their telescopes and declared there is no heaven. Many scientists do not believe in heaven, but they do believe in UFO's. Secularists do not believe in heaven, but they do believe there are other worlds. Educators do not believe in Heaven, but they do believe complexity came out of a big bang!

It is not that they love facts so much, it is that they hate the possibility that a righteous God, who created all men, will judge all men, and will sentence all men.

27.2 Theological Definitions and Considerations

There are at least three heavens.

✓ The first heaven.

The first Heaven is what we see when we look up. It encompasses the clouds and the blue sky of the day. We call it our atmosphere.

(Acts 14:17) *Nevertheless he left not himself without witness, in that he did good, and gave us rain from heaven, and fruitful seasons, filling our hearts with food and gladness.*

The atmospheric heavens include the air that we breathe as well as the space that immediately surrounds the earth. The technical term for this is the "troposphere." It extends about twenty miles above the earth. The space above this is called the "stratosphere." The Scripture uses the term heaven to describe this area.

The first heaven, along with the earth, will be destroyed by God Himself and new a one created. Being that Hell is eternal and is in the center of this present earth, we assume that the new earth is created from the destroyed earth. No doubt the old earth will be without form and void.

The knowledge that heaven and earth would one day be recreated has been around since the days of Old Testament inspiration.

(Isaiah 65:17) *For, behold, I create new heavens and a new earth: and the former shall not be remembered, nor come into mind.*

(Isaiah 66:22) *For as the new heavens*

and the new earth, which I will make, shall remain before me, saith the LORD, so shall your seed and your name remain.

Peter knew of it and John was allowed a glimpse of it.

(2 Peter 3:13) *Nevertheless we, according to his promise, look for new heavens and a new earth, wherein dwelleth righteousness.*

(Revelation 21:1) *And I saw a new heaven and a new earth: for the first heaven and the first earth were passed away; and there was no more sea.*

✓ The second heaven

The second heaven is known as the stellar universe or the galaxies beyond earth's immediate atmosphere.

(Deuteronomy 4:19) *And lest thou lift up thine eyes unto heaven, and when thou seest the sun, and the moon, and the stars, even all the host of heaven, shouldest be driven to worship them, and serve them, which the LORD thy God hath divided unto all nations under the whole heaven.*

(Matthew 24:29) *Immediately after the tribulation of those days shall the sun be darkened, and the moon shall not give her light, and the stars shall fall from heaven, and the powers of the heavens shall be shaken:*

(Hebrews 11:3) Through faith we understand that the worlds were framed by the word of God, so that things which are seen were not made of things which do appear.

✓ The third Heaven

The Scripture speaks of heavenly spheres beyond that which is visible from the earth, but occupy a definite and literal place. It is called the heaven of heavens.

(Deuteronomy 10:14) Behold, the heaven and the heaven of heavens is the LORD'S thy God, the earth also, with all that therein is.

The third heaven is the abode of God. It is the seat of the divine Majesty, the habitation of angels and glorified saints. Its created magnificence might be thought of as the palace and city of the Almighty.

(Nehemiah 9:6) Thou, even thou, art LORD alone; thou hast made heaven, the heaven of heavens, with all their host, the earth, and all things that are therein, the seas, and all that is therein, and thou preservest them all; and the host of heaven worshippeth thee.

Class Discussion Questions

1. What do you remember about Solomon's palace?

Solomon's palace compounded in all its splendor would pale into dimness compared to the abode of God.

READ in class 1 Kings 10:1-13

In describing heaven, how can one possibly capture the majesty and wonder of it all? God said that we have insufficient imagination to comprehend.

(1 Corinthians 2:9) But as it is written, Eye hath not seen, nor ear heard, neither have entered into the heart of man, the things which God hath prepared for them that love him.

Herein is the very throne of God.

(Hebrews 12:2) Looking unto Jesus the author and finisher of our faith; who for the joy that was set before him endured the cross, despising the shame, and is set down at the right hand of the throne of God.

(Revelation 7:15) Therefore are they before the throne of God, and serve him day and night in his temple: and he that sitteth on the throne shall dwell among them.

(Hebrews 8:1) Now of the things which we have spoken this is the sum: We have such an high priest, who is set on the right hand of the throne of the Majesty in the heavens;

In this heaven exists God's Holy of Holies. It is here that Christ ascended up and applied His shed blood to the altar once for all time.

(Hebrews 9:10-12) Which stood only in meats and drinks, and divers washings, and carnal ordinances, imposed on them until the time of reformation. But Christ being come an high priest of good things to come, by a greater and more perfect tabernacle, not made with hands, that is to say, not of this building; Neither by the blood of goats and calves, but by his own blood he entered in once into the holy place, having obtained eternal redemption for us.

(Hebrews 9:24) For Christ is not entered into the holy places made with hands, which are the figures of the true; but into heaven itself, now to appear in the presence of God for us:

Because of what took place in the heavenly Holy of Holies, heaven's population now includes the saints of all the ages. They walk with the angels and celestial beings.

Where is the third heaven?

It cannot be far from earth being that the stairs of the celestial city will one day descend to the new earth. No doubt it is hidden from the view of man in some divine dimension. Satan certainly had no trouble finding it as he stood accusing Job nor did he have difficulty going between heaven and earth. (Job 1:6-12)

27.3 The New Jerusalem

What do we know about the new heaven and earth of Revelation 21?

(Revelation 21:1-8) And I saw a new heaven and a new earth: for the first heaven and the first earth were passed away; and there was no more sea. And I John saw the holy city, new Jerusalem, coming down from God out of heaven, prepared as a bride adorned for her husband. And I heard a great voice out of heaven saying, Behold, the tabernacle of God is with men, and he will dwell with them, and they shall be his people, and God himself shall be with them, and be their God. And God shall wipe away all tears from their eyes; and there shall be no more death, neither sorrow, nor crying, neither shall there be any more pain: for the former things are passed away. And he that sat upon the throne said, Behold, I make all things new. And he said unto me, Write: for these words are true and faithful. And he said unto me, It is done. I am Alpha and Omega, the beginning and the end. I will give unto him that is athirst of the fountain of the water of life freely. He that overcometh shall inherit all things; and I will be his God, and he shall be my son. But the fearful, and unbelieving, and the abominable, and murderers, and whoremongers, and sorcerers, and idolaters, and all liars,

shall have their part in the lake which burneth with fire and brimstone: which is the second death.

The New Jerusalem is a city that is very much a part of the new heaven.

The New Jerusalem is also called the "holy city", "that great city" and the "holy Jerusalem".

✓ The Physical Attributes

It is a city coming down out of the new heaven from God. It is a cube shaped city measuring 1,500 miles on every side. If you were to get on an elevator at the bottom and travel to the top at 60 mph, you would not get to the top for 25 hours! The same would be true of traveling from front to back or from side to side.

The walls are of jasper, the streets are of gold, the gates are of pearl, and the foundations are of precious stones. Heaven's light does not need sun, moon, or stars. The river is pure and clear as crystal. The Tree of Life is in the midst of the street and on both sides of the river. The throne of God is there.

✓ The Spiritual Attributes

Righteousness shall reign. (2 Pet 3:13) God's presence with His people shall be forever. (Rev 21:3) God shall wipe away all tears and there shall be no more death, sorrow, pain, or crying. (Rev 21:4) All former things are passed away and all things are made new. (Rev 21:4,5) Nothing shall ever enter Heaven that defileth, or worketh abomination, or maketh a lie. (Rev 21:27)

Review of the Tree of Life

Access to the Tree of Life is restored unto the saints. When God created it, He gave it both healing and life giving power. Our access to the tree was prevented after the fall of man in the garden. That access is restored to us in Glory.

(Revelation 2:7) He that hath an ear, let him hear what the Spirit saith unto the churches; To him that overcometh will I give to eat of the tree of life, which is in the midst of the paradise of God.

(Revelation 22:2) In the midst of the street of it, and on either side of the river, was there the tree of life, which bare twelve manner of fruits, and yielded her fruit every month: and the leaves of the tree were for the healing of the nations.

(Revelation 22:14) Blessed are they that do his commandments, that they may have right to the tree of life, and may enter in through the gates into the city.

A greater understanding of the Tree of Life warrants a look back at the Old

Testament.

(Genesis 3:22-24) And the LORD God said, Behold, the man is become as one of us, to know good and evil: and now, lest he put forth his hand, and take also of the tree of life, and eat, and live for ever: Therefore the LORD God sent him forth from the garden of Eden, to till the ground from whence he was taken. So he drove out the man; and he placed at the east of the garden of Eden Cherubims, and a flaming sword which turned every way, to keep the way of the tree of life.

(Ezekiel 47:12) And by the river upon the bank thereof, on this side and on that side, shall grow all trees for meat, whose leaf shall not fade, neither shall the fruit thereof be consumed: it shall bring forth new fruit according to his months, because their waters they issued out of the sanctuary: and the fruit thereof shall be for meat, and the leaf thereof for medicine.

It is important to understand that we have eternal life because it is promised to us, not because we will have access to the tree.

How God will maintain our glorious body in an eternal state is not yet revealed to us. While God is eternal because it is His nature, we will live forever because God ordained it and chooses to keep us by His power.

As Christians we will be with our God and Saviour forever and ever along with the saints of all the ages. We will know them and they will know us.

> *Well it's a great, great morning*
> *Your first day in Heaven*
> *When you stroll down the golden avenue.*
> *There are mansions left and right*
> *And you're thrilled at every sight*
> *And the saints are always smiling saying "How do you do?"*
> *Oh it's a great, great morning*
> *You're first day in Heaven*
> *When you realize your worrying days are through.*
> *You'll be glad you were not idle*
> *Took time to read your Bible*
> *It's a great morning for you.*

This Week's Memory Verse

But as it is written, Eye hath not seen, nor ear heard, neither have entered into the heart of man, the things which God hath prepared for them that love him. (1 Corinthians 2:9)

THE DOCTRINE OF HEAVEN, and the New Jerusalem.

1. Which heaven contains all the worlds and galaxies? _____

2. Which heaven contains the New Jerusalem? _____

3. Which heaven do you see when you look up? _____

4. What is the measurement of the New Jerusalem? _____
_____

5. What access is restored to the saints in Heaven? _____

Write out this week's Bible verse from memory.

1 Corinthians 2:9

_____
_____
_____
_____
_____

Finish the Phrase

For, behold, I create new heavens and a new earth: and the former shall not be remembered, nor _____

Nevertheless we, according to his promise, look for new heavens and a new earth, wherein dwelleth _____

Through faith we understand that the worlds were framed by _____

And I John saw the holy city, new Jerusalem, coming down from God out of heaven, prepared as a bride adorned

_____

To him that overcometh will I give to eat _____

And the LORD God said, Behold, the man is become as one of us, to know

_____

BEST POINT MADE

Proverbs Chapter Twenty-Seven

What were the main themes of this chapter?

_____

_____

_____

_____

What were the instructional points meant to bring you closer to God?

_____

_____

_____

_____

What were the instructional points meant to protect you from spiritual destruction?

_____

_____

_____

_____

What things in your life could use strengthening?

_____

_____

_____

_____

_____

Was there anything in this chapter that was of help in serving the LORD?

_____

_____

_____

_____

_____

Did you learn anything new about the LORD?

_____

_____

_____

_____

Were there any suggestions made whereby you can be a greater blessing to others?

_____

_____

_____

_____

_____

28.1 God's Program

God's only program described in the Bible for this present age is the local New Testament church. Christ loved the church and gave Himself for it.

(Ephesians 5:25) Husbands, love your wives, even as Christ also loved the church, and gave himself for it;

(1 Corinthians 3:9) For we are labourers together with God: ye are God's husbandry, ye are God's building.

(Matthew 16:13-18) When Jesus came into the coasts of Caesarea Philippi, he asked his disciples, saying, Whom do men say that I the Son of man am? And they said, Some say that thou art John the Baptist: some, Elias; and others, Jeremias, or one of the prophets. He saith unto them, But whom say ye that I am? And Simon Peter answered and said, Thou art the Christ, the Son of the living God. And Jesus answered and said unto him, Blessed art thou, Simon Barjona: for flesh and blood hath not revealed it unto thee, but my Father which is in heaven. And I say also unto thee, That thou art Peter, and upon this rock I will build my church; and the gates of hell shall not prevail against it.

To truly love Christ we must also love the church that He gave Himself for. It should be our heart, our focus, and our work. Christ is still building His church today through us.

We help build the church of the Lord Jesus Christ in many ways.

✓ **By being faithful attenders**

(Hebrews 10:25) Not forsaking the assembling of ourselves together, as the manner of some is; but exhorting one another: and so much the more, as ye see the day approaching.

In other words, we are not to forsake the churching of ourselves together. When someone says, "I'm a member of the true church", what they usually mean is that they do not attend church. They are disobedient to the commandment. One cannot be a good Christian and live in disobedience.

✓ **By being faithful servants**

The work of the local church relies upon many volunteers of many varieties. These volunteers mostly come from the membership of that church. Most would agree that simply occupying a pew every week is not serving the LORD. While there may be any number of ways to serve the LORD outside of the church, at least a portion of (if not all of) our serving needs to be directly impacting the ministry of our local church.

Class Discussion Questions

1. How many ministries in your church can you think of depend on volunteers?

✓ **By being faithful givers**

In both the Old and New Testaments, the tithes and offerings were given by the congregation to the church. In Acts 7:33, we see that God refers to Moses' congregation as the "church in the wilderness".

(Malachi 3:8-10) Will a man rob God? Yet ye have robbed me. But ye say, Wherein have we robbed thee? In tithes and offerings. Ye are cursed with a curse: for ye have robbed me, even this whole nation. Bring ye all the tithes into the storehouse, that there may be meat in mine house, and prove me now herewith, saith the LORD of hosts, if I will not open you the windows of heaven, and pour you out a blessing, that there shall not be room enough to receive it.

(1 Corinthians 16:2) Upon the first day of the week let every one of you lay by him in store, as God hath prospered him, that there be no gatherings when I come.

The tithe should not be misdirected by the giver to other projects deemed important to them. The tithe belongs to the local church. Let worthy projects be supported by offerings over and above the tithe.

✓ **By being faithful soul-winners**

Someone once said that the work of the church is to win them, baptize them, add them, and then teach them. This is a true and faithful saying.

(Matthew 28:19) Go ye therefore, and teach all nations, baptizing them in the name of the Father, and of the Son, and of the Holy Ghost:

(Acts 2:47) Praising God, and having favour with all the people. And the Lord added to the church daily such as should be saved.

(Ephesians 4:11-12) And he gave some, apostles; and some, prophets; and some, evangelists; and some, pastors and teachers; For the perfecting of the saints, for the work of the ministry, for the edifying of the body of Christ:

✓ **By being faithful encouragers**

(Romans 14:19) Let us therefore follow after the things which make for peace, and things wherewith one may edify another.

(1 Thessalonians 5:11) Wherefore comfort yourselves together, and edify one another, even as also ye do.

28.2 Terms and Definitions

The first terms you should know are the group terms used in the Bible. If you do not know these terms and their definitions, your doctrine and theology will be incorrect on other things in the New Testament.

Do you know the definitions and differences between the following terms?

- ✓ Church
- ✓ Family of God
- ✓ Body of Christ
- ✓ Kingdom of God
- ✓ Kingdom of Heaven

If you are going to carry on God's work in God's way, you must understand these terms and their applications.

The Term "Church"

Where does the word "church" in the King James Bible come from?

Each time you see the English word "church" in the New Testament the Greek word behind it is *ECCLESIA*. Ecclesia by its appropriate definition means "assembly, an assembly, or the assembly."

Many erroneously define this word as the "called out ones". However, this is an error made using the unsure science of etymology and attempting to declare the noun KLESIS ("a calling") as the root word of ECCLESIA and EK as "out". While good students of the Bible would never deny that Christians are "called out" of the world (2 Cor 6:17-18) and that local churches are made up of members who are "called out", this is not justification to alter the word's definition.

It is a mistake to translate ECCLESIA beyond its normal and customary usage during Biblical times. The simple meaning of the word must remain, "assembly".

Where did the English word "church" come from? The answer is uncertain because it was a relatively new word in the English language sometime before 1600 A.D. It appears to be a coined word rather than a literal translation.

The coined word "church" is a very good word for two reasons:

✓ First, it readily helps us to differentiate between God's divine assemblies and public assemblies like the one translated from the word ECCLESIA in Acts 19:39.

(Acts 19:39) But if ye enquire any thing concerning other matters, it shall be determined in a lawful assembly.

265

Secondly, the word "assembly" would have likely run contrary to Anglican church doctrine. They viewed their church as universal, rather than local. (Note: The Tyndale and Geneva translations used the word "congregation" for ecclesia.)

Regardless of its origin, the English word "church" is helpful and good.

A complete definition and descriptions of the term church are derived from numerous New Testament applications.

These applications help us to derive the following definition of the local church:

✓ An autonomous group of immersed believers in a single location

✓ A group which is organized together for three purposes: carrying out the Great Commission, observance of the LORD's supper, and the edification and spiritual encouragement of its members.

✓ A group which is administrated by one Biblical office: Pastor or Elder

✓ The group's physical needs, especially those of its widows, are watched over by special servants called Deacons.

✓ All of the above function within a delicate framework of theocracy and democracy.

The church is local in scope and is neither universal, nor invisible. God's program has always been and always will be a congregational one. God called Moses' congregation the "church in the wilderness". (Acts 7:38)

With the birth of Christ, not only was the foundation laid for the New Testament Church, but the cornerstone was set.

(1 Corinthians 3:11) For other foundation can no man lay than that is laid, which is Jesus Christ.

(Ephesians 2:19-22) Now therefore ye are no more strangers and foreigners, but fellowcitizens with the saints, and of the household of God; And are built upon the foundation of the apostles and prophets, Jesus Christ himself being the chief corner stone; In whom all the building fitly framed together groweth unto an holy temple in the Lord: In whom ye also are builded together for an habitation of God through the Spirit.

Some people believe that the "true" church is universal and invisible. What's wrong with that idea?

✓ Such a church could not have a pastor.

✓ Such a church could not carry out the two church ordinances.

✓ Such a church could not be self-governing, nor do things "decently and in order".

✓ Such a church could not fill a single New Testament need.

✓ Such a church could not edify nor care for its members.

✓ Such a church could not be defined nor described as "an assembly".

What about a universal church assembled in Heaven after the rapture? The answer is simple. There is no need for a church in Heaven. There is no need for the work of a church in Heaven.

The Term "Body of Christ"

If the church cannot be universal by definition or by description, how must we define the Body of Christ on earth? There is ample Biblical evidence that the Body of Christ is the church.

(Colossians 1:15-18) Who is the image of the invisible God, the firstborn of every creature: For by him were all things created, that are in heaven, and that are in earth, visible and invisible, whether they be thrones, or dominions, or principalities, or powers: all things were created by him, and for him: And he is before all things, and by him all things consist. And he is the head of the body, the church: who is the beginning,

the firstborn from the dead; that in all things he might have the preeminence.

(Ephesians 1:22-23) And hath put all things under his feet, and gave him to be the head over all things to the church, Which is his body, the fulness of him that filleth all in all.

If by New Testament DEFINITION the church can only be local, then each church is a body of Christ.

If by New Testament DESCRIPTION the church can only be local, then each church is a body of Christ.

Denominational groups and some non-denominational groups say that the body of Christ is the descriptive phrase used to describe all believers on earth. They say that 1 Cor 12:12,13 teaches this.

(1 Corinthians 12:12-13) For as the body is one, and hath many members, and all the members of that one body, being many, are one body: so also is Christ. For by one Spirit are we all baptized into one body, whether we be Jews or Gentiles, whether we be bond or free; and have been all made to drink into one Spirit.

The denominational premise is mistaken for the following reasons:

✓ 1 Corinthians is a letter written from Paul to the church at Corinth.

✓ The only "body" Paul is trying to correct is the body of Christ at Corinth.

✓ 1 Corinthians 12:23-28 makes it clear that the chapter is about the local church.

(1 Corinthians 12:23) And those members of the body, which we think to be less honourable, upon these we bestow more abundant honour; and our uncomely parts have more abundant comeliness. For our comely parts have no need: but God hath tempered the body together, having given more abundant honour to that part which lacked: That there should be no schism in the body; but that the members should have the same care one for another. And whether one member suffer, all the members suffer with it; or one member be honoured, all the members rejoice with it. Now ye are the body of Christ, and members in particular. And God hath set some in the church, first apostles, secondarily prophets, thirdly teachers, after that miracles, then gifts of healings, helps, governments, diversities of tongues.

The bodies of Christ that Paul speaks of always have specific members guided by specific leadership. Paul is quick to remind us that we are each and all members of only "one" body. Thus, membership in more than one church at the same time is unbiblical. Membership in a local church (the Body of Christ) requires both salvation and immersion. The fact that we are all members of "one body" (church), does not make us all members of the same body (church). Sixty-eight times the New Testament uses the phrase "the church". Not in a single case does that phrase speak of an invisible, universal church.

Illustration

One must also realize that within the bounds of proper grammar, single nouns are often used to describe plural things. We could say that "the automobile" is the greatest source of pollution in San Francisco. Would anyone take us to mean that one automobile did it all? Of course not. The single word "church" sometimes refers to all churches.

Since the local church is the Body of Christ, then all other organizations, regardless of their fundamental beliefs and good intentions, are not the Body of Christ. Remember, Christ's entire New Testament program is tied into and under the local church.

Jesus loved the church and gave Himself for it (Eph 5:25). Christ named Himself as the foundation and cornerstone of the church. Absolutely no other person could ever be this rock (1 Cor 3:11; Eph 2:20).

Ideally and biblically, ministries should be a part of and under the authority of a local N.T. church. This does not mean that ministries spinning outside of the church are not doing a good work. God alone will sort out and address these ministries. (see Lk 9:49-50)

The Term "Family of God"

The **Family of God** includes all the saved on earth and in Heaven. It includes both O.T. saints and N.T. saints.

(Ephesians 3:14-15) *For this cause I bow my knees unto the Father of our Lord Jesus Christ, Of whom the whole family in heaven and earth is named,*

The Terms "Kingdom of God" and "Kingdom of Heaven"

The **Kingdom of God** includes all of the saved on earth at any given time (Lk 16:16; Rom 14:17; Gal 3:26). When they die they pass into the **Kingdom of Heaven** (2 Tim 4:18; Mt 11:11; 16:19).

(Luke 16:16) *The law and the prophets were until John: since that time the kingdom of God is preached, and every man presseth into it.*

(Romans 14:17) *For the kingdom of God is not meat and drink; but righteousness, and peace, and joy in the Holy Ghost.*

(2 Timothy 4:18) *And the Lord shall deliver me from every evil work, and will preserve me unto his heavenly kingdom: to whom be glory for ever and ever. Amen.*

(Matthew 11:11) *Verily I say unto you, Among them that are born of women there hath not risen a greater than John the Baptist: notwithstanding he that is least in the kingdom of heaven is greater than he.*

(Matthew 16:19) *And I will give unto thee the keys of the kingdom of heaven: and whatsoever thou shalt bind on earth shall be bound in heaven: and whatsoever thou shalt loose on earth shall be loosed in heaven.*

Class Discussion Questions

1. What do you like best about your church?

2. In what ways do you enjoy the Family of God?

This Week's Memory Verse

Not forsaking the assembling of ourselves together, as the manner of some is; but exhorting one another: and so much the more, as ye see the day approaching. (Hebrews 10:25)

THE DOCTRINE OF THE LOCAL CHURCH

1. God's only program described in the Bible for this present age is the
_____ New Testament _____.

2. These applications help us to derive the following definition of the local
church:

An autonomous group of_____ believers in a single _____.

A group which is organized together for three purposes:

_____

_____

_____

A group which is administrated by one Biblical office: _____

The group's physical needs, especially those of its widows, are watched over
by special servants called _____.

All of the above functions within a delicate framework of _____
and _____.

Write out this week's Bible verse from memory.

Hebrews 10:25

_____

_____

_____

_____

_____

Finish the Phrase

But whom say ye that I am? And Simon Peter answered and said, Thou art the Christ, the _____

upon this rock I will build my _____

For other foundation can no man lay than that is laid, which is _____

And are built upon the foundation of the apostles and prophets, Jesus Christ himself being the _____

And hath put all things under his feet, and gave him to be the _____

Verily I say unto you, Among them that are born of women there hath not risen a greater than _____

BEST POINT MADE

Proverbs Chapter Twenty-Eight

What were the main themes of this chapter?

_____

_____

_____

_____

What were the instructional points meant to bring you closer to God?

_____

_____

_____

_____

What were the instructional points meant to protect you from spiritual destruction?

_____

_____

_____

_____

What things in your life could use strengthening?

_____

_____

_____

_____

Was there anything in this chapter that was of help in serving the LORD?

_____

_____

_____

_____

Did you learn anything new about the LORD?

_____

_____

_____

_____

Were there any suggestions made whereby you can be a greater blessing to others?

_____

_____

_____

_____

29.1 Introduction

The local church is the living, breathing organization entrusted by God to carry out the work of Jesus Christ on earth. It is made up of believers who are commissioned to this work. The Bible sets up both leadership positions and support positions within each congregation to ensure that God's work is carried out in God's way. A closer look at these positions will give us a greater understanding of the local church.

29.2 Leadership and Support Positions

The primary LEADERSHIP positions of the local church are all *pastoral*.

The Bible uses the following N.T. descriptive titles for this position with each emphasizing a different aspect of the pastor's ministry.

Bishop (Greek, episcopos): meaning "overseer."

Elder or Presbytery (Gk. presbuteros): meaning "ruler over affairs".

Pastor or Shepherd (Gk. poimain): meaning "guardian of the flock".

Prophet (Gk. prophetes): meaning "one who is called to preach God's words openly".

Churches generally use only one of these terms to describe their primary leader. This position, regardless of the title, is the ruling position in every church.

(1 Timothy 5:17-18) Let the elders that rule well be counted worthy of double honour, especially they who labour in the word and doctrine. For the scripture saith, Thou shalt not muzzle the ox that treadeth out the corn. And, The labourer is worthy of his reward.

In cases of plurality where a church is large enough to have more than one man on their pastoral staff (Jas 5:14), it is necessary that one serves as head over the others. He is usually referred to as head pastor.

In simple terms, assistant pastors are assistants to the head pastor and work for him. Were it not for the growth of his work, he would not need their assistance. I Corinthians 14:40 instructs us to do all things "decently and in order".

Assistant pastors must meet all the same standards and requirements as head pastors. They should not be allowed a lesser spiritual life than that of the pastor. He should manifest a servant's heart, a good work ethic, a self-starting character, and a loyal philosophy. If there is a weakness on the part of head pastors, it is usually a failure to hire the right kind of men to assist him.

Independent, fundamental, Baptist churches typically will allow the pastor to choose his own staff after the congregation has approved the need for additional staff. Imagine what might happen if the congregation appointed an assistant pastor who was not matched well with the head pastor or did not share his vision for the church.

The primary SUPPORT positions of the local church are *ministerial*.

While all pastoral positions are ministerial, not all ministerial positions are pastoral.

The Bible divides the support positions under the following names.

Evangelist (Gk. euangelistes): meaning "soul-winner" or "gospel preacher". He is *authorized and commissioned*.

Deacons (Gk. diaconos): meaning "servant". They are *elected and directed*.

Teachers (Gk. didaskalos): meaning "one who disciples". They are *appointed and assigned*.

Each of these servants are under the guidance and leadership of the pastor. He appoints the work of the deacons. Deacons do not oversee nor appoint the pastor's work. The pastor appoints the work of teachers. Teachers do not oversee nor appoint the pastor's work.

The same is true of evangelists. In the early church, it appears that evangelists were full-time soul-winners and street preachers. There is no indication that their commission was to revive churches and church members. They do not seem to have traveled from church to church holding meetings. This idea is one that evolved through the centuries since then. It is probably best concluded that the main responsibility of an evangelist is to evangelize the lost.

Apostle (Gk. apostolos): this title is the title given to the twelve men personally commissioned by Jesus to help serve as foundations in establishing N.T. doctrine and church policy (Eph 2:20). When Judas died, his position was given to Paul. The position of Apostle ceased

275

with the death of the last Apostle. They were never replaced by our Lord.

29.3 A Biblical Look at the Position of Pastor

The pastor is dedicated solely to ministering to and the oversight of one flock. That flock is a local church.

Most church members do not realize that the pastor's duties are immense. He is "on call" twenty-four hours a day seven days a week. Even if he takes a day off every week, he does not cease to be "on call".

(1 Peter 5:1-4) The elders which are among you I exhort, who am also an elder, and a witness of the sufferings of Christ, and also a partaker of the glory that shall be revealed: Feed the flock of God which is among you, taking the oversight thereof, not by constraint, but willingly; not for filthy lucre, but of a ready mind; Neither as being lords over God's heritage, but being ensamples to the flock. And when the chief Shepherd shall appear, ye shall receive a crown of glory that fadeth not away.

(1 Timothy 3:5) For if a man know not how to rule his own house, how shall he take care of the church of God?

(2 Timothy 4:2-5) Preach the word; be instant in season, out of season; reprove, rebuke, exhort with all longsuffering and doctrine. For the time will come when they will not endure sound doctrine; but after their own lusts shall they heap to themselves teachers, having itching ears; And they shall turn away their ears from the truth, and shall be turned unto fables. But watch thou in all things, endure afflictions, do the work of an evangelist, make full proof of thy ministry.

The Pastor's Duties

✓ He guards the flock from spiritual destruction and outside enemies.

✓ He feeds the flock through preaching and teaching.

✓ He edifies the saints in all walks of life.

✓ He rules over and oversees every aspect of church work, ministry, and church government.

✓ He exhorts and rebukes in a spirit of love and concern.

✓ He ministers to his people in times of need. For example: sickness, funerals, weddings, or life's many problems which call for instruction, counseling, and wisdom.

The pastor is biblically kept from overstepping certain authoritative boundaries.

He is not a high priest nor a mediator

between you and God for your sins.

(1 Timothy 2:5) For there is one God, and one mediator between God and men, the man Christ Jesus;

(1 Peter 2:5-9) Ye also, as lively stones, are built up a spiritual house, an holy priesthood, to offer up spiritual sacrifices, acceptable to God by Jesus Christ. Wherefore also it is contained in the scripture, Behold, I lay in Sion a chief corner stone, elect, precious: and he that believeth on him shall not be confounded. Unto you therefore which believe he is precious: but unto them which be disobedient, the stone which the builders disallowed, the same is made the head of the corner, And a stone of stumbling, and a rock of offence, even to them which stumble at the word, being disobedient: whereunto also they were appointed. But ye are a chosen generation, a royal priesthood, an holy nation, a peculiar people; that ye should shew forth the praises of him who hath called you out of darkness into his marvellous light:

He is not a dictator or lord over the flock. He rules over church business and ministry, but he does not rule over the homes of his flock. The pastor is not the head of any household except his own. Each father or husband is the head of his own home. He leads the flock. He does not drive the flock.

(1 Peter 5:2-3) Feed the flock of God which is among you, taking the oversight thereof, not by constraint, but willingly; not for filthy lucre, but of a ready mind; Neither as being lords over God's heritage, but being ensamples to the flock.

Congregations have a special relationship to their pastor.

✓ They love, honor, and obey him. (Heb 13:7,17; 1 Tim 5:17-19; 2 Th 3:6-15)

✓ They allow his leadership over them as they serve the LORD in their church.

It is the pastor that must give an account to God for the local church's ministry, not the people. (Heb 13:17) Thus he is the chairman of every board and the overseer of every group.

The pastor is the "man of God" (God's anointed) given to the local church. The wise church member will consult this man of God before making major decisions. It is wise not to make these decisions without spiritual perspective and advice.

(Hebrews 13:17) Obey them that have the rule over you, and submit yourselves: for they watch for your souls, as they that must give account, that they may do it with joy, and not with grief: for that is unprofitable for you.

Biblical Standards for Pastors

Pastors are admonished in Scripture to abide by strict, Biblical, and personal standards. A sampling of these standards is listed in 1 Tim 3:1-8

(1 Timothy 3:1-8) This is a true saying, If a man desire the office of a bishop, he desireth a good work. A bishop then must be blameless, the husband of one wife, vigilant, sober, of good behaviour, given to hospitality, apt to teach; Not given to wine, no striker, not greedy of filthy lucre; but patient, not a brawler, not covetous; One that ruleth well his own house, having his children in subjection with all gravity; (For if a man know not how to rule his own house, how shall he take care of the church of God?) Not a novice, lest being lifted up with pride he fall into the condemnation of the devil. Moreover he must have a good report of them which are without; lest he fall into reproach and the snare of the devil.

✓ He must be blameless.

✓ He must be the husband of only one wife.

✓ He must be vigilant (meaning on guard with his eyes open) and sober (serious).

✓ He must be of good behavior and hospitable.

✓ He must be able to teach.

✓ He must absolutely abstain from alcoholic drinks.

✓ He must not be greedy, covetous, nor use the ministry for personal gain.

✓ He must be patient, not a fighter or striker.

✓ He must rule his wife and children well and wisely.

✓ He must not be a novice (untrained and inexperienced).

✓ He must have a good report (private and public reputation).

It is fair to assert that the pastor is expected to uphold any and all other Biblical standards as well.

The Appointment of Pastors to Churches

The first pastor of a new church is generally appointed by the church or missionary that started the church. Since churches are to start churches, it stands to reason that God may have intended churches to be started by churches (or at least commissioned by one).

Paul and his team were commissioned and sent out by the church at Antioch to start churches. As churches were started and grew, Paul and his team eventually appointed and ordained the first pastors of those churches.

(Titus 1:5) For this cause left I thee in Crete, that thou shouldest set in order the things that are wanting, and ordain elders in every city, as I had appointed thee:

This is how Bible-believing, missionary church planters do it today.

The Bible gives no specific instruction to churches concerning replacing a previous pastor. Most independent church congregations elect their next pastor when a vacancy occurs. The specific process to accomplish this varies from church to church.

It is interesting to note that pastors in Apostolic times did not change churches or jump from church to church. This does not mean it did not happen, but it was not demonstrated in the New Testament pattern. If people cannot grow by church hopping, then it must also be true that pastors cannot grow the people by church hopping himself.

Pastors ought to commit themselves to an honest effort to stay with one church per life time. It takes at least 25 years for a life's work to be built. While the Holy Spirit does move other pastors to other churches, the hard truth is that most pastors move because they are discouraged with one thing or another. It is usually better to deal with the discouragement than to run from it. The common misconception is that the "grass is greener" elsewhere. One humorous theologian suggested that the grass is only greener elsewhere when it grows above a septic system.

Providing for Pastors

The pastor is ultimately to be supported by the tithes and offerings of the church. Sometimes a new church planter will raise monthly support from existing churches. Sometimes he will work a temporary job while the new church is being started. Paul did this sometimes. He worked as a tentmaker. As soon as the church is able, it should become the pastor's provider.

(Luke 10:3-7) Go your ways: behold, I send you forth as lambs among wolves. Carry neither purse, nor scrip, nor shoes: and salute no man by the way. And into whatsoever house ye enter, first say, Peace be to this house. And if the son of peace be there, your peace shall rest upon it: if not, it shall turn to you again. And in the same house remain, eating and drinking such things as they give: for the labourer is worthy of his hire. Go not from house to house.

Removing an Unfit Pastor From His Position

Because pastors are men and not gods, they can fall into sin of such as would require their removal from office. This can only be done by the congregation he oversees. There is no such thing as an outside counsel of bishops, pastors, or men who have the Biblical authority or divine permission to do this. The only record of such a counsel in church history is that of the Apostles. However, they are all dead and have never been replaced.

The Bible gives us these sad guidelines for church discipline.

An accusation must come from more than one person.

(1 Timothy 5:19-21) Against an elder receive not an accusation, but before two or three witnesses. Them that sin rebuke before all, that others also may fear. I charge thee before God, and the Lord Jesus Christ, and the elect angels, that thou observe these things without preferring one before another, doing nothing by partiality.

Upon the evidence, it is decided by the church members if the pastor is guilty or innocent. If guilty, the church may decide to rebuke the pastor or dismiss him from office. Serious charges will generally bring about a pastor's dismissal. Most churches remove an unfit pastor by vote of the church using a set procedure in the church's bylaws. It is refreshing to know that only a very tiny number of pastors have ever needed to be disciplined.

This Week's Memory Verse

Remember them which have the rule over you, who have spoken unto you the word of God: whose faith follow, considering the end of their conversation. (Hebrews 13:7)

THE DOCTRINE OF THE LOCAL CHURCH, It's Leadership

1. The primary LEADERSHIP positions of the local church are all _____.

2. The primary SUPPORT positions of the local church are _____.

3. The Bible uses the following N.T. descriptive titles for pastors.

Bishop (Gk. episcopos): meaning _____.

Elder or Presbytery (Gk. presbuteros): meaning _____.

Pastor or Shepherd (Gk. poimain): meaning _____.

Prophet (Gk. prophetes): meaning _____.

4. The Bible divides the support positions under the following names.

Evangelist (Gk. euangelistes): meaning "soul-winner" or "gospel preacher". He is _____.

Deacons (Gk. diaconos): meaning "servant". They are _____.

Teachers (Gk. didaskalos): meaning "one who disciples". They are _____.

Write out this week's Bible verse from memory.

Hebrews 13:7

_____
_____
_____
_____
_____

Finish the Phrase

For if a man know not how to rule his own house, how shall he take care of

_____

Let the elders that rule well be counted worthy of double _____

Preach the word; be instant in season, out of season; reprove, rebuke, exhort with all longsuffering and _____

(Hebrews 13:17) Obey them that have the _____, and submit yourselves: for they watch for your _____, as they that must give _____, that they may do it with joy, and not with _____.

BEST POINT MADE

Proverbs Chapter Twenty-Nine

What were the main themes of this chapter?

_____

_____

_____

_____

_____

What were the instructional points meant to bring you closer to God?

_____

_____

_____

_____

_____

What were the instructional points meant to protect you from spiritual destruction?

_____

_____

_____

_____

_____

What things in your life could use strengthening?

_____

_____

_____

_____

_____

Was there anything in this chapter that was of help in serving the LORD?

_____

_____

_____

_____

_____

Did you learn anything new about the LORD?

_____

_____

_____

_____

Were there any suggestions made whereby you can be a greater blessing to others?

_____

_____

_____

_____

_____

_____

30.1 Introduction

There are two ordinances given solely to the local church and put under its immediate authority. This authority extends to missionaries sent out of those churches and the churches being planted by those missionaries until such time as those churches become independent and self-governing. These two ordinances are Baptism and the Lord's Table. Each shows a different aspect of our redemption.

Foot washing is not an ordinance of the church and was never practiced by the early church as anything other than a humble act of washing the dirty feet of a house guest as they entered the house. Imagine how dirty feet became being shod with nothing but sandals.

30.2 The Ordinance of Baptism

(Acts 10:42-48) And he commanded us to preach unto the people, and to testify that it is he which was ordained of God to be the Judge of quick and dead. To him give all the prophets witness, that through his name whosoever believeth in him shall receive remission of sins. While Peter yet spake these words, the Holy Ghost fell on all them which heard the word. And they of the circumcision which believed were astonished, as many as came with Peter, because that on the Gentiles also was poured out the gift of the Holy Ghost. For they heard them speak with tongues, and magnify God. Then answered Peter, Can any man forbid water, that these should not be baptized, which have received the Holy Ghost as well as we? And he commanded them to be baptized in the name of the Lord. Then prayed they him to tarry certain days.

The main elements of baptism can be remembered in a simple acrostic spelling the word baptism.

Bible commanded for all believers
A local church ordinance
Public testimony of faith in Christ
The first step of obedience
Immersion under the water
Salvation's picture of death, burial, and resurrection
Meant only for those who have already been saved

The word baptism comes from a Greek word meaning "to dip under". Baptism by sprinkling or pouring fails to dip under, does not follow Biblical example, and does not picture salvation.

How was Christ baptized?

(Matthew 3:16) And Jesus, when he was baptized, went up straightway out of the water: and, lo, the heavens were opened unto him, and he saw the Spirit of God descending like a dove, and lighting upon him:

How was the Ethiopian Eunuch baptized?

(Acts 8:39) And when they were come up out of the water, the Spirit of the Lord caught away Philip, that the eunuch saw him no more: and he went on his way rejoicing.

What do we see in the following text?

(Romans 6:2-6) God forbid. How shall we, that are dead to sin, live any longer therein? Know ye not, that so many of us as were baptized into Jesus Christ were baptized into his death? Therefore we are buried with him by baptism into death: that like as Christ was raised up from the dead by the glory of the Father, even so we also should walk in newness of life. For if we have been planted together in the likeness of his death, we shall be also in the likeness of his resurrection: Knowing this, that our old man is crucified with him, that the body of sin might be destroyed, that henceforth we should not serve sin.

The N.T. never teaches nor implies baptism by sprinkling or pouring.

Baptism is Commanded

While baptism is not a part of salvation, neither is it optional. It is commanded of us. All believers are required to be baptized.

✓ This requirement is seen in what is known as the great commission.

(Matthew 28:19-20) Go ye therefore, and teach all nations, baptizing them in the name of the Father, and of the Son, and of the Holy Ghost: Teaching them to observe all things whatsoever I have commanded you: and, lo, I am with you alway, even unto the end of the world. Amen.

✓ This requirement is seen in the direct command of Scripture.

(Acts 2:38) Then Peter said unto them, Repent, and be baptized every one of you in the name of Jesus Christ for the remission of sins, and ye shall receive the gift of the Holy Ghost.

✓ This requirement is seen in solid Biblical example.

(Acts 2:41) Then they that gladly received his word were baptized: and the same day there were added unto them about three thousand souls.

(Acts 8:12) But when they believed Philip preaching the things concerning the kingdom of God, and the name of

Jesus Christ, they were baptized, both men and women.

(Acts 18:8) And Crispus, the chief ruler of the synagogue, believed on the Lord with all his house; and many of the Corinthians hearing believed, and were baptized.

The thief on the cross cannot be used as an example of a Christian who was never baptized. He was accepted of Christ before the death, burial, and resurrection of Christ, and went to paradise. In other words, he was an Old Testament believer.

Christians who refuse to be biblically baptized are living in disobedience to the command.

They cannot biblically join a New Testament church. They cannot biblically partake of the Lord's Table because they are not members of the local church. Christians who refuse to be obedient in baptism might well expect chastisement. (Heb 12:5-11)

While salvation and baptism are not the same, they hold hands together in such a way as to appear to be a single command. Let us take another look at Acts 2:38.

(Acts 2:38) Then Peter said unto them, Repent, and be baptized every one of you in the name of Jesus Christ for the remission of sins, and ye shall receive

the gift of the Holy Ghost.

We have already established in previous lessons that salvation is not by baptism or any work of man and that water does not wash away sin. We see this truth established in the story of Cornelius.

READ Acts 10:1-48

Class Discussion Questions

1. What is in the story of Cornelius that tells us he was saved before he was baptized?

30.3 The Ordinance of The Lord's Table

There are only two local church ordinances: the second being the Lord's Table (sometimes called communion).

(1 Corinthians 11:23) For I have received of the Lord that which also I delivered unto you, That the Lord Jesus the same night in which he was betrayed took bread: And when he had given thanks, he brake it, and said, Take, eat: this is my body, which is broken for you: this do in remembrance of me. After the same manner also he took the cup, when he had supped, saying, This cup is the new testament in my blood: this do ye, as oft as ye drink it, in remembrance of me. For as often as ye eat this bread, and drink this cup, ye

do shew the Lord's death till he come.

The occasion of the first Lord's Table is the one that Christ instituted.

(Matthew 26:26-30) And as they were eating, Jesus took bread, and blessed it, and brake it, and gave it to the disciples, and said, Take, eat; this is my body. And he took the cup, and gave thanks, and gave it to them, saying, Drink ye all of it; For this is my blood of the new testament, which is shed for many for the remission of sins. But I say unto you, I will not drink henceforth of this fruit of the vine, until that day when I drink it new with you in my Father's kingdom. And when they had sung an hymn, they went out into the mount of Olives.

It was the occasion of the Passover Feast that Jesus was celebrating with his twelve disciples. (Read Exodus 11 and 12) The feast was a remembrance of the shed blood and deliverance from the death angel when the Jews were slaves in Egypt.

Jesus used the occasion of this feast to institute a type of "Christian" Passover that would cause us to remember Christ's shed blood and our deliverance from death through Him.

As the Lord taught the Apostles to observe this supper, the Apostles taught the New Testament church to observe it in the same manner.

Paul continued this careful instruction to church members in his epistles.

(1 Corinthians 10:16) The cup of blessing which we bless, is it not the communion of the blood of Christ? The bread which we break, is it not the communion of the body of Christ?

(1 Corinthians 11:17-30) Now in this that I declare unto you I praise you not, that ye come together not for the better, but for the worse. For first of all, when ye come together in the church, I hear that there be divisions among you; and I partly believe it. For there must be also heresies among you, that they which are approved may be made manifest among you. When ye come together therefore into one place, this is not to eat the Lord's supper. For in eating every one taketh before other his own supper: and one is hungry, and another is drunken. What? have ye not houses to eat and to drink in? or despise ye the church of God, and shame them that have not? What shall I say to you? shall I praise you in this? I praise you not. For I have received of the Lord that which also I delivered unto you, That the Lord Jesus the same night in which he was betrayed took bread: And when he had given thanks, he brake it, and said, Take, eat: this is my body, which is broken for you: this do in remembrance of me. After the same manner also he took the cup, when he had supped, saying, This cup is the new testament in my blood: this do ye, as oft as ye

drink it, in remembrance of me. For as often as ye eat this bread, and drink this cup, ye do shew the Lord's death till he come. Wherefore whosoever shall eat this bread, and drink this cup of the Lord, unworthily, shall be guilty of the body and blood of the Lord. But let a man examine himself, and so let him eat of that bread, and drink of that cup. For he that eateth and drinketh unworthily, eateth and drinketh damnation to himself, not discerning the Lord's body. For this cause many are weak and sickly among you, and many sleep.

The Symbols of the Lord's Table

The individual elements were symbols. The unleavened bread represents the broken body of Christ given for us.

The cup of unfermented wine represents both the shed blood of Jesus and our redemption.

The absence of leaven in the bread and the absence of fermentation in the wine symbolized the absence of corruption in Jesus' blood and body. Both leaven and fermentation are corrupting factors.

The carnal Corinthian church abused the Lord's table by corrupted elements, by drunkenness and by the fellowship of eating. This was the one church no one wants to pattern after.

The supper itself was symbolic. The greatest significance lies in its nature as a memorial feast.

The two ordinances together cause us to see the complete picture of our redemption.

In Baptism we see the picture of the **death**, **burial**, and **resurrection of Christ**. The Lord's Supper gives us the remaining two parts of the picture. The unleavened bread pictures the **broken body of Christ**. The cup pictures the **shed blood of Christ**.

In both ordinances we see the results of our redemption. In baptism we see that we are raised to walk in the newness of life.

(Romans 6:3-4) Know ye not, that so many of us as were baptized into Jesus Christ were baptized into his death? Therefore we are buried with him by baptism into death: that like as Christ was raised up from the dead by the glory of the Father, even so we also should walk in newness of life.

In the Lord's Table we see that we are to "examine" ourselves for sin. After this we are to walk in the newness of life.

(1 Corinthians 11:27-29) Wherefore whosoever shall eat this bread, and drink this cup of the Lord, unworthily, shall be guilty of the body and blood of the Lord. But let a man examine himself, and so let him eat of that

bread, and drink of that cup. For he that eateth and drinketh unworthily, eateth and drinketh damnation to himself, not discerning the Lord's body.

The Corinthian believers profaned the Lord's Table and treated the ordinance shabbily. The above Scripture text is Paul's harsh rebuke to them.

How often should we observe the Lord's Table?

(1 Corinthians 11:26) For as often as ye eat this bread, and drink this cup, ye do shew the Lord's death till he come.

It appears that it should be observed on a regular basis in remembrance of these things, but not so often that it becomes a meaningless ritual. The Passover was observed once per year by commandment. God considered this enough to keep the remembrance.

Does the 1 Corinthians 11:26 text give the New Testament Church permission to observe the Lord's Table more often? Most theologians believe the permission is implied. What do you think?

Many churches observe the ordinance once every month and usually on the same Sunday of the month. Other churches observe the ordinance far fewer times. Neither practice is wrong. The best philosophy is to let each local church decide this under their own authority.

Special Observations

The Lord's Supper holds several other important things for us to observe. Other than the first one, no Lord's Supper was held outside of the authority of the local church. It is always administered by the local church. We conclude that it cannot be administered privately or as a casual, social event.

(Acts 20:7-8) And upon the first day of the week, when the disciples came together to break bread, Paul preached unto them, ready to depart on the morrow; and continued his speech until midnight. And there were many lights in the upper chamber, where they were gathered together.

There is an ongoing debate about who should be invited to the Lord's Table within each church. Some churches invite only their members. This is called "closed". Other churches invite those of like faith and practice to participate who might happen to be in their service. This is called "close". Still, others invite all Christians in their service to participate in the Lord's Table with them. This is called "open". Without getting into the debate we note that the supper in the upper room with Jesus and His disciples is not a pattern for any given argument. Why?

✓ They were not a local church.

290

✓ One was invited to participate who was not even a believer.

✓ The disciples were leaders within the group. They were not the group.

It is best concluded that each local church has the authority to observe the Lord's Table as they wish on the matter of participation.

This Week's Memory Verse

Then they that gladly received his word were baptized: and the same day there were added unto them about three thousand souls. (Acts 2:41)

THE DOCTRINE OF THE LOCAL CHURCH, Its Ordinances

1. Finish the acrostic:

B _____
A _____
P _____
T _____
I _____
S _____
M _____

2. In Baptism we see the picture of the _____
_____

The Lord's Supper gives us the remaining two parts of the picture. The unleavened bread pictures the _____

The cup pictures the _____

Write out this week's Bible verse from memory.

Acts 2:41

_____
_____
_____
_____
_____

Finish the Phrase

And Jesus, when he was baptized, went up straightway _____

And when they were come up out of the water, the Spirit of the Lord caught away _____

Then Peter said unto them, Repent, and be baptized every _____

For he that eateth and drinketh unworthily, eateth and drinketh _____

For as often as ye eat this bread, and drink this cup, ye do shew _____

BEST POINT MADE

Proverbs Chapter Thirty

What were the main themes of this chapter?

_____

_____

_____

_____

What were the instructional points meant to bring you closer to God?

_____

_____

_____

What were the instructional points meant to protect you from spiritual destruction?

_____

_____

_____

What things in your life could use strengthening?

_____

_____

_____

_____

Was there anything in this chapter that was of help in serving the LORD?

_____

_____

_____

_____

Did you learn anything new about the LORD?

_____

_____

_____

_____

Were there any suggestions made whereby you can be a greater blessing to others?

_____

_____

_____

_____

_____

We begin the chapter with a reminder that this book is not written on an advanced seminary level. It should be understood that there is not enough space in this chapter to answer every question, make every argument, or prove every point in reference to the inspiration and preservation of the Bible. This material will, however, form an excellent foundation for your understanding and further studies.

31.1 Introduction

For centuries Satan has tried to destroy the Bible. He has orchestrated many schemes to try to achieve that end. The Bible has been ridiculed, outlawed, and burned. All of these efforts have inflicted little damage on the printing, distribution, and preaching of the Bible. But Satan's latter day scheme is the brilliant one and has inflicted much damage. What is this scheme? It is to change the inspired words of God and corresponding "translations", then rechange them again and again. Today, there are so many different Bibles in print that it is often quipped that one can join a "Bible of the Month Club". What is the result of this mess? A great number of confused Christians no longer have the confidence that the Bible represents every word of God and that endless translations have failed to preserve these words in their own language. Add to this the fact that unscrupulous publishers have inserted political correctness into their contemporary translations on a wide range of contemporary moral issues.

Is the Bible the final rule of faith and practice for Christians? Not for most Christians. They have come to believe that Bible truth is just a matter of translation or personal interpretation.

The Bible's authority will never be fully restored in the eyes of men until we return to an authoritative translation. This is especially true for English speakers.

31.2 Revelation from God

From the beginning it was of paramount importance that God communicate with man. Why? Because man needed to know that he was created by God and not just birthed out of some burst of gas in the universe somewhere. Man needed to know that there was rhyme and reason for his existence. If God did create us, there must have been a reason for it. If God did create us then we are wholly obligated to God's wishes. God would have a right to certain expectations of us.

A leading and world renowned evolutionist said that he believed in evolution, not because it was plausible, but because the alternative was unthinkable. What was so unthinkable? It was that Divine Law would take precedence over human law and the idea that he was "his own man" would be baseless. It is the accounting we must give to God that offends evolutionists.

God did communicate with man. Not only did He communicate with man, but he did it on three different fronts.

✓ **First, God communicated to man through creation.**

Note the strong wording in the following text.

(Romans 1:19-20) Because that which may be known of God is manifest in them; for God hath shewed it unto them. For the invisible things of him from the creation of the world are clearly seen, being understood by the things that are made, even his eternal power and Godhead; so that they are without excuse:

The evidence of creation by design and designer is so solid that God allows no excuses at the Great White Throne Judgement. No one will get by with saying that they did not know God existed. They will literally be without excuse.

✓ **Secondly, God communicated to man through an innate knowledge of God put into every man's conscience.**

Whether by Divine endowment or by intuitive knowledge, the point is that every man ever born has this in him. Atheists are not born, they are made. They are indoctrinated by others who have rejected the truth of God. Their minds and hearts have been seared with a hot iron. God commands believers directly on this matter.

(Proverbs 19:27) Cease, my son, to hear the instruction that causeth to err from the words of knowledge.

✓ **Thirdly, God communicated to man in writing.**

This writing is the verbally inspired, supernaturally preserved Word of God. We call it the Bible.

Think about the necessity of such a writing.

✓ **If we are going to know about God, He must tell us about Himself.**

✓ **If we are going to be saved, we must be told the way.**

✓ **If we are going to serve God and please God, we must be told how to do that.**

31.3 The Inspiration

Christian fundamentalists have always required that its adherents believe in a verbally inspired, perfect Word of God. Thus, to avoid blatant hypocrisy, they must believe that such a Word of God exists.

By <u>INSPIRATION</u>, we mean the very breath of God.

(2 Timothy 3:16-17) All scripture is given by inspiration of God, and is profitable for doctrine, for reproof, for correction, for instruction in righteousness: That the man of God may be perfect, throughly furnished unto all good works.

(Job 32:8) But there is a spirit in man: and the inspiration of the Almighty giveth them understanding.

The words of God came down from Heaven via the breath of the Holy Spirit and through the hand of holy men in such completeness that no words were authored by men.

Inspiration is the word that the Bible uses to describe the <u>MODE</u> of delivery. God could have sent an angel to deliver a pre-written copy of the Word of God. God did not choose this mode. He chose to use holy men to record every word of the Divine dictation. For an interesting personal study, find out what plenary means.

(2 Peter 1:21) For the prophecy came not in old time by the will of man: but holy men of God spake as they were moved by the Holy Ghost.

By <u>VERBAL</u>, we mean that every word of the Scripture is inspired, not just the idea.

By <u>PERFECT</u>, we mean that what these men wrote down, through the inspiration of the Holy Spirit, was absolutely perfect in every respect. The words were right. The grammar was correct. The accent marks were right. In other words, it was the perfect Word of God without error.

(Psalm 12:6) The words of the LORD are pure words: as silver tried in a furnace of earth, purified seven times.

English speaking people call the compilation of these inspired and perfect words by several names: the Bible, the Scripture, and the Word of God.

Think about it. The 66 books of the Bible were recorded by 40 different men over a period of 1,500 years. Written down in Hebrew, Greek, and Aramaic, the books and words of the Bible never contradict each other even once. Most of these men never knew each other. It is a miracle that serves further proof of one author, the Holy Spirit.

Because the Bible is verbally inspired and supernaturally preserved, it alone is the final rule of faith and practice. It is the final authority for all fields of knowledge including the sciences, histories, and philosophies of men. We say the philosophies of men because God has no philosophies.

31.4 The Preservation

We believe in the miracle of Divine preservation for two reasons.

✓ **We believe in Divine preservation because of what the Bible says about itself.**

(1 Peter 1:25) *But the word of the Lord endureth for ever. And this is the word which by the gospel is preached unto you.*

(Matthew 5:18) *For verily I say unto you, Till heaven and earth pass, one jot or one tittle shall in no wise pass from the law, till all be fulfilled.*

Some say that it is only preserved in Heaven. They base their statement on Psalm 119:89. This is a shallow belief considering the wording of the text and that no one in Heaven needs to be saved. The Word was written to man, not those in Heaven. It is man that needs a perfect Word of God.

✓ **We believe in Divine preservation because inspiration without preservation is pointless.**

God has never done anything that was pointless. Yet, some teach that the perfect words of God were lost throughout the antiquity of time, thus changes occurred.

Question. Why would God meticulously inspire every word only for those words to suffer loss, changes, additions, and subtractions? It is very clear that God is not the least bit interested in the thoughts and changes of men on this subject.

(Isaiah 55:8-11) *For my thoughts are not your thoughts, neither are your ways my ways, saith the LORD. For as the heavens are higher than the earth, so are my ways higher than your ways, and my thoughts than your thoughts. For as the rain cometh down, and the snow from heaven, and returneth not thither, but watereth the earth, and maketh it bring forth and bud, that it may give seed to the sower, and bread to the eater: So shall my word be that goeth forth out of my mouth: it shall not return unto me void, but it shall accomplish that which I please, and it shall prosper in the thing whereto I sent it.*

God's words have never been lost as some erroneously teach. The Bible has never needed to be re-inspired as some falsely claim. Such a claim flies in the face of God's promise of preservation.

We will look closer at this promise later in the chapter.

God's perfect plan for the Bible has been and is now being fulfilled. Every people from every tribe in every generation has had and now has the opportunity to have the perfect words of God translated into their own language.

Under secular liberalism, public education's textbooks have suffered tremendous deletions, deliberate alterations, and an undaunted execution of historical truth. Today's textbooks are filled with half-truths and whole lies. Their goal is to destroy patriotism, redefine democracy, antiquate the U.S. Constitutional protections while erasing Christianity. New World Order masterminds know that the end result will be anarchy, distrust, and loss of faith in freedom. The collapse of sovereignty in every nation will tumble the world head-long into the dictatorship of the Antichrist.

Under theological liberalism, fundamentalism has been directly assaulted by assaulting their one and only authority, the Bible. Knowing that fundamentalists stood strong on the authority of the Bible, where liberalism aimed its attack was not on the doctrine of inspiration of the Bible, but on the doctrine of preservation.

Liberals began with a simple premise:

that only the "originals" are inspired. Since the originals are all lost, we have only imperfect copies. Without computers and copiers, they say it was only natural for scribes to make scribal errors in the hand copied reproductions.

Today, these copies are called "manuscripts". They number about five-thousand. Liberals say that these all differ from one another, so we have to sort of average them. By the way, that premise is less than true.

This is where the liberals have their claim to contemporary fame and scholarship. They have a hay day with revising Bible history, rewriting God's words into what they think God might have said or meant to say. They then print and mass market their error with great financial profit. When the profits run out, they come out with a new Bible and another one after that and another one after that one.

If liberalism is right, then Christianity has some very major problems. If some words were lost or changed from the original autographs which words were changed? The answer is that we cannot know. If we do not know which words are changed, then we can count on none of them! If the very first hand copies suffered changes, then copies of those copies would not only repeat those errors, but in time add to them. Scholars cannot rightly say that agreement between the manuscripts proves authenticity.

Many years ago, as the author of this book sat in a Christian university Bible course, he heard his freshman doctrines teacher say that we only "essentially" have the Word of God.

If we only essentially have the Word of God than the Bible does not correct us, we must correct it! Thus, liberalism would effectively reduce the authority of the Word of God to something much less than absolute. This is why so much of historic and Biblical Christianity has lost its way.

Endless questions of doubt now prevail. Questions like:

✓ Did God literally create the world or is there room for theistic evolution?

✓ Was Jesus really born of a virgin by the Holy Ghost?

✓ Was Mary Magdalene a humble servant to Jesus or was she his lover?

✓ Did he bodily raise from the dead, or was it a divine idea that arose?

✓ Is Hell a real place of torment or is it just an eternal separation from God?

The serpent brought down Eve with one strategy: questions purposed in planting doubt and confusion about what God really said.

(Genesis 3:1) Now the serpent was more subtle than any beast of the field which the LORD God had made. And he said unto the woman, Yea, hath God said, Ye shall not eat of every tree of the garden?

The serpent knew exactly what God said to Eve. But he knew that he could confuse Eve.

(Genesis 3:2-3) And the woman said unto the serpent, We may eat of the fruit of the trees of the garden: But of the fruit of the tree which is in the midst of the garden, God hath said, Ye shall not eat of it, neither shall ye touch it, lest ye die.

If the words of God are not preserved, then yes, we only essentially have the word of God. Therefore, the Bible would be merely a matter of private interpretation.

Is this what you believe about the Bible?

You must admit that without Divine Preservation, the Bible is not the pure Word of God, it only contains the word of God. Is this what you believe? We sincerely hope not!

31.6 What the Bible Said about Itself

(Matthew 5:18) For verily I say unto you, Till heaven and earth pass, one jot

or one tittle shall in no wise pass from the law, till all be fulfilled.

(2 Peter 1:19-20) We have also a more sure word of prophecy; whereunto ye do well that ye take heed, as unto a light that shineth in a dark place, until the day dawn, and the day star arise in your hearts: Knowing this first, that no prophecy of the scripture is of any private interpretation.

For EVERY act of God, there seems to be a CONTRARY act of Satan.

With the Son of God risen from the dead and the Word of God written, the Lord was glad and the Devil was mad.

With the ink of the Apostle barely dry on the sacred pages, Paul's most rebellious church, the church at Corinth began its assault on the authority of God's words. The most harshly written, corrective, and chastising letters of Paul are those of 1 and 2 Corinthians. We wish that the church of Corinth had heeded; however, their poison continued.

With the deviate doctrines of Corinth, the foundation for Bible revision was laid. Unscrupulous men changed the words of God in the years to come. Instead of adjusting their doctrine to fit the words of God, they adjusted the words of God to fit their false doctrines. Roman Catholic theologians were among them. Thus, born into the family of sacred writings were corrupted manuscripts. No one denies the existence of ancient, erroneous, and contaminated Bible manuscripts. Today, among the five-thousand-thirty-nine Greek manuscripts or fractions of manuscripts the corrupted manuscripts stick out like an infected big toe.

Fast forward to the year 1611. World Evangelism had skidded close to a halt. The uttermost was not being reached as commanded Acts 1:8. Pure doctrine was harder to come by. It was during those days that King James of England ordered groups of scholars to sort out the corrupted texts from the sacred texts and translate into English an authoritative Bible. It is very clear that God's hand was in this effort. If you have trouble accepting this, consider the following foundational truths.

✓ Consider the INTENT OF GOD found in *Psalm 100:5.*

"For the LORD is good; his mercy is everlasting; and his truth endureth to all generations."

✓ Consider the PURPOSE OF GOD found in 2 Timothy 3:16-17.

"All scripture is given by inspiration of God, and is profitable for doctrine, for reproof, for correction, for instruction in righteousness: That the man of God may be perfect, thoroughly furnished unto all good works."

✓ Consider the <u>PROMISE OF GOD</u> found in *Luke 21:33*.

"Heaven and earth shall pass away: but my words shall not pass away."

✓ Consider the <u>INTERVENTION OF GOD</u> found in *Psalm 12:6-7*.

" The words of the LORD are pure words: as silver tried in a furnace of earth, purified seven times. Thou shalt keep them, O LORD, thou shalt preserve them from this generation for ever."

31.7 The King James Bible

It has been taught by some that since we lost the originals, God had to re-inspire the Bible and that this re-inspired Bible is the KJV. If this is true and God really did this, then we have some obvious questions.

✓ To whom did God tell this idea and when did God tell it to them?

✓ What did every generation do for the Word of God during the hundreds of years it was lost?

✓ Were the KJV translators "holy men of God"?

Strong admonition: Do not speak for God the things He did not speak for Himself!

In truth, the King James translation team was made up of great men of honesty, integrity, and scholarship. However, they certainly were not "holy men of God" of the type found in 2 Peter 1:21!

Where did the KJV scholarship team start? They started by rooting out the corrupted manuscripts.

Did they succeed? If you will do the right research, a complete research, and an honest research, you will discover that they did successfully do this. Further advanced studies will help you understand the development of the Textus Receptus (from which our KJV is correctly translated). If you are in possession of a King James Bible, you are in possession of the words of God in English and you can have faith in every word of it.

31.8 Corrupted Texts

What effect do the corrupted texts have on contemporary English translations? Nearly every doctrine of the Word is either marred, insulted, or deleted all together,

Here is just one among a great many examples:

(Micah 5:2 KJV) "But thou, Bethlehem Ephratah, *though* thou be little among the thousands of Judah, *yet* out of thee shall he come forth unto me *that is* to be ruler in Israel; whose goings forth *have been* from of old, from everlasting."

(Micah 5:2 NIV) But you, Bethlehem Ephratah, though you are small among the clans of Judah, out of you will come for me one who will be ruler over Israel, whose origins are from old, from ancient times.

The NIV inserted the word "origins" and deleted the word "everlasting". This makes the Son of God a created being with origin.

Over and over and over again, modern translations do this sort of thing. These comparisons are very easy to find on the present day internet.

Conclusion:

The KJV stands all alone in preservation and permanence. All contemporary versions of the Bible either disappeared from use or will disappear. The life span of modern translations is always short and then they die. Death proves counterfeit!

Do you want a Bible that is easier to read or do you want to know what God said in His own words?

This Week's Memory Verse

The words of the LORD are pure words: as silver tried in a furnace of earth, purified seven times. Thou shalt keep them, O LORD, thou shalt preserve them from this generation for ever. (Psalm 12:6-7)

THE DOCTRINE OF INSPIRATION AND PRESERVATION

1. By Inspiration we mean _____

2. By Verbal we mean _____

3. By Perfect we mean _____

4. We believe in Divine preservation for two reasons. What are they?

_____

_____

_____

_____

5. The KJV stands all alone in _____ and _____.

6. The death of modern Bibles proves _____.

Write out this week's Bible verse from memory.

Psalm 12:6-7

_____

_____

_____

_____

_____

Finish the Phrase

For the invisible things of him from the creation of the world are clearly seen, being understood by the things that are made, even his eternal power and Godhead; so that they are without

_____

Cease, my son, to hear the instruction that causeth to err from the _____

All scripture is given by _____

For verily I say unto you, Till heaven and earth pass, one jot or one tittle shall in no _____

We have also a more sure word of _____

Heaven and earth shall pass away: but my words shall not _____

The words of the LORD are pure words: as silver tried in a furnace of earth, purified seven times. Thou shalt keep them, O LORD, thou shalt _____

BEST POINT MADE

Proverbs Chapter Thirty-One

What were the main themes of this chapter?

_____

_____

_____

_____

What were the instructional points meant to bring you closer to God?

_____

_____

_____

_____

What were the instructional points meant to protect you from spiritual destruction?

_____

_____

_____

_____

What things in your life could use strengthening?

_____

_____

_____

_____

_____

Was there anything in this chapter that was of help in serving the LORD?

_____

_____

_____

_____

Did you learn anything new about the LORD?

_____

_____

_____

_____

Were there any suggestions made whereby you can be a greater blessing to others?

_____

_____

_____

_____

_____

1

Study to shew thyself approved unto God, a workman that needeth not to be ashamed, rightly dividing the word of truth. (2 Timothy 2:15)

2

Fear ye not, neither be afraid: have not I told thee from that time, and have declared it? ye are even my witnesses. Is there a God beside me? yea, there is no God; I know not any. (Isaiah 44:8)

3

Am I a God at hand, saith the LORD, and not a God afar off? Can any hide himself in secret places that I shall not see him? saith the LORD. Do not I fill heaven and earth? saith the LORD. (Jeremiah 23:23-24)

4

Jesus saith unto him, Have I been so long time with you, and yet hast thou not known me, Philip? he that hath seen me hath seen the Father; (John 14:9a)

5

Beware lest any man spoil you through philosophy and vain deceit, after the tradition of men, after the rudiments of the world, and not after Christ. For in him dwelleth all the fulness of the Godhead bodily. (Colossians 2:8-9)

6

For he hath made him to be sin for us, who knew no sin; that we might be made the righteousness of God in him. (2 Corinthians 5:21)

7

But he that shall blaspheme against the Holy Ghost hath never forgiveness, but is in danger of eternal damnation: (Mark 3:29)

8

Know ye not that ye are the temple of God, and *that* the Spirit of God dwelleth in you? (1 Corinthians 3:16)

9

Charity never faileth: but whether there be prophecies, they shall fail; whether there be tongues, they shall cease; whether there be knowledge, it shall vanish away. (1 Corinthians 13:8)

10

Likewise the Spirit also helpeth our infirmities: for we know not what we should pray for as we ought: but the Spirit itself maketh intercession for us with groanings which cannot be uttered. (Romans 8:26)

11

So God created man in his *own* image, in the image of God created he him; male and female created he them. (Genesis 1:27)

12

Let no man say when he is tempted, I am tempted of God: for God cannot be tempted with evil, neither tempteth he any man: (James 1:13)

13

Therefore to him that knoweth to do good, and doeth *it* not, to him it is sin. (James 4:17)

14

The eyes of the LORD are in every place, beholding the evil and the good. (Proverbs 15:3)

15

Jesus saith unto him, I am the way, the truth, and the life: no man cometh unto the Father, but by me. (John 14:6)

16

Therefore if any man be in Christ, he is a new creature: old things are passed away; behold, all things are become new. (2 Corinthians 5:17)

17

For by one offering he hath perfected for ever them that are sanctified. (Hebrews 10:14)

18

For we must all appear before the judgment seat of Christ; that every one may receive the things done in his body, according to that he hath done, whether it be good or bad. (2 Corinthians 5:10)

19

And, behold, I come quickly; and my reward is with me, to give every man according as his work shall be. (Revelation 22:12)

20

Beloved, now are we the sons of God, and it doth not yet appear what we shall be: but we know that, when he shall appear, we shall be like him; for we shall see him as he is. (1 John 3:2)

21

Many will say to me in that day, Lord, Lord, have we not prophesied in thy name? and in thy name have cast out devils? and in thy name done many wonderful works? And then will I profess unto them, I never knew you: depart from me, ye that work iniquity. (Matthew 7:22-23)

22

Therefore be ye also ready: for in such an hour as ye think not the Son of man cometh. (Matthew 24:44)

23

Brethren, my heart's desire and prayer to God for Israel is, that they might be saved. (Romans 10:1)